SPECIAL NEEDS IN ORDINARY SCHOOLS
General Editor: Peter Mittler

Children with Learning Difficulties

Special Needs in Ordinary Schools

General editor: Peter Mittler
Associate editors: James Hogg, Peter Pumfrey, Tessa Roberts, Colin Robson
Honorary advisory board: Neville Bennett, Marion Blythman, George Cooke, John Fish, Ken Jones, Sylvia Phillips, Klaus Wedell, Phillip Williams

Titles in this series

Meeting Special Needs in Ordinary Schools: An Overview
Reappraising Special Needs Education

Concerning pre- and primary schooling:

Primary Schools and Special Needs: Policy, Planning and Provision

Developing Mathematical and Scientific Thinking in Young Children
Encouraging Expression: The Arts in the Primary Curriculum
Pre-School Provision for Children with Special Needs

Concerning secondary schooling:

Secondary Schools for All? Strategies for Special Needs

Humanities for All: Teaching Humanities in the Secondary School
Responding to Adolescent Needs: A Pastoral Care Approach
Science for All: Teaching Science in the Secondary School
Shut Up! Communication in the Secondary School

Concerning specific difficulties:

Children with Hearing Difficulties
Children with Learning Difficulties
Children with Physical Disabilities
Children with Speech and Language Difficulties
Improving Classroom Behaviour: New Directions for Teachers and Pupils
The Visually Handicapped Child in Your Classroom

Forthcoming:

Communication in the Primary School
Teaching Mathematics in the Secondary School

Children with Learning Difficulties

Diane Montgomery

CASSELL

Published in Great Britain by **Cassell Educational Limited**
Villiers House, 41/47 Strand, London WC2N 5JE

© Cassell Educational Limited 1990

First published 1990
Reprinted 1993

British Library Cataloguing in Publication Data
Montgomery, Diane
    Children with learning difficulties. – (Special needs in ordinary schools)
    1. Learning disordered children
    I. Title   II. Series
    362.3′088054

Library of Congress Cataloging-in-Publication Data
Montgomery, Diane.
    Children with learning difficulties / Diane Montgomery.
        p.   cm.
    Bibliography: p.
    1. Learning disabled children – Education.   I. Title.
    LC4704.M66   1989
    371.91 – dc20   89–8635
                                                              CIP

ISBN 0–304–31472–2 (Cassell)

Typeset by Input Typesetting Ltd, London
Printed and bound in Great Britain by
Biddles Ltd, Guildford and King's Lynn

Contents

Acknowledgements

My thanks to all the teachers of children with learning difficulties mentioned in this book and to those others and their pupils who have contributed to my work in this area.

Especial thanks to the editors Professor Peter Mittler and James Hogg for their kind and constructive advice and comments on the drafts during a difficult period of writing.

To Pullus

If education is viewed as a process for self discovery which gives freedom to individuals to experience and explore according to their own potentialities, they will be totally involved with life itself, and grow to contribute their best to society as well as to their own happiness.

Dr Madhuri Shah (1985) President of the World Education Fellowship

Foreword: Towards education for all

AIMS

This series aims to support teachers as they respond to the challenge they face in meeting the needs of all children in their school, particularly those identified as having special educational needs.

Although there have been many useful publications in the field of special educational needs during the last decade, the distinguishing feature of the present series of volumes lies in their concern with specific areas of the curriculum in primary and secondary schools. We have tried to produce a series of conceptually coherent and professionally relevant books, each of which is concerned with ways in which children with varying levels of ability and motivation can be taught together. The books draw on the experience of practising teachers, teacher trainers and researchers and seek to provide practical guidelines on ways in which specific areas of the curriculum can be made more accessible to all children. The volumes provide many examples of curriculum adaptation, classroom activities, teacher –child interactions, as well as the mobilisation of resources inside and outside the school.

The series is organised largely in terms of age and subject groupings, but three 'overview' volumes have been prepared in order to provide an account of some major current issues and developments. Seamus Hegarty's *Meeting Special Needs in Ordinary Schools* gives an introduction to the field of special needs as a whole, whilst Sheila Wolfendale's *Primary Schools and Special Needs* and John Sayer's *Secondary Schools for All?* address issues more specifically concerned with primary and secondary schools respectively. We hope that curriculum specialists will find essential background and contextual material in these overview volumes.

In addition, a section of this series will be concerned with examples of obstacles to learning. All of these specific special needs can be seen on a continuum ranging from mild to severe, or from temporary and transient to long-standing or permanent. These include difficulties in learning or in adjustment and behaviour, as well as problems resulting largely from sensory or physical impairments or from difficulties of communication from whatever cause. We hope that teachers will consult the volumes in this section for guidance on working with children with specific difficulties.

The series aims to make a modest 'distance learning' contribution to meeting the needs of teachers working with the whole range of pupils with special educational needs by offering a set of resource materials relating to specific areas of the primary and secondary curriculum and by suggesting ways in which learning obstacles, whatever their origin, can be identified and addressed.

We hope that these materials will not only be used for private study but be subjected to critical scrutiny by school-based inservice groups sharing common curricular interests and by staff of institutions of higher education concerned with both special needs teaching and specific curriculum areas. The series has been planned to provide a resource for Local Education Authority (LEA) advisers, specialist teachers from all sectors of the education service, educational psychologists, and teacher working parties. We hope that the books will provide a stimulus for dialogue and serve as catalysts for improved practice.

It is our hope that parents will also be encouraged to read about new ideas in teaching children with special needs so that they can be in a better position to work in partnership with teachers on the basis of an informed and critical understanding of current difficulties and developments. The goal of 'Education for All' can only be reached if we succeed in developing a working partnership between teachers, pupils, parents, and the community at large.

ELEMENTS OF A WHOLE-SCHOOL APPROACH

Meeting special educational needs in ordinary schools is much more than a process of opening school doors to admit children previously placed in special schools. It involves a radical re-examination of what all schools have to offer all children. Our efforts will be judged in the long term by our success with children who are already in ordinary schools but whose needs are not being met, for whatever reason.

The additional challenge of achieving full educational as well as social integration for children now in special schools needs to be seen in the wider context of a major reappraisal of what ordinary schools have to offer the pupils already in them. The debate about integration of handicapped and disabled children in ordinary schools should not be allowed to overshadow the movement for curriculum reform in the schools themselves. If successful, this could promote the fuller integration of the children already in the schools.

If this is the aim of current policy, as it is of this series of unit texts, we have to begin by examining ways in which schools and school policies can themselves be a major element in children's difficulties.

Can schools cause special needs?

Traditionally, we have looked for causes of learning difficulty in the child. Children have been subjected to tests and investigations by doctors, psychologists and teachers with the aim of pinpointing the nature of the problem and in the hope that this might lead to specific programmes of teaching and intervention. We less frequently ask ourselves whether what and how we teach and the way in which we organise and manage our schools could themselves be a major cause of children's difficulties.

The shift of emphasis towards a whole-school policy is sometimes described in terms of a move away from the deficit or medical model of special education towards a more environmental or ecological model. Clearly, we are concerned here with an interaction between the two. No one would deny that the origins of some learning difficulties do lie in the child. But even where a clear cause can be established – for example, a child with severe brain damage, or one with a serious sensory or motor disorder – it would be simplistic to attribute all the child's learning difficulties to the basic impairment alone.

The ecological model starts from the position that the growth and development of children can be understood only in relation to the nature of their interactions with the various environments which impinge on them and with which they are constantly interacting. These environments include the home and each individual member of the immediate and extended family. Equally important are other children in the neighbourhood and at school, as well as people with whom the child comes into casual or closer contact. We also need to consider the local and wider community and its various institutions – not least, the powerful influence of television, which for some children represents more hours of information intake than is provided by teachers during eleven years of compulsory education. The ecological model thus describes a gradually widening series of concentric circles, each of which provides a powerful series of influences and possibilities for interaction – and therefore learning.

Schools and schooling are only one of many environmental influences affecting the development and learning of children. A great deal has been learned from other environments before the child enters school and much more will be learned after the child leaves full-time education. Schools represent a relatively powerful series of environments, not all concerned with formal learning. During the hours spent in school, it is hard to estimate the extent to which the number and nature of the interactions experienced by any one child are directly concerned with formal teaching and learning. Social interactions with other children also need to be considered.

Questions concerned with access to the curriculum lie at the heart of any whole-school policy. What factors limit the access of certain children to the curriculum? What modifications are necessary to ensure fuller curriculum access? Are there areas of the curriculum from which some children are excluded? Is this because they are thought 'unlikely to be able to benefit'? And even if they are physically present, are there particular lessons or activities which are inaccessible because textbooks or worksheets demand a level of literacy and comprehension which effectively prevent access? Are there tasks in which children partly or wholly fail to understand the language which the teacher is using? Are some teaching styles inappropriate for individual children?

Is it possible that some learning difficulties arise from the ways in which schools are organised and managed? For example, what messages are we conveying when we separate some children from others? How does the language we use to describe certain children reflect our own values and assumptions? How do schools transmit value judgements about children who succeed and those who do not? In the days when there was talk of comprehensive schools being 'grammar schools for all', what hope was there for children who were experiencing significant learning difficulties? And even today, what messages are we transmitting to children and their peers when we exclude them from participation in some school activities? How many children with special needs will be entered for the new General Certificate of Secondary Education (GCSE) examinations? How many have taken or will take part in Technical and Vocational Education Initiative (TVEI) schemes?

The argument here is not that all children should have access to all aspects of the curriculum. Rather it is a plea for the individualisation of learning opportunities for all children. This requires a broad curriculum with a rich choice of learning opportunities designed to suit the very wide range of individual needs.

Curriculum reform

The last decade has seen an increasingly interventionist approach by Her Majesty's Inspectors of Education (HMI), by officials of the Department of Education and Science (DES) and by individual Secretaries of State. The 'Great Debate', allegedly beginning in 1976, led to a flood of curriculum guidelines from the centre. The garden is secret no longer. Whilst Britain is far from the centrally imposed curriculum found in some other countries, government is increasingly insisting that schools must reflect certain key areas of experience for all pupils, and in particular those concerned with the world of work (*sic*), with science and technology, and with economic awareness. These priorities are also reflected in the prescriptions for teacher education laid down with an increasing degree of firmness from the centre.

There are indications that a major reappraisal of curriculum content and access is already under way and seems to be well supported by teachers. Perhaps the best known and most recent examples can be found in the series of Inner London Education Authority (ILEA) reports concerned with secondary, primary and special education, known as the Hargreaves, Thomas and Fish Reports (ILEA, 1984, 1985a, 1985b). In particular, the Hargreaves Report envisaged a radical reform of the secondary curriculum, based to some extent on his book *Challenge for the Comprehensive School* (Hargreaves, 1982). This envisages a major shift of emphasis from the 'cognitive–academic' curriculum of many secondary schools towards one emphasising more personal involvement by pupils in selecting their own patterns of study from a wider range of choice. If the proposals in these reports were to be even partially implemented, pupils with special needs would stand to benefit from such a wholesale review of the curriculum of the school as a whole.

Pupils with special needs also stand to benefit from other developments in mainstream education. These include new approaches to records of achievement, particularly 'profiling' and a greater emphasis on criterion-referenced assessment. Some caution has already been expressed about the extent to which the new GCSE examinations will reach less able children previously excluded from the Certificate of Secondary Education. Similar caution is justified in relation to the TVEI and the Certificate of Pre-Vocational Education (CPVE). And what about the new training initiatives for school leavers and the 14–19 age group in general? Certainly, the pronouncements of the Manpower Services Commission (MSC) emphasise a policy of provision for all, and have made specific arrangements for young people with special needs, including those with disabilities. In the last analysis, society and its institutions will be judged by their success in preparing the majority of young people to make an effective and valued contribution to the community as a whole.

A CLIMATE OF CHANGE

Despite the very real and sometimes overwhelming difficulties faced by schools and teachers as a result of underfunding and professional unrest, there are encouraging signs of change and reform which, if successful, could have a significant impact not only on children with special needs but on all children. Some of these are briefly mentioned below.

The campaign for equal opportunities

First, we are more aware of the need to confront issues concerned with civil rights and equal opportunities. All professionals concerned with human services are being asked to examine their own attitudes and practices and to question the extent to which these might unwittingly or even deliberately discriminate unfairly against some sections of the population.

We are more conscious than ever of the need to take positive steps to promote the full access of girls and women not only to full educational opportunities but also to the whole range of community resources and services, including employment, leisure, housing, social security and the right to property. We have a similar concern for members of ethnic and religious groups who have been and still are victims of discrimination and restricted opportunities for participation in society and its institutions. It is no accident that the title of the Swann Report on children from ethnic minorities was *Education for All* (Committee of Inquiry, 1985). This too is the theme of the present series and the underlying aim of the movement to meet the whole range of special needs in ordinary schools.

The equal opportunities movement has not itself always fully accepted people with disabilities and special needs. At national level, there is no legislation specifically concerned with discrimination against people with disabilities, though this does exist in some other countries. The Equal Opportunities Commission does not concern itself with disability issues. On the other hand, an increasing number of local authorities and large corporations claim to be 'Equal Opportunities Employers', specifically mentioning disability alongside gender, ethnicity and sexual orientation. Furthermore, the 1986 Disabled Persons Act, arising from a private member's Bill and now on the statute book, seeks to carry forward for adults some of the more positive features of the 1981 Education Act – for example, it provides for the rights of all people with disabilities to take part or be represented in discussion and decision-making concerning services provided for them.

These developments, however, have been largely concerned with children or adults with disabilities, rather than with children already in ordinary schools. Powerful voluntary organisations such as MENCAP (The Royal Society for Mentally Handicapped Children and Adults) and the Spastics Society have helped to raise political and public awareness of the needs of children with disabilities and have fought hard and on the whole successfully to secure better services for them and for their families. Similarly, organisations of adults with disabilities, such as the British Council of Organisations for Disabled People, are pressing hard for better quality, integrated education, given their own personal experiences of segregated provision.

Special needs and social disadvantage

Even these developments have largely bypassed two of the largest groups now in special schools: those with moderate learning difficulties and those with emotional and behavioural difficulties. There are no powerful pressure groups to speak for them, for the same reason that no pressure groups speak for the needs of children with special needs already in ordinary schools. Many of these children come from families which do not readily form themselves into associations and pressure groups. Many of their parents are unemployed, on low incomes or dependent on social security; many live in overcrowded conditions in poor quality housing or have long-standing health problems. Some members of these families have themselves experienced school failure and rejection as children.

Problems of poverty and disadvantage are common in families of children with special needs already in ordinary schools. Low achievement and social disadvantage are clearly associated, though it is important not to assume that there is a simple relation between them. Although most children from socially disadvantaged backgrounds have not been identified as low achieving, there is still a high correlation between social-class membership and educational achievement, with middle-class children distancing themselves increasingly in educational achievements and perhaps also socially from children from working-class backgrounds – another form of segregation within what purports to be the mainstream.

The probability of socially disadvantaged children being identified as having special needs is very much greater than in other children. An early estimate suggested that it was more than seven times as high, when social disadvantage was defined by the presence of all three of the following indices: overcrowding (more than 1.5 persons per room), low income (supplementary benefit or free school meals) and adverse family circumstances (coming from a single-parent home or a home with more than five children) (Wedge and Prosser, 1973). Since this study was published, the number of families coming into these categories has greatly increased as a result of deteriorating economic conditions and changing social circumstances.

In this wider sense, the problem of special needs is largely a problem of social disadvantage and poverty. Children with special needs are therefore doubly vulnerable to underestimation of their abilities: first, because of their family and social backgrounds, and second, because of their low achievements. A recent large-scale study of special needs provision in junior schools suggests that while teachers' attitudes to low-achieving children are broadly positive, they are pessimistic about the ability of such children to derive much benefit from increased special needs provision (Croll and Moses, 1985).

Partnership with parents

The Croll and Moses survey of junior school practice confirms that teachers still tend to attribute many children's difficulties to adverse home circumstances. How many times have we heard comments along the lines of 'What can you expect from a child from that kind of family?' Is this not a form of stereotyping at least as damaging as racist and sexist attitudes?

Partnership with parents of socially disadvantaged children thus presents a very different challenge from that portrayed in the many reports of successful practice in some special schools. Nevertheless, the challenge can be and is being met. Paul Widlake's recent books (1984, 1985) give the lie to the oft-expressed view that some parents are 'not interested in their child's education'. Widlake documents project after project in which teachers and parents have worked well together. Many of these projects have involved teachers visiting homes rather than parents attending school meetings. There is also now ample research to show that children whose parents listen to them reading at home tend to read better and to enjoy reading more than other children (Topping and Wolfendale, 1985; see also Sheila Wolfendale's *Primary Schools and Special Needs*, in the present series).

Support in the classroom

If teachers in ordinary schools are to identify and meet the whole range of special needs, including those of children currently in special schools, they are entitled to support. Above all, this must come from the headteacher and from the senior staff of the school; from any special needs specialists or teams already in the school; from members of the new advisory and support services, as well as from educational psychologists, social workers and any health professionals who may be involved.

This support can take many forms. In the past, support meant removing the child for considerable periods of time into the care of remedial teachers either within the school or coming from outside. Withdrawal now tends to be discouraged, partly because it is thought to be another form of segregation within the ordinary school, and therefore in danger of isolating and stigmatising children, and partly because it deprives children of access to lessons and activities available to other children. In a major survey of special needs provision in middle and secondary schools, Clunies-Ross and Wimhurst (1983) showed that children with special needs were most often withdrawn from science and modern languages in order to find the time to give them extra help with literacy.

Many schools and LEAs are exploring ways in which both teachers and children can be supported without withdrawing children from ordinary classes. For example, special needs teachers increasingly are working alongside their colleagues in ordinary classrooms, not just with a small group of children with special needs but also with all children. Others are working as consultants to their colleagues in discussing the level of difficulty demanded of children following a particular course or specific lesson. An account of recent developments in consultancy is given in Hanko (1985), with particular reference to children with difficulties of behaviour or adjustment.

Although traditional remedial education is undergoing radical reform, major problems remain. Implementation of new approaches is uneven both between and within LEAs. Many schools still have a remedial department or are visited by peripatetic remedial teachers who withdraw children for extra tuition in reading with little time for consultation with school staff. Withdrawal is still the preferred mode of providing extra help in primary schools, as suggested in surveys of current practice (Clunies-Ross and Wimhurst, 1983; Hodgson, Clunies-Ross and Hegarty, 1984; Croll and Moses, 1985).

Nevertheless, an increasing number of schools now see withdrawal as only one of a widening range of options, only to be used where the child's individually assessed needs suggest that this is indeed the most appropriate form of provision. Other alternatives are now being considered. The overall aim of most of these involves the development of a working partnership between the ordinary class teacher and members of teams with particular responsibility for meeting special needs. This partnership can take a variety of forms, depending on particular circumstances and individual preferences. Much depends on the sheer credibility of special needs teachers, their perceived capacity to offer support and advice and, where necessary, direct, practical help.

We can think of the presence of the specialist teacher as being on a continuum of visibility. A 'high-profile' specialist may sit alongside a pupil with special needs, providing direct assistance and support in participating in activities being followed by the rest of the class. A 'low-profile' specialist may join with a colleague in what is in effect a team-teaching situation, perhaps spending a little more time with individuals or groups with special needs. An even lower profile is provided by teachers who may not set foot in the classroom at all but who may spend considerable periods of time in discussion with colleagues on ways in which the curriculum can be made more accessible to all children in the class, including the least able. Such discussions may involve an examination of textbooks and other reading assignments for readability, conceptual difficulty and relevance of content, as well as issues concerned with the presentation of the material, language modes and complexity used to explain what is required, and the use of different approaches to teacher–pupil dialogue.

IMPLICATIONS FOR TEACHER TRAINING

Issues of training are raised by the authors of the overview works in this series but permeate all the volumes concerned with specific areas of the curriculum or specific areas of special needs.

The scale and complexity of changes taking place in the field of special needs and the necessary transformation of the teacher-training curriculum imply an agenda for teacher training that is nothing less than retraining and supporting every teacher in the country in working with pupils with special needs.

Although teacher training represented one of the three major priorities identified by the Warnock Committee, the resources devoted to this priority have been meagre, despite a strong commitment to training from teachers, LEAs, staff of higher education, HMI and the DES itself. Nevertheless, some positive developments can be noted (for more detailed accounts of developments in teacher education see Sayer and Jones, 1985 and Robson, Sebba, Mittler and Davies, 1988).

Initial training

At the initial training level, we now find an insistence that all teachers in training must be exposed to a compulsory component concerned with meeting special needs in the ordinary school. The Council for the Accreditation of Teacher Education (CATE) and HMI seem set to enforce these criteria; institutions that do not meet them will not be accredited for teacher training.

Although this policy is welcome from a special needs perspective, many questions remain. Where will the staff to teach these courses come from? What happened to the Warnock recommendations for each teacher-training institution to have a small team of staff specifically concerned with this area? Even when a team exists, they can succeed in 'permeating' a special needs element into initial teacher training only to the extent that they influence all their fellow specialist tutors to widen their teaching perspectives to include children with special needs.

Special needs departments in higher education face similar problems to those confronting special needs teams in secondary schools. They need to gain access to and influence the work of the whole institution. They also need to avoid the situation where the very existence of an active special needs department results in colleagues regarding special needs as someone else's responsibility, not theirs.

Despite these problems, the outlook in the long term is

favourable. More and more teachers in training are at least receiving an introduction to special needs; are being encouraged to seek out information on special needs policy and practice in the schools in which they are doing their teaching practice, and are being introduced to a variety of approaches to meeting their needs. Teaching materials are being prepared specifically for initial teacher-training students. Teacher trainers have also been greatly encouraged by the obvious interest and commitment of students to children with special needs; optional and elective courses on this subject have always been over-subscribed.

Inservice courses for designated teachers

Since 1983, the government has funded a series of one-term full-time courses in polytechnics and universities to provide intensive training for designated teachers with specific responsibility for pupils with special needs in ordinary schools (see *Meeting Special Needs in Ordinary Schools* by Seamus Hegarty in this series for information on research on evaluation of their effectiveness). These courses are innovative in a number of respects. They bring LEA and higher-education staff together in a productive working partnership. The seconded teacher, headteacher, LEA adviser and higher-education tutor enter into a commitment to train and support the teachers in becoming change agents in their own schools. Students spend two days a week in their own schools initiating and implementing change. All teachers with designated responsibilities for pupils with special needs have the right to be considered for these one-term courses, which are now a national priority area for which central funding is available. However, not all teachers can gain access to these courses as the institutions are geographically very unevenly distributed.

Other inservice courses

The future of inservice education for teachers (INSET) in education in general and special needs in particular is in a state of transition. Since April 1987, the government has abolished the central pooling arrangements which previously funded courses and has replaced these by a system in which LEAs are required to identify their training requirements and to submit these to the DES for funding. LEAs are being asked to negotiate training needs with each school as part of a policy of staff development and appraisal. Special needs is one of nineteen national priority areas that will receive 70 per cent funding from the DES, as is training for further education (FE) staff with special needs responsibilities.

These new arrangements, known as Grant Related Inservice Training (GRIST), will change the face of inservice training for all teachers but time is needed to assess their impact on training opportunities and teacher effectiveness (see Mittler, 1986, for an interim account of the implications of the proposed changes). In the meantime, there is serious concern about the future of secondments for courses longer than one term. Additional staffing will also be needed in higher education to respond to the wider range of demand.

An increasing number of 'teaching packages' have become available for teachers working with pupils with special needs. Some (though not all) of these are well designed and evaluated. Most of them are school-based and can be used by small groups of teachers working under the supervision of a trained tutor.

The best known of these is the Special Needs Action Programme (SNAP) originally developed for Coventry primary schools (Muncey and Ainscow, 1982) but now being adapted for secondary schools. This is based on a form of pyramid training in which co-ordinators from each school are trained to train colleagues in their own school or sometimes in a consortium of local schools. Evaluation by a National Foundation for Educational Research (NFER) research team suggests that SNAP is potentially an effective approach to school-based inservice training, providing that strong management support is guaranteed by the headteacher and by senior LEA staff (see Hegarty, *Meeting Special Needs in Ordinary Schools*, this series, for a brief summary).

Does training work?

Many readers of this series of books are likely to have recent experience of training courses. How many of them led to changes in classroom practice? How often have teachers been frustrated by their inability to introduce and implement change in their schools on returning from a course? How many heads actively support their staff in becoming change agents? How many teachers returning from advanced one-year courses have experienced 'the re-entry phenomenon'? At worst, this is quite simply being ignored: neither the LEA adviser, nor the head nor any one else asks about special interests and skills developed on the course and how these could be most effectively put to good use in the school. Instead, the returning member of staff is put through various re-initiation rituals ('Enjoyed your holiday?'), or is given responsibilities bearing no relation to interests developed on the course. Not infrequently, colleagues with less experience and fewer qualifications are promoted over their heads during their absence.

At a time of major initiatives in training, it may seem churlish to raise questions about the effectiveness of staff training. It is necessary to do so because training resources are limited and because the morale and motivation of the teaching force depend on satisfaction with what is offered – indeed, on opportunities to negotiate what is available with course providers. Blind faith in training for training's sake soon leads to disillusionment and frustration.

For the last three years, a team of researchers at Manchester University and Huddersfield Polytechnic have been involved in a DES funded project which aimed to assess the impact of a range of inservice courses on teachers working with pupils with special educational needs (see Robson, Sebba, Mittler and Davies, 1988, for a full account and Sebba and Robson, 1987, for a briefer interim report). A variety of courses was evaluated; some were held for one evening a week for a term; others were one-week full time; some were award-bearing, others were not. The former included the North-West regional diploma in special needs, the first example of a course developed in total partnership between a university and a polytechnic which allows students to take modules from either institution and also gives credit recognition to specific Open University and LEA courses. The research also evaluated the effectiveness of an already published and disseminated course on behavioural methods of teaching – the EDY course (Farrell, 1985).

Whether or not the readers of these books are or will be experiencing a training course, or whether their training consists only of the reading of one or more of the books in this series, it may be useful to conclude by highlighting a number of challenges facing teachers and teacher trainers in the coming decades.

1. We are all out of date in relation to the challenges that we face in our work.
2. Training in isolation achieves very little. Training must be seen as part of a wider programme of change and development of the institution as a whole.
3. Each LEA, each school and each agency needs to develop a strategic approach to staff development, involving detailed identification of training and development needs

with the staff as a whole and with each individual member of staff.

4. There must be a commitment by management to enable the staff member to try to implement ideas and methods learned on the course.

5. This implies a corresponding commitment by the training institutions to prepare the student to become an agent of change.

6. There is more to training than attending courses. Much can be learned simply by visiting other schools, seeing teachers and other professionals at work in different settings and exchanging ideas and experiences. Many valuable training experiences can be arranged within a single school or agency, or by a group of teachers from different schools meeting regularly to carry out an agreed task.

7. There is now no shortage of books, periodicals, videos and audio-visual aids concerned with the field of special needs. Every school should therefore have a small staff library which can be used as a resource by staff and parents. We hope that the present series of unit texts will make a useful contribution to such a library.

The publishers and I would like to thank the many people – too numerous to mention – who have helped to create this series. In particular we would like to thank the Associate Editors, James Hogg, Peter Pumfrey, Tessa Roberts and Colin Robson, for their active advice and guidance; the Honorary Advisory Board, Neville Bennett, Marion Blythman, George Cooke, John Fish, Ken Jones, Sylvia Phillips, Klaus Wedell and Phillip Williams, for their comments and suggestions; and the teachers, teacher trainers and special needs advisers who took part in our information surveys.

SOME IMPLICATIONS OF THE EDUCATION REFORM ACT: AN EDITORIAL POSTSCRIPT

Full access to the curriculum is the central theme of this series of books and the fundamental challenge posed by the 1988 Education Reform Act. What are the implications of this Act for children with special educational needs? Will it help or hinder access to the national curriculum? How will they fare under the proposed assessment arrangements? What degree of priority will be given to these children by the new governing bodies, by headteachers, by LEAs and by the community? Will the voice of parents be heard when priority decisions are being taken on how the schools' resources will be used? What are the implications of local management, financial delegation and open enrolment? Is there a risk that children in ordinary schools will be denied access to the national curriculum? Will there be increased pressure to provide them with the 'protection of a statement' and to press for them to be sent to special schools? Will ordinary schools welcome children whose needs call for additional resources and for a fully accessible curriculum? Will they be welcome in grant-maintained schools? What is the future of the strong links which have been established between special and ordinary schools during the last few years and which are enabling an increasing number of special school pupils to be timetabled to spend periods in a neighbouring ordinary school? Will the Act make it harder for children in special schools to be integrated into ordinary schools?

These and many other questions have been asked with growing urgency ever since the publication of the first consultation paper on the national curriculum. There was concern and anger that the government appeared to have overlooked children with special educational needs both in its consultation document and in the early versions of the Bill and because it appeared to be ignoring the strong representations on this subject which were being made during the consultation process. The early Bill contained only one special needs clause concerned with exclusion from the national curriculum, accompanied by reiterated official references to the need to be able to exempt children from a second language when they had not yet mastered English.

There seemed to be little recognition of the risks to the principles and practice of the 1981 Education Act, to the needs of the 18 per cent of children in ordinary schools and to the dangers of inappropriate exclusion. For many months it was not clear whether grant-maintained schools would be subject to the 1981 Act. At a general level, there was concern over the reduced powers of LEAs, given their key role in consultation with parents and their overview of planning and monitoring of special needs provision over the authority as a whole. This last concern was most acutely reflected in relation to the abolition of the ILEA, which had not only developed good authority-wide provision but had published far-reaching plans for improved integrated provision in ordinary and special schools. Where are these reports today?

The extent to which these anxieties are justified will depend in part on the way in which the legislation is interpreted in the schools and LEAs, and on the kind of guidance issued from the centre. In this latter respect, there are grounds for optimism. Although it was only when the Bill was in its final parliamentary stages that there was evidence that special needs issues were beginning to be considered, there is increasing evidence that these special needs concerns are receiving a much higher degree of priority. New members with special needs interests were added to the National Curriculum Council and the Schools Examination and Assessment Council. Clear statements of policy and principle from ministers, from the DES and from HMI are establishing the rights of all children to the national curriculum. Exceptions, exclusions, disapplications and modifications can only be made in individual cases for children with statements, with the full participation of parents and professionals and subject to appeal. There will be no blanket exemptions for groups of children, far less for types of school. Each modification will have to be fully justified by reference to the needs of the individual child, and against the background of a policy which is designed to ensure the fullest possible access to the curriculum. Exemptions for children not on statements can only be temporary. In all cases, schools have to indicate what kind of alternative provision is to be made. Modifications can be made in respect of single attainment targets, programmes of study or assessment arrangements. For example, it seems that children may be on programmes of study leading to attainment targets but might need a modified approach to assessment – e.g. oral instead of written, computer-aided rather than oral, etc. All these issues will need to be debated in relation to individual children rather than to 'categories' of pupils.

The national curriculum documents in science, maths and English as well as interim reports on design and technology and Welsh are all firmly committed to the principle of the fullest possible access for all children. The Report of the Task Group on Assessment and Testing (TGAT) went a long way towards meeting special needs concerns with its suggestion that attainment targets should be reported in terms of ten levels and that they should be formative, criterion-referenced and in profile form. These ten levels, which are linked to programmes of study, are designed to ensure progression and continuity and to avoid children being seen to 'fail the tests'. Children will be able to progress from one level to another for any of the attainment targets, even though they may be several years behind the attainments of other children of the same age. Finally, the specifications and terms of reference given to the development agencies charged with producing Standard Assessment Tasks (SATs) – initially for Key Stage 1 at the age of about seven –

clearly specify that SATs must be suitable or adaptable for pupils with special educational needs.

Although the emphasis so far has been largely on children in ordinary schools, the challenge of implementing the national curriculum in all special schools will also need to be addressed. It is clear that special schools are without exception subject to the national curriculum and to the assessment arrangements but a great deal of work needs to be done to develop programmes of study and assessment arrangements which are suitable and age-appropriate for the whole range of pupils with special needs in special schools, without departing in principle from the framework provided by the national curriculum.

At the beginning of 1989, special needs provision is clearly at a highly critical stage. A pessimistic forecast would be that children with special needs, whether in ordinary or special schools, could be marginalised, isolated and excluded from developments in mainstream education. They might be less welcome because priorities may lie with children whose needs are easier and cheaper to meet and who will not adversely affect the school's public performance indicators. Such progress as has been made towards integration of special school pupils could be halted or reversed and an increasing number of children already in ordinary schools could become educationally and socially segregated in their own schools or inappropriately sent to special schools. The ethos of schools could become divisive and damaging to vulnerable children.

Because these remain real and potentially disastrous possibilities, it is essential to develop determined advocacy at all levels to ensure that the national curriculum and the new legislation are exploited to the full in the interests of all children, particularly those with special educational needs. Such advocacy will need to be well informed as well as determined and will be most effective if it is based on a partnership between professionals, parents and the pupils themselves.

Professor Peter Mittler
University of Manchester
February 1989

REFERENCES

Clunies-Ross, L. and Wimhurst, S. (1983) *The Right Balance: Provision for Slow Learners in Secondary Schools*. Windsor: NFER/Nelson.

Committee of Inquiry (1985) *Education for All*. London: HMSO (The Swann Report).

Croll, P. and Moses, D. (1985) *One in Five: The Assessment and Incidence of Special Educational Needs*. London: Routledge & Kegan Paul.

Farrell, P. (ed.) (1985) *EDY: Its Impact on Staff Training in Mental Handicap*. Manchester: Manchester University Press.

Hanko, G. (1985) *Special Needs in Ordinary Classrooms: An Approach to Teacher Support and Pupil Care in Primary and Secondary Schools*. Oxford: Blackwell.

Hargreaves, D. (1982) *Challenge for the Comprehensive School*. London: Routledge & Kegan Paul.

Hodgson, A., Clunies-Ross, L. and Hegarty, S. (1984) *Learning Together*. Windsor: NFER/Nelson.

Inner London Education Authority (1984) *Improving Secondary Education*. London: ILEA (The Hargreaves Report).

Inner London Education Authority (1985a) *Improving Primary Schools*. London: ILEA (The Thomas Report).

Inner London Education Authority (1985b) *Equal Opportunities for All?* London: ILEA (The Fish Report).

Mittler, P. (1986) The new look in inservice training. *British Journal of Special Education* **13**, 50–51.

Muncey, J. and Ainscow, M. (1982) Launching SNAP in Coventry. *Special Education: Forward Trends* **10**, 3–5.

Robson, C., Sebba, J., Mittler, P. and Davies, G. (1988) *Inservice Training and Special Needs: Running Short School-Focused Courses*. Manchester: Manchester University Press.

Sayer, J. and Jones, N. (eds) (1985) *Teacher Training and Special Educational Needs*. Beckenham: Croom Helm.

Sebba, J. and Robson, C. (1987) The development of short, school-focused INSET courses in special educational needs. *Research Papers in Education* **2**, 1–29.

Topping, K. and Wolfendale, S. (eds) (1985) *Parental Involvement in Children's Reading*. Beckenham: Croom Helm.

Wedge, P. and Prosser, H. (1973) *Born to Fail?* London: National Children's Bureau.

Widlake, P. (1984) *How to Reach the Hard to Teach*. Milton Keynes: Open University Press.

Widlake, P. (1985) *Reducing Educational Disadvantage*. London: Routledge & Kegan Paul.

Preface

This book is written with class and subject teachers in mind who every day have to cope with children with learning difficulties and who have no support teachers, whole-school policy or programmes to help them. It explains how children with learning difficulties may be identified and helped. Identification is illustrated through classroom observation of performance on the curriculum task in daily lessons without special tests and screening devices.

 The different patterns of needs shown by children with learning difficulties are discussed, and distinctions are made between general and specific learning difficulties. Main learning needs of each of these groups are identified and suggestions are made to try to help them. The links between learning difficulties and behavioural problems are explored, and there are suggestions for interventions during class teaching rather than in withdrawal and small-group situations.

Experience and research teaching examples are drawn together to show how stimulating and cognitively challenging work may be developed for children with learning difficulties which will enable them through collaborative learning to reach new levels, in ways not previously deemed possible. It shows them reaching out towards and beyond their previously conceived potentials. A whole-curriculum approach is outlined for children with general learning difficulties and this is linked to an underlying cognitive-process methodology. Specialist tutorials are suggested for remediation of specific learning difficulties. Nevertheless the cognitive process theme is taken up in the final chapter in first-level classroom intervention and shows strategies for identifying, diagnosing and remediating specific and general difficulties in reading, writing and number.

Teachers in North America use the term 'learning disabilities' more frequently than 'learning difficulties'. Use of the words 'disability', 'disabling' and 'disabled', however, can suggest that one has to live with a handicap and only special measures can surmount it. Thus preference is given to the term 'learning difficulties' in order to suggest that students can be *enabled* and teachers *empowered* to help them overcome what may be regarded as transient problems. Empowering teachers is an important consideration, it is complex and involves the enhancement of teaching skills rather than giving programmes of instruction for the classroom technician to follow.

The subject of learning difficulties is extraordinarily wide and many volumes would be required to do it justice. This book is an introduction and represents the author's particular perspective on helping such children. These views are based upon experience and grounded research and as such cannot represent a survey of the field. It is, however, a genuine attempt to change practice and has been well received and successful in courses on special needs in initial and inservice training.

—1———————————————

Who are the children with learning difficulties?

INTRODUCTION

Learning difficulties can encompass a very wide range of problems, each of which may result in a failure to learn in a particular individual. In order to make the subject manageable within the confines of a single book, the term 'learning difficulties' will be used to refer to those children whose main difficulties are in the area of intellectual functioning (DES, 1978; Brennan, 1979, 1985). Such learning difficulties appear to lie on a continuum from mild through moderate to severe. The children with moderate to severe learning difficulties had previously been termed 'educationally subnormal' and educational provision was offered for them in separate 'special' schools, units or classes. Children with mild learning difficulties, and some with moderate difficulties, were to be found in ordinary classrooms. Since the publication of the Warnock Report (DES, 1978) and the implementation of the 1981 Education Act, many Local Education Authorities (LEAs) have pursued a policy of integration in which many or, in some cases, almost all pupils are supported in mainstream schools.

Whereas previously teachers seemed mostly to offer pupils with learning difficulties extra time (Hegarty et al., 1981; Croll et al., 1985), attention is now being more directly focused upon their special needs among a wider and more disparate group entering ordinary schools. This book concentrates on the learning needs of pupils with mild to moderate learning difficulties who may be found in ordinary schools. It seeks to help teachers identify these difficulties and attempts to construct a pedagogy and practice to overcome them.

In the British 1981 Education Act a child was defined as having 'special educational needs' if 'he has a learning difficulty which calls for special educational provision to be made for him' (1981 Act, s. 1). Learning difficulty was defined in the following manner:

A child has a 'learning difficulty' if –
a) he has significantly greater difficulty in learning than the majority of children of his age; or
b) he has a disability which either prevents or hinders him from making use of educational facilities of a kind generally provided in schools, within the area of the local authority concerned, for children of his age (1981 Act, s. 1).

As can be seen in these extracts, the definitions of special educational needs and learning difficulty are relative ones. 'Special educational provision' is defined as 'Educational provision which is additional to, or otherwise different from, the educational provision made generally for children in schools maintained by the local authority concerned' (1981 Act, s. 1). The 1981 Education Act replaced sections 33 and 34 of the 1944 Education Act as the law governing special education and came into force in April 1983.

Although the Act defines 'learning difficulty' as though it were a single entity, children so defined generally have a range of difficulties. These often become apparent only when children enter formal education. This chapter is concerned with the identification of children with learning difficulties by the teacher in the ordinary classroom and with outlining assessment procedures which may be helpful. Although this chapter is directed to identifying the manifestations of learning difficulties, suggesting that it is the children who have the problems, the rest of the chapters in this book show how it is in fact more often the curriculum and pedagogy that they are offered which results in the problems and the failures.

CHILDREN WITH LEARNING DIFFICULTIES

Although at birth children normally have all ten billion brain cells and many neural patterns and pathways already established, three developmental processes occur over time to change the neonate brain. These three processes are growth, maturation and learning. To the observer, children with learning difficulties seem slower to mature and slower to learn everyday things than children of the same age, and so they are often referred to as 'slow learners'. However, once these slow learners have learnt and perhaps have a structure for recall, they seem no less able than other children to demonstrate their capacities.

Children with learning difficulties are thus those who tend to have poorer attainments than other children of their age. This failure to progress at the same rate as the majority of their peers can permeate all areas of their attainment in the pre-school years, during formal education and then later in the search for employment and occupation. These children will most often be noted to be slower to attain the 'developmental milestones' in walking and talking and to fall further and further behind with the 'developmental tasks' of the school, such as reading and writing. In the majority of instances, mild to moderate learning difficulties become apparent only after these children enter primary, and in some cases secondary, schools. Teachers become aware of these difficulties when they note the pupil's inability to keep up with peers in school tasks. They might then observe an inability to use expressive language as well as peers, together with poorer comprehension of directions, stories and instructions. They may also note slow progress in reading and writing, and poor strategies for organising and using knowledge and skills, including social skills. Galloway and Goodwin (1987) linked poor social skills with behavioural difficulties in which the pupils lacked the inter-personal skills to ease themselves out of difficult or tense situations in class and became labelled as 'disruptives'. Common links between learning difficulties and behavioural difficulties were noted by Rutter *et al.* (1970) in the Isle of Wight survey and by a number of researchers since (Williams, 1970; Rutter, 1975; Chazan *et al.*, 1980, Laslett, 1982).

More recently, teachers in junior schools surveyed by Croll and Moses (1985) described 7.7 per cent of pupils as having special needs associated with behavioural difficulties. Two-thirds of this group also had learning difficulties and nearly a quarter had physical or health problems. The teacher attributed the learning difficulties to mainly 'within-child' factors, and behavioural difficulties to causal factors related to home and parental circumstances. The researchers concluded that with both kinds of difficulty there was considerable overlap between the causal factors. It was interesting to note that in only 3 per cent of cases analysed were difficulties seen as arising from the school or teacher. This point will be taken up in later chapters. Whether some behavioural difficulties were a response to hidden or undiagnosed learning difficulties was not clear. This pattern of response is commonly observed in the classroom observation studies undertaken in appraisal research (Montgomery, 1984a, 1985, 1988). Other behavioural difficulties are often provoked by a seeming lack of relevance of the curriculum being offered. At times of personal or family stress some children may 'act out' their distress whilst others tend to repress it. Both groups can then fail to make progress in learning. The results presented here confirm Moses's hypothesis that there is a distinctive set of behavioural characteristics among children with learning difficulties, a 'slow learner behaviour pattern'.

> This involves lower levels of engagement in work, particularly work directly on a curriculum task, high levels of fidgeting and much more time than other children spent on their own, distracted from work. Teachers spend considerably more time with these children on an individual basis than they do with other pupils, but, like the rest of the class, the children with learning difficulties have most experience of interaction with the teacher as part of a class audience. The children with behaviour problems share most of the characteristics of children with learning difficulties (and half of them are also in the learning difficulties group). Differences include teachers being rather less likely to work with them as members of a small group and a higher level of distraction from work in interaction with other pupils than is found among the children with learning difficulties (Croll and Moses, 1985, pp. 133–4).

In addition to reading, writing and behavioural difficulties, other factors – such as poor attention, poverty of experience, and sensory and perceptual difficulties – can contribute to learning difficulties observed. Children with multiple difficulties of this kind are referred to as children with 'complex learning difficulties'. It is this group who were the most likely, prior to the 1981 Education Act, to have been referred for special education, together with those exhibiting behavioural problems particularly of a disruptive nature. These behaviour problems are those which 'prevent other pupils from learning and cause undue stress to their teachers' (HMI, 1979). It is not surprising that teachers still want to have these pupils removed from their classrooms, and referrals are increasing for special education in segregated provision such as special 'units'. Special schools for children with learning difficulties are becoming refuges for children with behavioural and learning difficulties. Nevertheless it is a common phenomenon that certain teachers possess qualities and teach in such a way that few children, if any, become disruptive in their classrooms.

Besides links and overlaps between groups of children with learning difficulties and those with behavioural difficulties, Galloway and Goodwin (1987), Hargreaves (1984) and Rutter and Maughan *et al.* (1979) found that there were also a number of predisposing contextual factors. They found that in unpropitious circumstances, with stress and disturbance at home coupled with stress from learning failure at school, pupils could become disruptive. The disruption arose as a response to an authoritarian school ethos and didactic teaching.

Prior to this a profile and pattern of minor learning and behavioural difficulties could be traced which represented distress signals from the pupils. This is in contrast to the group of pupils with mild learning difficulties who become depressed, anxious and isolated (Laslett 1977b, 1982; Kolvin *et al.*, 1981). These children are more often tolerated by teachers in ordinary classrooms because they do not disrupt lessons. They share, however, a number of characteristics with children with overt behavioural problems, including a diminished sense of self-worth and self-esteem. Those children with the severest behavioural difficulties, according to Wilson and Evans (1980), are those with the lowest self-esteem. The term 'behavioural difficulties' will be used in this text to represent the continuum from withdrawal and isolation to attention-seeking and disruption, for each pattern should be of concern to the teacher. Even in their mildest forms they should be considered as signs of distress which need to be investigated before 'failure to thrive' in the educational environment sets in.

Another important factor to emerge from the Croll and Moses (1985) study was that the most frequent terms used by teachers to describe children with learning difficulties were 'poor reader' and 'slow learner'. These expressions usually referred to the same child – the reading difficulties seen as part of the overall pattern of slow learning. There were, however, just over 10 per cent of children who were poor readers without being slow learners – pupils who will be referred to as having 'specific learning difficulties' (DES, 1978) – and 14 per cent who were considered to be slow learners but not slow readers (p. 136).

The group of children with learning difficulties is therefore a heterogeneous one. Whilst some schools offer separate provision for slow learners and their 'able underachievers' (Gains and McNicholas, 1979) others do not (Clunies-Ross and Wimhurst, 1983).

THE HISTORICAL CONTEXT OF LEARNING DIFFICULTIES IN BRITAIN

People with learning difficulties have been the group who have suffered the greatest indignities over a millennium from cruel, derogatory labels. Edward I distinguished between the 'born fool' and the 'lunatic' – an interesting distinction and one which the 'man or woman in the street' does not always make. This lack of distinction is also noted when someone who is physically disabled or hearing-impaired is treated as though he or she were mentally impaired too. The adult with learning difficulties is often treated like a child. This treatment could have arisen from the segregation policy hitherto endorsed (Barton and Tomlinson, 1984) and a lack of experience and contact with people with disabilities. By the sixteenth century, the term 'idiot' had been coined not only for anyone with learning difficulties but also for anyone who was ignorant and uneducated. This definition must have included the large mass of the population, for there was little access for them to education of any kind. In the nineteenth century, the term 'idiot' was reserved for those with the lowest intellectual ability, 'imbecile' for those at the next level and 'feeble-minded' or 'moron' for the upper level.

The Education Act of 1921 defined four categories for special education, blind, deaf, epileptic and defective. 'Defective' included all those with physical and mental disabilities, and the LEAs had to 'certify' all those children who were born defective but were not idiots or imbeciles. They were to be made to attend special schools from 7 to 16. It was the 1944 Education Act which enshrined the concept of ESN, although it did abolish 'certification of defectives' and made access to schooling a right if the children were 'still educable'. The severest cases still had to be reported under the Mental Deficiency Act of 1913. Under the Handicapped Pupils and School Health Service Regulations of 1945, the four original categories were increased to eleven: blind, partially sighted, deaf, partially deaf, delicate, diabetic, epileptic, maladjusted, physically handicapped, speech defects and ESN. The ESN group were defined as children of limited ability with other retarding conditions – such as ill-health, lack of education and lack of continuity of education – and those who were 20 per cent retarded for their age, although not so low as to be considered ineducable. It was estimated that this group would make up some 10 per cent of the whole school population. There would be 1 to 2 per cent needing special schooling and 0.2 per cent needing boarding schools, and the remaining 8 to 9 per cent would be in ordinary schools. It was recommended that this group should be 'taught in small groups in attractive accommodation by sympathetic teachers'.

In 1959 the category of 'SSN', 'severely sub-normal', was also established and it was these children who were considered ineducable and were reported under the Mental Deficiency Act of 1913. The care and treatment of these individuals rested in the hands of the Health Authorities. It was not until 1971, following the 1970 Education Act (Handicapped Children), that the responsibility for these individuals was transferred from the Health Authorities to the Education Authorities. They were 'the last to come in'. In this Act it was considered that all children were likely to benefit from education and so the categories of handicaps were retitled 'ESN(M)' – moderate – and 'ESN(S)' – severe. More progress was made following the publication of the Warnock Report (1978), where it was suggested that stigmatising labels be phased out and the subject of integrated education for all became a key issue.

The Warnock Committee was established in 1973 and over a period of five years it collected evidence from a wide variety of sources on the special educational needs of children. In a sense it was the culmination of all the trends and developments of previous decades and set the agenda for the next ten years in the special education field. In the Warnock Report (DES, 1978) it was suggested that 20 per cent of pupils were in need of special educational provision of some kind at some time in their school careers. Of this group, some 18 per cent were to be found in ordinary schools and were generally children with mild learning difficulties. Children with moderate and severe learning difficulties formed the group who had previously been called 'ESN', that is, educationally sub-normal (moderate or severe). These terms were justifiably abandoned. The thinking behind the Warnock groupings was to try to remove all potentially stigmatising labels and to substitute instead something which would define the child's special need and *indicate suitable educational provision*. Presumably the committee also rejected the category of 'slow learner' on the same grounds, although it is arguably less unpleasant than being considered 'sub-normal'.

There seems always to have been a difficulty of definition surrounding the 'slow learner'. Gulliford (1969) suggested that the slow learner was a pupil in an ordinary rather than a special school, reflecting the current perspective when children in a special school were labelled 'ESN'. Williams (1970) used the term 'slow learner' for pupils found to be of 'limited intelligence', and Brennan (1974) defines the group as those who are unable to cope with school work normal for their age-group but 'whose failure to do so cannot be explained by any handicapping condition'. Both these authors exclude able pupils with specific learning difficulties and, although many schools and teachers do not do so, this lead will be followed here (Clunies-Ross and Wimhurst, 1983).

The notion of 20 per cent retardation for referral for special education became a guiding principle in many LEAs, such that no children with learning difficulties were considered to be in special need unless they had the required 20 per cent decrement between age and ability. A critical borderline of 20 per cent, however, is an administrative concept or tool rather than a definition of need, and there are considerable problems of mis-classification which can ensue from holding to such guidelines (Leach, 1983). Fortunately, the implementation of the 1981 Education Act statementing procedures and the development of special educational needs services in LEAs has brought about a broadening of the identification procedures that many use.

The 1981 Education Act imposed a duty upon LEAs, that they should have regard 'to the need for securing that special educational provision is made for pupils who have special educational needs' (1944 Act as amended). Moreover, it imposed upon school governors responsibilities to use their 'best endeavours' to secure that provision. Duties were also imposed upon LEAs to educate pupils with special educational needs in ordinary schools on condition that the parents' views had been taken into account and that the education in the ordinary school was compatible with:

a) his receiving the special educational provision that he requires;
b) the provision of efficient instruction for the children with whom he will be educated; and
c) the efficient use of resources.

As can be seen, the duty to *integrate* could easily be circumvented by an LEA in its interpretation of the 'efficient' use of resources. Condition (b) allows for the segregated provision for those who are disruptive. In the same section of the Act (s. 2) a duty is placed upon 'those responsible for the child in school':

> to secure, so far as is both compatible with the (conditions listed above) and reasonably practicable, that the child engages in the activities of the school together with children who do not have special educational needs.

The interpretation of 'activities' in this section can be taken to mean either the ordinary curriculum in full or a selection of those activities contained in it which are deemed appropriate. Here again, the definitions will be seen to be relative. It has to be hoped that LEAs will comply with the spirit of the Act.

Once such duties have been imposed, to make special educational provision, integrate into ordinary school and offer the same curriculum, it is incumbent upon LEAs to *assess* pupils and to try to identify their special educational needs. Thus it is that their assessment procedures have come under close scrutiny and many useful procedures have been developed and previous methods revised. A key participant in assessment is the teacher.

Teachers, although they may not be aware of it, have extensive opportunities for observing, identifying and assessing children with learning difficulties. These opportunities are to be found during every classroom activity whilst the pupil is 'on-' or 'off-task'. There is, however, limited opportunity for recording and analysing their observations whilst they are teaching. This is where checklists, tests and observation tallies are particularly useful. Teachers can, however, incorporate screening and assessment exercises into curriculum activities and note success or failure in their records *post hoc*. In this way a detailed profile can be compiled over a long period of time which can provide valuable information in the assessment procedure.

THE CHARACTERISTICS OF CHILDREN WITH LEARNING DIFFICULTIES (MILD TO MODERATE) BASED UPON CLASSROOM OBSERVATION

Children with mild to moderate learning difficulties are most often to be found in the ordinary classroom, particularly in the early years of primary school. They include many who come from disadvantaged social and cultural environments where their linguistic skills and competencies have been held back by limiting experiences. For example, they may have been kept in a severely unstimulating environment in early childhood – locked alone in a room for hours in a day or looked after by incompetent childminders, au pairs who speak no English or parents who do not speak to them. The National Society for the Prevention of Cruelty to Children (NSPCC, 1986) reported the case of Sarah who, at three and a half, did not know her own name since the family, when they wanted her, merely shouted 'Oi!'.

Parents who are themselves of limited ability cannot always provide the stimulating language environment necessary for their young children, and slower learners suffer from this lack of stimulation to a much greater degree than other, more able children. Knowing a little of the family circumstances and meeting the parents could indicate to an observant teacher that, although the child obtains a poor score in the lower range of IQ or in school attainments, he or she could in the right kind of educational nurturing environment make marked progress, such that the original assessment results were an underestimate of the real potential. Although the IQ scores of groups do not appear to change substantially over time (Eysenck, 1966), the scores of a few individuals within such groups appear to do so for various reasons, particularly on group-administered tests (Good and Brophy, 1972). Some of these reasons are to be found in the changes in literacy skills over time of the individuals taking particular tests. On orally presented tests, increasing linguistic competence can play a part.

Without some form of special provision many of these children may not develop sufficiently to realise their potential. For this reason a number of education authorities have been running 'nurture groups' for children in groups smaller than usual class size. Attention is directed to providing the necessary learning experiences which these disadvantaged children may have missed, ranging from play to talk and social skills. Some children may even need to be taught to play, speak, interact with others and look after themselves. When this is done, a marked extension of those children's potential results. Most important, the attitude of teachers towards them changes to produce higher expectations: the relationship between pupil performance and teacher expectation is well established (Rosenthal and Jacobson, 1968; Bennett, 1976).

The core problems in learning difficulties which the teacher may observe

Memory

Slow learners show poor retention of ideas. For example, an average 10-year-old will remember about six unrelated items but slower learners remember only three or four such items. This means that they easily become confused by lengthy instructions, remembering only the first or last items. Younger children remember only one or two items instead of three or four at 5 years old.

The problems arising from limited memory span may also mean that, if reading skills are not yet fluent, energy and attention during reading are directed entirely towards the act of reading or the mechanics of the process and away from the meaning or content. The more that is read in a session, the greater the tendency to lose the thread and 'bark at print'. To avoid this, the readers need to read shorter segments and to be stopped and questioned for comprehension. They need to be given time to reflect on what has been read, to retell the story in their own words, and to reread it several times or record themselves reading and listen to this whilst following the text.

Language

The slow learner's poor retention of ideas leads to limited language comprehension and this may be observed in:

- a limited vocabulary;
- limited powers of expression, both oral and written.

The limited vocabulary of a child with learning difficulties will be noticeable only if the teaching strategies encourage talking about the learning task and if the teacher is close by to listen. If the teacher requires mainly one-word answers to closed questions or reinforces brief responses, the poor vocabulary may not be noted so easily. If the writing includes mainly copy writing or single-sentence writing of news, the problems and limitations may again not be apparent until late infant and early junior school, especially if the copy writing is neat.

The typical kinds of response to questions and to verbal interaction will tend to be monosyllabic and more like what one would expect of younger children. There may be immature grammatical constructions, such as an over-generalisation in the use of plurals, from dogs and cats to sheeps and moneys, and so on. Similar immature forms of verbs may be noted, such as 'we runned home', 'we swimmed' and 'I gotted one'. When describing the nature of objects like tools, slower learners will often describe what one does with them rather than the category to which they belong – for example, 'Hammer?' 'Hit with it. Bang, Bang!' (performs actions). These children's language structures typify the problems of language delay which are by far the most commonly found in ordinary-school populations (Webster and McConnell, 1987).

Learning experiences are best understood and internalised when the children *discuss as they experience* and put their ideas into words. The discussions do not have to be channelled through the teacher but are between children and structured by the task. The teacher listens to and draws the whole together. The children are then in a better position to *express their ideas more formally*, in writing, through drama or in pictures. It is so often true that, even as adults, we do not know what we actually think until we try to explain something to someone else; this is particularly true of children with learning difficulties. Didactic and formal 'chalk and talk' methods of teaching fail these children, who need learning methods of participative language experience.

Thinking

Not only have slow learners limited receptive and expressive language but, as has been indicated, their powers of comprehension are also limited. This means they need more support and structure imposed on their environment so that they can learn more easily.

Lack of facility for understanding in both language and spatial functions is termed 'general cognitive difficulty', and manifests itself to the observant teacher and parent in a number of ways. Early on the child *lacks a spontaneous curiosity*, tending to be passive and unresponsive. This is sometimes welcomed by busy parents, for to have an undemanding, passive baby can be something of a relief at first. This is not typical, however, of average babies, who gurgle and cry, push, pull, eat and shake things, and explore everything in their immediate environment. When they reach toddling stage, their curiosity can lead them into danger as well as provide interest and learning experiences. At school there is a tendency for children with learning difficulties not to notice mismatches that would lead to independent learning. At older school age and into adulthood, it is characteristic for such children to be continually bored, not to find current school work interesting or relevant, and to need strong external stimulation. For a time, videos and television can provide this stimulation and may be the only stimulation sought. Later, it may be the company of peers, in football supporters' groups, clubs and the like. These provide interest but there is always a problem when slower learners have to entertain themselves. There is a failure to develop deep and absorbing interests which will fill spare time, and they can easily suffer from boredom and depression, especially at puberty. Depression is a serious condition, for the slower learner often has not the necessary mental capacity to overcome frustrations and anger by logical action and argument. Anger therefore builds up and either can flare in an uncontrolled way at any moment or is suppressed, leading to depression.

Rutter (1975) discusses examples of children with learning difficulties who also suffer from behaviour problems. He finds that these slow learners are much more likely to respond to difficult situations in an aggressive and violent manner than their more able peers. Their behavioural strategies and emotional and cognitive resources are more limited. Croll and Moses (1985) also find a large group of slow learners who also show behavioural difficulties.

Children with learning difficulties show *an inability to generalise from their observations.* Not only do they fail to notice key features but they also need very often to be taught what other children learn incidentally by being in contact with the environment. For example, without necessarily being taught, most of us infer that the numbers on a bus indicate it travels a particular route, that the same letters can be used to make up different words, that money has to be saved and put into a bank before you can go and take some out again. Slower learners take longer to grasp these essentials than other children, and severely slow and some moderately slow learners need specifically to be taught such things and require a great deal of experiential learning incorporating these concepts. This inability to generalise from observations, to deduce simple and more complex rules, applies to concept formation in general.

Learning tends to remain situation- or task-specific. Children with learning difficulties find *difficulty in transferring learning* from one situation and applying it to another. At junior or middle school and early secondary stages, they may learn in science that when they heat a metal ball it will no longer pass through the ring as before, but they cannot explain why railway lines can buckle in summer, how telephone wires must be put up slackly in summer, or why they must open a tin of beans before cooking its contents. They argue that it is the weight of the engine and the wires which causes problems and that the tin must be opened first because 'your Mum tells you' or 'you get wrong if you don't'.

When considering children with learning difficulties within Piaget's framework (1952), what can be observed is that they move through the Piagetian stages at a developmentally slower rate than other children. Intellectually, they are less mature than their peers and tend to seek the company of younger children. It is important, therefore, to note which other children they play with or mix with in the playground as this can be an important clue. At the opposite extreme, very bright young children often sound like quaint little old men and women, and seek the company of much older pupils and adults.

A useful Piagetian primer is that of Phillips (1975). The capacity to estimate whether a pupil is in pre-operational, concrete operational or even abstract levels of thinking can be helpful when designing tasks or worksheets and in marking individual work. The level of mental operations can be determined in particular by listening to pupils' oral reasoning whilst engaged in a range of problem-resolving activities.

When the ability to write has been developed, copying skills may be good but the intellectual limitations are again seen in open-ended or so-called 'creative' writing. Children with learning difficulties tend to write about a third as much as their average peers (Myklebust, 1965). When the stories of younger slow learners are analysed, they lack the logical sequential structure the task demands. Although they may begin well, the story line deteriorates as they progress, repetitions of words and phrases occur, the sentence construction loses its coherence, words and phrases may be omitted, and bits of story are inserted out of apparent sequence:

> Once upon a time there was a three bear and she eat the thing they has for eats (cannot remember the word 'breakfast', when given decided not to try and spell it or ask for the spelling) (Tracy, aged 8).

Teacher asks about what else happened in the story. Tracy continues, 'She sleep in the bed in the bed'. Tracy puts her pencil down and resumes the conversation with her friend until it is time to pack up.

Before Tracy tries to write anything even as familiar as the story of 'Goldilocks and the Three Bears', she probably needs a chance to act out the story in a small group, so confirming its significant events in her memory, and then she needs a chance to tell the story sequence in words as a group activity, sentence by sentence round the group, and as an individual to her partner or the teacher. One needs also to question whether, in fact, even after the drama-work group, the story-telling group and pairs work, this particular story needs to be written down at all, since it is already in a book. Tracy clearly finds a nursery story somewhat unmotivating at this age. Much better that her own learning experiences and story ideas should be recorded, for these are not written down anywhere. These could be reviewed with her at intervals so that she can observe the progress she is making.

THE VALUE OF TESTS AND OTHER ASSESSMENT TECHNIQUES IN IDENTIFYING LEARNING AND SPECIFIC LEARNING DIFFICULTIES

Specific learning difficulties

The term 'specific learning difficulties' refers to problems in reading, writing, spelling and number work, sometimes called the 'developmental tasks' of the school-age child. These difficulties are unexpected when the general intellectual ability of the pupil is taken into account (Frith, 1980). Pupils with reading difficulties also have, in the majority of cases, an even more severe spelling difficulty (Naidoo, 1972; Pollack, 1979; Miles, 1983a; Snowling, 1985).

This group was once subsumed under the general umbrella of 'slow learners'. Now it is recognised that children of average and even high intelligence can also have the severest difficulties with literacy skills. It is considered that these pupils also need special help to overcome their problems and that this help can be different in nature and shorter term from that needed by slower learners with reading and spelling problems. In research literature (Vellutino, 1979; Miles, 1981), pupils with specific learning difficulties are identified as those with a reading age or reading quotient 20 per cent lower than their 'mental age' (derived from intelligence quotient) or IQ. Thus, at chronological age 10, a pupil with a reading age of 8 and below is said to have *specific learning difficulties* if he or she has a mental age of 10 (average intellectual ability for age). If he or she has a mental age of 8 (lower intellectual ability for age) then the pupil is said to have *mild to moderate learning difficulties*. Some assessment profiles using age, ability and attainment are given in Figure 1.1.

Most referrals for specialist remedial help may take place only at the end of junior school, when the school's non-specialist remedial provision and the LEA peripatetic input have failed. By this time there have been five years of halting or halted progress and much in the way of errors to unlearn. If a pupil at 7 is one year behind in reading, this would not qualify for specialist help if the administrative guideline of 20 per cent is applied; by the age of 10, with that degree of problem, he or she will be likely to show at least two years' decrement. This is observed in children with both specific and general learning difficulties when their reading progress sticks at about the 7- to 8-year-old level. This seems to be the limit of most children's capacity to remember words from visual recall without the necessary word-attack skills and meaning-accessing strategies which they should have been building. This is the time when the process in school changes, often as they change schools, from 'learning to read' to 'reading to learn' and the vocabulary required suddenly becomes extensive.

The reading age–chronological age relation is quite frequently inadvisedly used as a means of determining those with specific learning difficulty for whom remedial provision should be made. If instead reading age and mental age (derived from the

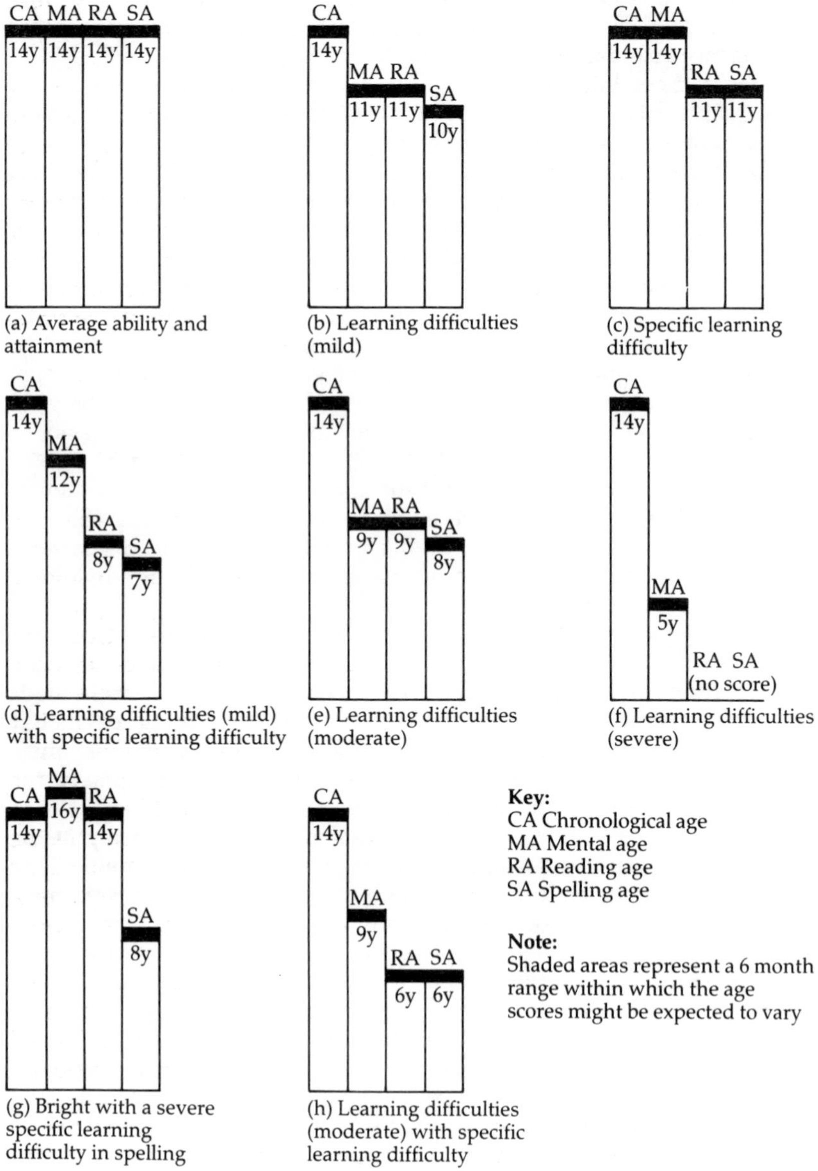

Figure 1.1 *Some general patterns of learning difficulties derived from age-norm data*

intelligence quotient formula ($IQ = MA/CA \times 100$) are compared, a number of children who have a high IQ and who read only at their chronological age level will be uncovered. It can be argued that they should be reading at a more competent level than this, even when one allows for regression to the mean (Yule, 1967). High ability is not necessarily correlated with very good reading skills (Ogilvie, 1973), although many very able individuals do learn to read at the ages of two or three and are, relatively speaking, self-taught. Some, however, do not, and some have specific learning difficulties (NAGC, 1984; Freeman, 1985). Reading age itself is also unsatisfactory as a guide to reading ability, for any test should be regarded only as an estimate of function. A more detailed analysis of the value of reading tests in the assessment of learning difficulties will be offered in Chapter 5.

Attitudinal issues and problems in the identification of children with learning difficulty

Now that, under the 1981 Act, a duty has been placed upon LEAs to identify children with special needs, procedures have begun to be tightened, waiting lists shortened and test procedures probed and reviewed. There is, however, much progress to be made and much inertia still to be removed from the system. Not the least of these problems are the blocks imposed by those who cannot, or will not, see children's problems as real; the headteachers who will not refer pupils because they do not 'have' children with reading problems or learning difficulties in their schools. They view such children as merely the lazy or careless, who must 'simply sort themselves out' if they are to become anybody or achieve anything. There are still the class teachers who feel that to make a referral or ask someone else to look at a child means that they have failed as a professional and equally view others who do so as failures. Their view, too, is that the child owns the problem and must 'wake his or her ideas up', or that 'they will never catch up so there is no use upsetting them'. Formal screening can rescue these children but, unless it is carefully done and is itself followed up by a detailed and rounded assessment, it can sacrifice them as well.

There are, of course, some LEAs which do not recognise a separate category of specific learning difficulties. They may not test IQ and therefore, as in the past, all children who are low in attainment in basic and academic skills are treated as one group of retarded, backward or slow learners. Both slow learners and able slow readers may be put in the same 'remedial' groups or non-academic forms (Clunies-Ross and Wimhurst, 1983), to receive the same, and often wholly inappropriate, educational diet.

To a large extent there is also a social psychology of learning difficulty (Thomas, 1978). In other words, if the learning difficulty is highly visible, and even the most unobservant person could not fail to notice it, then something is likely to be done. The problem is that the most highly visible difficulties are not necessarily the most severe and disadvantaging. Thus a child who is wheelchair-bound, though most often able to maintain a place in an ordinary school as well as any other, for non-educational reasons is often confined to a special school quite unjustifiably. Children with partial deafness may go undiagnosed for much of school life, falling further and further behind their peers, and are treated as less able because of their failure to understand and respond.

The category of the less able and 'dull' carries with it a social stigma (Thomas, 1978), and is often used as a term of abuse. Children with learning difficulties are subject to a great deal of attitudinal prejudice and social stigma which, as will be seen, can be created more by teaching failure than failure or unwillingness to learn. They are also subject to discriminatory treatment and attitudes in the hidden curriculum.

The contribution of assessment and testing procedures to the identification of learning difficulties

Assessment

Assessment is a more broadly-based evaluation of aptitudes and attainments, which includes the collection, recording and evaluation of a variety of test scores, the screening of information, case study material and observational report. The assessor draws upon this range of information to make an assessment, for example, of special educational needs.

Testing

Testing involves giving individuals a series of tasks to do or items to respond to, usually in a given time span but not always, so that their responses may be recorded and later analysed. The analysis may take the form of quantifying the results and arriving at scores which may be compared to those of a typical age or developmental band. These types of test are called *norm-referenced.* In the area of reading, for example, a reading age can be looked up in the test manual that corresponds to the score calculated from the errors or omissions made in reading the set of words or sentences, or the passage. Not that this is particularly helpful to the individual being tested. The tester, however, discovers that Jan has a reading age typical of an 8-year-old although he is only 6, whereas Tracy has a reading age of 6 when she is, in fact, 8 years old. Jan is doing very well; Tracy may be – other information is required in order to judge this. Norm-referenced data are useful to administrators, for it could be shown that a cohort of children entering a particular school had a poor reading profile which hampered progression in their academic pursuits, accounting in part for a fall in the level of public examination results generally achieved. Data could also be used to monitor a particular teacher's progress, for it might be apparent that pupils entering his or her class each year showed a slower rate of reading progress than those of other teachers in the same school, even though the children were randomly assigned to classes on entry to the year. Norm-referenced data can be of use to the individual if they are used as part of the diagnostic profile.

Norm-referenced testing

The norm-referenced test most frequently given in schools is the reading test. Schonell's Graded Word Recognition Test is still very popular with primary school teachers as a quick check on an individual basis or for school records as part of a more all-round assessment of reading. The most popular reading test in secondary and middle schools surveyed by Clunies-Ross and Wimhurst (1983) was the Daniels and Diack (1958) Reading Test 12, which is group-administered. Some LEAs have introduced a *screening survey* of all their pupils at 7-plus using norm-referenced tests. The tests are usually of intellectual abilities, reading and number. This enables LEAs to record estimates of IQ, RQ and MQ. The data help enable LEAs to identify children who have learning difficulties, and those with specific learning difficulties, and this information has been used to initiate referrals for special education. In the case of pupils whose IQ (intelligence quotient) fell two standard deviations below the mean, that is, at about 70–72 to 55 IQ or below, a review would take place and consideration would be given as to whether they would benefit from a place in special school for children with learning difficulties. Since the implementation of the 1981 Act, it is more likely that such pupils would be supported in mainstream schools where possible and only be considered for special schooling if there were other, more complicating difficulties, such as emotional and severe behavioural difficulties, leading to disruption in class. Thus it is that the nature of the population in those special schools that have been retained is changing.

As the 'Great Education Reform Bill' is implemented, with its proposals for a National Curriculum and National Assessments, there will be assessment and testing procedures developed on a wide scale, and some have argued that the formal and academic curriculum which might result will lead to greater disruption and disaffection in schools amongst the lower attainers (Peter, 1988). The report of the Task Group on Assessment and Testing (TGAT, 1988) gave an excellent analysis of the form that such a national system should take, and stressed the diagnostic and formative nature of 'good' systems.

Norm-referenced data can also be of use to the pupil if it is used as part of the assessment profile (Figure 1.2). Although not constructed for the purpose, the recording and analysis of a pupil's response to individual test items can also give a range of assessment information. Thus if the pupil's attempts to read the words on the word-recognition test *are noted*, they can be analysed for the level of word-attack skills and determine the intervention mode. On an IQ test, analysis of errors can enable vocabulary knowledge and types of linguistic and other skills to be taught or remediated. Spelling tests which give age norms (Daniels and Diack, 1958; Schonell and Schonell, 1946; Robertson *et al.*, 1983) also provide written evidence of handwriting co-ordination and diagnostic spelling information. Adding spelling tests to the screening inventory would thus enable an additional group of pupils with learning difficulties to be identified (Cowdery *et al.*, 1983). These pupils are those with severe spelling problems without reading problems, and those with handwriting and spelling problems.

It is usual to regard a discrepancy between test scores of one standard deviation, or 15 points, as of significance and requiring further consideration. Particular LEAs would put those pupils on a list for regular review and call for a report from the school. Pupils with discrepancies of 20–25 or more points between scores would be listed for a further and immediate diagnostic assessment in conjunction with reports from the school. Under the new proposed system of testing at 7, 11, 14 and 16 many more LEAs will have test data in language, mathematics and science available, and might well use this information for intervention purposes. It could, unfortunately, also be used predictively to select pupils for 'streaming' and ability grouping.

When considering the identification of pupils with learning difficulties and specific learning difficulties with a view to providing education for their special needs, the concept of critical IQ borderlines for referral should be and is being questioned. In some LEAs it has become only a small part of the information which is collected and considered when a pupil's special needs are being assessed. However, many secondary schools still use mainly norm-referenced group tests of ability and attainment to select pupils for various types of provision within the school. Some schools still use only attainment tests in English, reading and spelling, and so cannot distinguish between those who are slow and those who are able learners. This can cause difficulties for the special needs department.

LEAs may still set arbitrary borderlines and percentages for special educational provision which are determined by their resourcing levels. This can be detected in the covert messages built into statements of children's needs. Others may eschew borderlines and percentages, preferring a full assessment profile to be drawn up on the basis of which special provision may then be made according to need. As has recently been recorded (Davie, 1988), interpretations of these needs can lead to some local authorities making special provision for as few as five pupils, whereas others of the same size provide for many hundreds. Borderlines and, equally, the lack of them can lead to system abuse. What is required is a positive attitude to provision for pupils with special educational needs, and a determination to secure that provision through positive action.

Under the provisions of the 1981 Education Act, statements have to be drawn up for all pupils considered to have special educational needs. The tendency in some cases, however, has been for the statement to be drawn up only where special education provision is to be made outside mainstream schooling rather than within it. The statement should also be used to obtain additional resourcing for pupils already in mainstream. A clear identification of children with learning difficulties and specific learning difficulties in ordinary school, the 18 per cent referred to in the Warnock Report (DES, 1978), should enable statements to be drawn up to attract additional funding. This could then reduce the size of the teaching groups, improve facilities, enhance the training of teachers and provide learning aids and resources. Agreement on a theory and practice of education for children with low attainments would make this easier, but at present no such agreement exists (HMI, 1986).

Borderlines do have their uses, however, even if derived from group tests, as long as they are used as estimates and guidelines to identify different patterns of ability and difficulty and to obtain resources. They can be used as rough screening tests which direct attention, but should be followed up in particular cases by individual investigations to determine the form of help needed.

The notions of critical borderlines, such as 115 for selection for selective schooling, 70 for referral for special education, or 20 per cent decrement, are not entirely reliable because of tests having standard errors of at least three to four points, making an IQ of 115 range between 111 and 119. In addition, such factors as classroom performance and school attainment must be taken into account. Very nervous children most often fail to perform well on timed tests, particularly in the recall of digit items or immediate memory span tests. Coaching, fatigue and stress can also have marked effects on test scores and affect individuals' performance at borderlines, leading to incorrect administrative referrals.

Group tests are those which are administered to groups of pupils at one time, and usually require paper and pencil for the pupils to record their responses. Inattention and inability to read and write can seriously affect group-test scores and thus handicap even further pupils with learning difficulties.

Group tests are more reliable in estimating middle rather than extreme scores (Smith *et al.*, 1972). At the extreme ends of the distribution, group tests have higher 'floors' and lower 'ceilings' or top scores than many individual tests, and fail to discriminate satisfactorily between pupils. Regrettably, many schools and LEAs rely heavily on such tests for assessing and grouping pupils for a variety of purposes, without considering the reservations about, and the limitations of, the nature of these tests. Figure 1.2 shows the normal distribution curve for measured intelligence, indicating the proportions of the population who can be predicted to fall under different parts of the curve. Note that the terms 'measured intelligence' and 'estimate' are used: arguments on the validity of the concept of intelligence and how scores are achieved abound (Wiseman, 1972). In considering the range of possible scores of a class of pupils of mixed ability, it can be helpful to look at the percentages in each area of the curve and relate these to proportions of a class of 30 children.

The expected frequency of pupils with mild to moderate learning difficulties in a randomly selected population is approximately 15 per cent. In a mixed-ability class group of 30 pupils, about 20 pupils will be 'average' in ability, 5 will be more 'able' learners and about 5 will be slower learners. Slightly more than 50 per cent of a randomly selected group would fall below the

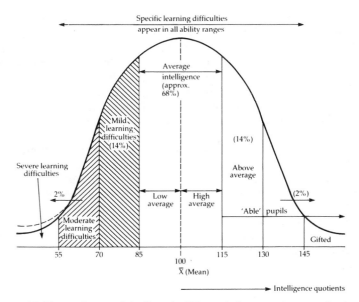

Figure 1.2 *The continuum of intellectual ability and the approximate predicted proportions of the population between different intelligence quotient (IQ) ranges*

mean of 100 IQ, for there is an inflation or secondary peak (dotted line) reflecting severe organic damage. Children's school attainments in reading and spelling, however, may show a somewhat different distribution (Rutter and Yule, 1973), with some very poor attainments in reading and spelling indicating specific learning difficulties across the ability range. Children's other qualities, such as personality, persistence, sociability, leadership and empathy, may show quite a different pattern. It is all of these which a teacher needs to take into account. In Terman's longitudinal study of gifted children, two consistent factors contributed to their achievement in addition to high ability (IQ 140 plus): emotional stability and persistence. Teachers of all pupils might find these significant personal attributes worthy of recording in pupil portfolios.

Norm-referenced tests given by the educational psychologist

A child who is 'failing to thrive' under the normal educative processes of the school is likely to be referred to the Special Educational Needs co-ordinator or peripatetic SEN teacher for observation and assessment. If they need additional help, the pupil will be referred for individual assessment by the educational psychologist who, amongst other things, will most often still administer the Wechsler Intelligence Scale for Children (WISC-R; Wechsler, 1974). But many educational psychologists will these days prefer to observe the child in the classroom and base their recommendations upon this (Quicke, 1984). Two major groups of scores are revealed by WISC-R, Verbal Intelligence and Performance Intelligence. These can broadly be considered to indicate the abilities in mental functioning of the two cerebral hemispheres.

Children who are intellectually slow will usually show a pattern of even development, but slower than average across both verbal and performance functions. There are those who may be revealed as having a disparity between the two functions of 15 or more points, and this would indicate some dysfunction (Kinsbourne and Warrington, 1963). For example, the following patterns of abilities might be observed in three children with mild learning difficulties:

Child 1	IQ (Full)	75	{ Verbal IQ Performance IQ	65 85
Child 2	IQ (Full)	75	{ Verbal IQ Performance IQ	76 74
Child 3	IQ (Full)	75	{ Verbal IQ Performance IQ	85 65

Each of these is a child with learning difficulties thought to be of a mild kind according to the global IQ on WISC-R. What is revealed by looking at the patterns of these scores is three very different patterns of difficulty which classroom observation would substantiate. In fact, only Child 2 can be truly said to have mild learning difficulty. The other two have specific learning difficulties in entirely different areas in the presence of low-average ability. Child 1 has specific language problems in the presence of potentially low-average intellectual ability. In each of these two cases, the higher score can be assumed to be the level of potential. If one looks at what happens to each of these children in school, one will no doubt find that:

Child 2 is quietly falling further behind with school work but is likely to be retained in the ordinary classroom unless he or she develops a behaviour problem.

Child 1 fails to learn to read and write, fails to follow stories and instructions, has poor powers of verbal expression, spends much time playing with toys, climbing and running about, does well in PE and games, but is a 'great handful'. He or she becomes an early candidate for referral to special school. With support from speech-therapy services and a language-development/language-experience method for teaching, it is likely that this child could maintain his or her place quite satisfactorily in ordinary primary school and need not finish up in a special school for children with learning difficulties or a special school for those with emotional and behavioural difficulties.

Child 3 will probably learn to read and spell fairly satisfactorily but has difficulty in writing his or her own thoughts down and actually understanding all he or she reads, especially in more complex sentences in later years. In constructional work and play activities, the child becomes at a loss for ideas on what to do. Figure drawing is very limited and in painting he or she generally makes a mess, producing little of imaginative value or of what is recognisable. Child 3 enjoys copying from the board and other rote activities, unless he or she also has handwriting co-ordination problems, and maintains a place in ordinary class since the ability is acquired to read and write at a 'satisfactory' level.

Criterion-referenced tests

Criterion-referenced tests are useful as part of the assessment profile, for they are assessments in which test items also constitute teaching objectives, as distinct from psychometric tests in which intelligence *per se* is ostensibly assessed with no presumption made about the educational relevance of items. The assessor can check off those items the pupil 'can do'. This principle of 'can do' is enshrined in CPVE (Certificate of Pre-Vocational

Table 1.1 *Example of criterion-referenced assessment items*

Can work with other members of group to achieve common aims	Can understand own position and results of own actions within a group	Can be an active and decisive member of a group	Can lead a group	
Can follow instructions for a simple task and carry it out independently	Can follow a series of instructions and carry them out independently	Can carry out a series of tasks effectively given minimal guidance	Can assume responsibility for delegated tasks and take initiatives	SOCIAL ABILITIES
Can carry out client's requests under supervision	Can carry out client's requests without supervision	Can recognise client's needs	Can anticipate and respond to client's needs	

Source: From an example Profile Report, 'Attainments in basic abilities', City and Guilds of London Institute, 1982.

Education) and GCSE (General Certificate of Secondary Education), which have sought to identify *core competencies* which, after training, the individuals can accomplish.

Marshall and Wolfendale (1977) argue for a failure rate on a criterion-referenced scale of 6 to 15 per cent, so that the test is most sensitive where children with learning difficulties are likely to score. Such tests, they argue, still involve judging children with reference to others, and so are not entirely divorced from normative values, but they are more advantageous than the many screening inventories used by LEAs. In the TGAT Report (1988), recommendations are made regarding both profiling and criterion-referencing systems. They are regarded as preferable and a fairer means of recording the achievements of pupils over a range of subjects and skills areas.

Diagnostic tests

Diagnostic tests are ones which may give age-norm or criterion-referenced data but in addition give information which indicates areas of strength and areas of weakness. Areas of weakness might then be given special attention and training in order to bring the person's performance to the level thought appropriate. The test manual might suggest how, or supplementary materials for training may be provided. There are mixed views on this. If the pupil was found to be weak in visual discrimination skills, then instead of training in that modality, some manuals might suggest it would be better to use another modality, such as the auditory one, to help compensate and bring about the required reading results. As can be seen, there are inbuilt assumptions about what causes reading difficulty and about the links between visual and auditory training methods and cognitive processing, none of them proven (Vellutino, 1979).

Diagnostic tests not only test broad areas of *ability*, such as co-ordination, language, memory, perception and intelligence. They can also be made to test *attainment* in specific skills areas within movement, reading, writing and number, for example. In the area of learning difficulties, it is an important part of the diagnosis to uncover both the level of intellectual abilities, the strengths and weaknesses, and also the levels of skill development and educational attainments. The case of Tracy, who was 8 years old but reading at the level of a 6-year-old, exemplifies this. If Tracy is found to be a child with mental capacities of a 5-year-old, then to be reading at that age level might be appropriate. If she was 8 years old, and had the average intellectual ability of an 8-year-old, then her reading was not near enough to this standard and she would be classed as having a specific learning difficulty which would need remediation to bring her reading to at least chronological age or grade level. Diagnostic tests and other assessment techniques would be required to determine the nature of her word-attack skills, reading strategies and comprehension, so that a remedial programme could be drawn up to help her.

The key feature of diagnosis is that it *should lead to some form of successful intervention*, and herein lies the difficulty. It often depends upon which test is used as to which training programme is likely to be followed, and not all prove equally successful in remediating the same difficulties.

A multidimensional assessment of children's learning abilities and skills, using a range of techniques rather than a few tests, is thus to be preferred. As teachers' time is limited and has to be apportioned between individuals in groups of 30 or more, *diagnostic teaching*, which incorporates observation, analysis, testing and evaluation, can be both the means of identification of learning difficulties and direct the planning and teaching to overcome them. Between identification and intervention, the information so obtained can be studied, patterned and analysed, then set against the general information derived from screening inventories and diagnostic testing to obtain broad but detailed case information where this is needed to make the diagnostic teaching inputs more specific.

DIAGNOSTIC TEACHING

The diagnostic information which is available to the teacher, the therapist or the parent is far greater than in tests. Each has the opportunity to observe the individual's performance on tasks in numerous curriculum, social and developmental areas. If the observer is well informed about developmental stages in the area under consideration, then it is very straightforward to collect a mass of useful information which will fill in most of the gaps in the standard test profile and over a much wider range of items than can be included in a test. For example, the tools or test instruments could be the children's own reading books in the school scheme and their copy writing or 'news' books. From these their misreading, misspelling and handwriting co-ordination problems can be diagnosed better than any test currently available. How this may be done will be indicated in Chapter 5.

For children who have more general, rather than specific,

learning difficulties, a broader diagnosis would include observing, recording and diagnosing their listening and speaking skills, their drawings, their social and behavioural interactions in the playground, play area and formal setting, their gross and fine motor co-ordination in movement, dance, drama, games and PE, their physical skills in hopping, skipping, dancing, throwing and catching, and so on. Anyone who works or lives with children can be in the position of having a vast source of untapped information, all waiting to be noted and acted upon in a developmental training or teaching programme.

What is important in all of this is knowing how to look, how to listen and how to intervene to derive more information to clarify a particular point. In Chapter 4 some examples are given of how teachers do this.

SCREENING INVENTORIES AND EARLY SCREENING TECHNIQUES IN THE IDENTIFICATION OF LEARNING DIFFICULTIES

When pupils have been in their reception class for a few months and have settled down somewhat, some local authorities ask teachers to use an informal checklist or a screening inventory to identify their pupils' areas of learning, social and personal difficulties, and abilities. Inventories such as COP, a Classroom Observation Procedure produced by the Inner London Education Authority (ILEA), or those of Wolfendale and Bryans (1979) and McNicholas (1981) are often used for these purposes. Many LEAs have produced their own screening inventories. Their powers of discrimination vary and those reviewed by Leach (1983) were found to have a major problem with respect to *validity*. He found screening inventories unreliable instruments, especially when used in the early years, for they failed to predict accurately later achievement or learning problems. For the purposes of identification he found that they screened in 12 per cent who should have been left out and screened out one-third who should have been included. This produced almost 50 per cent misclassification, which is equally achievable by randomising methods. The problems seemed to stem from the inventory items and their somewhat global and all-embracing nature. There were often too small a number of them to identify some complex difficulties (Smith *et al.*, 1972).

Screening inventory cut-off points were also found debatable by Leach, for although there is a continuum from 'no difficulties' to learning difficulties, at some point the inventory manufacturers had set an 'at risk' line. This meant that they had defined a problem cut-off point. If their items were of questionable validity and they failed to demonstrate prediction to later learning difficulties, if they failed to demonstrate concurrent validity (the ability to distinguish at the test between good and poor performers and between those 'at risk' and not 'at risk') as Arter and Jenkins (1979) and Leach (1980) demonstrated, then the item validity and cut-off points also come into question. Wedell (1977) has also discussed this aspect; in asking 'What is a problem?' he considers whether we can draw a line between what is a problem and what is not.

Inventories also often have only the crudest and most generalised of scoring systems from, for example, 'good' to 'average' to 'poor'. What is lacking is any detailed explanation and objective method of determining good, average and poor scores. Recent studies by Kingslake (1983) support Leach's findings, as does the study of one of our teachers (Forsyth, 1987) in the Learning Difficulties Project. She evaluated the results of her school's early screening inventory by following up after a two-year gap the cohort tested in reception classes. The inventory was partly based on the Aston Index (Newton and Thomson, 1976), and partly on the LEA screening inventory. After two years the only items which appeared capable of predicting which children would develop learning difficulties were:

- knowledge of letter sounds and names (Golinkoff, 1978);
- phoneme segmentation (Liberman *et al.*, 1977; Snowling, 1985);
- emergent spelling skills (Read, 1986).

None of these items is normally included in screening tests for 5-year-olds.

An even more recent study of pre-school children (Tizard, 1987) supports these findings. Lindsay (1984) and Lindsay and Pearson (1986) also question early screening. They suggest that if it is to be carried out at the age of 5 the diverse nature of pre-school children leads to great variation in abilities recorded. Early screening by health visitors at 2 years, for example, has a higher predictive validity than educational screens, for many of the tests are on a physical basis (e.g. of motor, auditory and visual functions). Nevertheless children still arrive at school with undetected mild co-ordination difficulties, and hearing and visual impairment.

The assumption that there is a borderline between children with and without learning difficulties is somewhat relative and arbitrary. It gives rise to the notion that the child's difficulty lies ultimately with the child, and concerns itself with mainly intrinsic factors. It excludes the extrinsic variables (school, home, culture, environment, etc.) which play a vital role in a child's holistic development. Arter and Jenkins (1979) tend to suggest that the problem lies not with the child but with the pedagogy to which he or she is subject. They conclude from their research that direct instruction and precision teaching, focusing upon an immediate intervention strategy, is more effective than one general philosophy which revolves around the notion that there exist reliable predictive structures which cause later achievements in schools. It has been suggested that the tests were effective if employed with an emphasis on immediate identification and intervention – the here and now – rather than for their predictive quality.

The value of early screening procedures is as a vehicle for finding a child's current level of performance. They will also serve as a means of proving to the LEA that aids to learning are required, and thus that financial assistance is essential. However, early screening procedures indicate that a child is either 'at risk' or 'not at risk', a differentiation, as we have said, that is likely to be somewhat arbitrary. Children tend to fluctuate in and out of areas in which they find difficulty depending upon their interactions with specific features of the educational environments they encounter. Ideally, therefore, the special needs of individual children should immediately be met. Continual monitoring of a child's educational development would indicate his or her problems in every aspect of learning.

The current attempt to identify, diagnose and intervene is what Watzlawick et al. (1974) have called 'first-order change', that is, the individual being made to change in order to suit his or her educational system. The suggestion of a 'second-order' change, whereby the pedagogy itself changes to become more conducive to the children's learning needs as they continually encounter ease and difficulty in their education, could prove to be more effective. This pedagogy should, it is suggested, reflect continuous assessment of changes in individual performance, rapid changes in teaching tactics and materials in response to difficulties, and the accurate assessment of children in terms of well-sequenced curricula. Ultimately, therefore, an answer lies with revised teaching methods and thus, when presenting a case to an LEA about the advantages and disadvantages of screening procedures, one should encourage the educational authority to review its own philosophy rather than just the screening techniques which, after all, are a vehicle for the philosophy. The discussion about appropriate pedagogy will be taken up in a subsequent chapter.

STATEMENTING UNDER THE 1981 EDUCATION ACT (ENGLAND AND WALES)

Under the 1981 Education Act LEAs are required to draw up statements for all pupils considered to have special educational needs and to identify the provision which will satisfy these needs. The final assessment is based upon reports drawn from class teachers in the school, educational psychologists, medical and social authorities, and the parents. A number of books and guides (Welton *et al.*, 1982; ILEA, 1984; NUT, 1984; Cox, 1985; Lindsay and Pearson, 1986) are now available to help participants in this process, together with local guidelines produced by many LEAs and schools for their own use. An example follows of typical LEA guidelines for producing an educational report from which, with the other contributors' reports, a statement can be compiled.

Information which may be collected for educational advice

A large amount of information will be required as background from which to write advice. For example:

(1) Existing school records should contain useful information to give a description of the child's functioning, history, physical problems, emotional problems, etc. In addition all of the following may need to be consulted:

- infant record;
- literacy record;
- test results (results of *recent* reading, spelling and mathematics tests);
- levels achieved in other areas of the curriculum (drama, PE, art, design problem-solving, science, project work, etc.);
- behavioural and social record or report from class teacher;
- medical record (if appropriate).

(2) In addition to the above records the headteacher will need to ask the appropriate class teacher for a comprehensive, up-to-date report on the pupil. This should include details of the child's present strengths and weaknesses and the 'needs' of the pupil as the teacher sees them. It should *not* be necessary for the class teacher to rewrite information already available.

(3)   Use of the LEA recommended screening checklist by the class teacher can assist in compiling the pupil record.

Assessment procedure

Informal stage

(1)   The teacher identifies pupil with learning difficulty.
(2)   The teacher notifies the headteacher and the school has informal talks with the parents.
(3)   The teacher tries to deal with problem, calling upon help from inside the school – support teaching, help from schools co-ordinator for special needs, colleagues' advice.
(4)   If the problem persists, the school seeks informal advice from other agencies, e.g. school medical officer, peripatetic teacher, speech therapist, specialist teacher of the hearing-impaired, language support services, adviser for special needs.
(5)   If the problem appears to be of a more serious nature, further advice may be sought from the educational psychologist.
(6)   The headteacher should again talk to the parents and obtain their agreement for the child to be seen by the educational psychologist.
(7)   Prior to the formal assessment by the educational psychologist, the LEA should be informed and the headteacher will have further discussions with the parents which will include an explanation of the assessment procedures.

Formal stage

(8)   The decision to advise the LEA that a pupil is likely to be in need of Special Education Provision will be taken by the headteacher and the educational psychologist.
(9)   The educational psychologist will inform the LEA of a pupil likely to have a special educational need requiring a full assessment.
(10)   A letter of Notification of Assessment will be sent to parents by the LEA. This letter will include reference to the fact that discussions have already taken place between the parents and the headteacher.
(11)   Parents have 29 days in which to submit any representations.

(12) After any representations have been received, or the parents have indicated that they do not wish to make any representations, the LEA will request advice from agencies in the following areas:

- educational (normally the headteacher)
- psychological
- medical

Any parental representations and advice received from professional agencies will be circulated to professionals from whom advice is being sought.

In addition to drawing up a statement of a child's particular educational needs, the LEA must keep the statement under annual review and vary the provision as the child's needs change. At 13+, under regulation 4(1) (a) of the Education (Special Educational Needs) Regulations (1983), there must be a formal reassessment of the pupil's needs. One school's list of assessments for producing the educational report at 13+ is as follows:

- school records and reports
- Neale's Analysis of Reading
- Bristol Social Adjustment Scale
- speech therapist's report

The school records in this case included language and numeracy records and a diary of social and personal attainment.

THE NEW NATIONAL CURRICULUM AND ITS ASSESSMENT FOR ENGLAND AND WALES

Following the publication of the consultation document, *The National Curriculum 5–16* by the British Government in 1987, legislation has been introduced to implement it. Scottish education is separately controlled and legislated. The document sets out the Government's reasons for wishing to introduce a National Curriculum and traces the movement back to Prime Minister Callaghan's speech in 1976. Since then, it is claimed, substantial agreement has been reached on policies which 'will develop the potential of all pupils and equip them for the responsibilities of citizenship and for the challenges of employment in tomorrow's world' (p. 2). Nowhere was it evidenced that the majority of schools were not fulfilling these functions or the aims in education set out in previous papers, *The School Curriculum* (HMI, 1981) and *Better Schools* (DES, 1985).

According to the consultation document, the pace of development in achieving a 'good curriculum' had been too slow: pupils should 'be entitled to the same opportunities wherever they go to school' (p. 3). It is surprising, therefore, that the proposed legislation excluded the private-sector schools for the time being and applied only to maintained schools. Was it assumed that private-sector schools already had a 'good curriculum', and if so on what evidence was this based, for there were no published accounts of these schools' inspections as there had been in the maintained sector? If these schools already had the 'good curriculum', then it should not have been necessary to exclude them. It undermined the principle of equal opportunities.

The National Curriculum consists of 'foundation' and 'additional' subjects; mathematics, English and science will form the core and occupy at least 30 per cent of pupils' time. The table illustrating this in the document (p. 7) lays down the allocation of curriculum time in the ten foundation subjects as follows: English, maths, combined sciences, technology, modern foreign language, history/geography (or history or geography) and art/music/drama/design are each allocated 10 per cent of curriculum time and physical education allocated 5 per cent of time. The total commitment adds up to 75 per cent of a pupil's time, or 85 per cent if combined sciences receive a 20 per cent allocation. This all refers to pupils between years 4 and 5 of secondary school. It recognises the concern there has been for a number of years that pupils at the end of the third year are faced with an option choice which is often narrow and (Brennan, 1979, 1985) even narrower for children with learning difficulties.

One cannot help feeling, however, that these concerns, although well justified, have been the 'tail which has wagged the dog'. Subjects have become the overriding preoccupation of the document rather than 'education' or 'curriculum'. In section 40 there is the following reference to children with special needs:

> There will not be any general provision for the exemption of individual pupils attending county, voluntary or grant maintained schools. But for a pupil who has a statement of special need under the Education Act 1981, it is proposed that the statement should specify any national curriculum requirements which should not apply. In addition, the Secretaries of State will be empowered to define in regulations circumstances in which the application of the national curriculum provisions might be modified for any foundation subject. For example, the modern languages regulations might indicate that pupils with severe difficulties in English should be introduced to a foreign language later than or on a different basis from most children.

Children with specific learning difficulties may not have significantly greater difficulties than pupils of their own age, but in achievements in literacy skills, they may be far behind what could be expected from their ability in other areas. Their difficulties in phonological and linguistic skills cause them even greater problems when trying to learn a foreign language. These able pupils with linguistic difficulties would be disadvantaged under the provisions of the National Curriculum.

Section 41 is of grave concern to early childhood educators and also teachers of children with special needs:

> The provisions will not apply to nursery schools, nor to nursery classes in primary schools; the focus will be on children of compulsory school age. In practice the provisions could be applied to four year olds in classes mainly for children of compulsory school age, but the subject working groups will be able specifically to recommend otherwise.

Roberts (1986) suggests that it is highly questionable that children in the 4-year-old group, the rising fives, should be offered the same curriculum as children in reception classes. Their needs are different and are not taken into account in such a setting. Educators should try to secure the needs of rising fives by ensuring that they are *not* incorporated into reception classes and into the system of curricular provision and assessment offered to those of compulsory school age.

Whilst it is acknowledged that every child has the right to have access to both a core and an extended curriculum, it is of considerable concern that this document assumes by implication that they do not enjoy this right. Primary teachers in particular offer a broad-based curriculum. It is mainly where withdrawal from the ordinary curriculum occurs for specialist teaching, or where in secondary schools pupils opt for particular curriculum routes in the later years, that there can be a serious narrowing of studies.

HMI surveys have shown that lower-attaining pupils in secondary schools are exposed to a narrow and restrictive curriculum and that average and more able pupils are forced to opt out of key subjects at the end of the third year. This is in contrast to what happens in other European countries and is a matter of concern in the harmonisation of community concerns.

Evidence from the primary sector shows that a broad-based curriculum is enjoyed by almost all children but that opportunities for the study of sciences and design technology are often much narrower than desirable. Despite newspaper 'investigations' and headlines, research has shown (Barker-Lunn, 1986) that there is a heavy emphasis upon teaching basic skills and there has been an increase in standards of reading and writing over the last two decades.

It would seem therefore that once again a genuine concern for the ills of secondary education has resulted in blanket provision which incorporates primary education. This has been to its detriment and has damaged the motivation of primary teachers. Primary education in England and Wales is held in high regard throughout the world and a more careful analysis of its nature and needs would have resulted in the improvement of its provision and would have given the required broad curriculum base which in educational terms is unlikely to be achieved by splitting children's learning into subject-defined compartments. This strategy is once again a secondary-school device to secure efficient staffing, administrative and rooming procedures, and has little to do with enhancing knowledge and understanding.

The divisive separation of subjects into percentage blocks of time presents organisational problems, for there are always subjects needing more substantial study than the time available allows. Division of curriculum time into separate subject blocks is one of the least efficient systems for organising learning (Hemming, 1987). Research over a number of years has shown that where staff have to integrate subjects and develop knowledge and skills across subject boundaries there is an increased level of conceptual understanding achieved in both or several areas.

It is important to affirm that the quality of much primary education is already high; studies should be made to enhance what already exists rather than reducing the argument to one of how much time is to be spent upon separate subjects. The same knowledge and skills can be represented in many subject fields. The Curriculum document's preoccupation with subject is at the expense of levels of knowledge and hierarchies of learning. For example, a particular subject content may be presented in such a way that one group of pupils knows, understands and can repeat the gist of it. Another method of teaching the same content involving practical activity can ensure that the knowledge is transferable to different situations. A third method of teaching can ensure the elements are analysed and the relations between them are understood, and these can then be used to construct new products and hypotheses. By this last means creative problem-solving and evaluative intellectual processes are developed and used. It is these higher forms of intellectual functioning which a country needs in its workforce, but no amount of simple subject teaching and knowledge acquisition can further them. A few individuals naturally have flexible and advanced intellects and require little in the way of encouragement to develop them, but for the vast majority this potential is latent and can deteriorate or never emerge unless directly encouraged by explicit teaching. Unless the interested public have access to this kind of information they will not be able to encourage and promote such activities in the ways that the document suggests. The standards monitored will thus be alien or secondary to the nature of that which was sought to be raised.

The strengths of education as an integrating force and as a means for the development of higher-order intellectual operations at a young age can be reinforced through assessment. Paragraph 47 of the TGAT report (1988) observes that 'Standard assessments need not only be in written form', and quotes presentation, operation and response variants including oral, written and practical responses. It is of supreme importance for children with learning difficulties that oral and practical assessments are included in the final systems of assessment. The written form of assessment has hitherto been too frequently and extensively used and is responsible for wide discrimination against many pupils, in particular those with the 'hidden handicaps' of specific learning difficulties.

A mixture of standardised assessment instruments, including tests, practical tasks and observations, are recommended in paragraph 59 as being of prime importance for all pupils. Assessment should also be both *formative* and *summative*: formative meaning that positive achievements of a pupil are recognised and discussed and the appropriate next steps planned; summative meaning that overall achievement is recorded in a systematic way (para. 23). Paragraph 27 recommends that the national assessment system should be essentially formative, especially at 7, 11 and 14.

It is essential to specify not only the curriculum that should not apply, but also the types of assessment that *must* apply: oral, practical and formative methods should be specified if the profile is not to be biased. Without a balanced assessment of this kind, children with learning difficulties will be denied the equal opportunities to demonstrate their achievements and their potential. The Task Group on Assessment and Testing proposed that a sequence of levels should be defined in each profile component:

For a profile component which applies over the full age range 7–16, there should be ten such levels . . .

Levels 1 to 3 should be used for national assessments at age 7 . . .

At age 7 the standard assessment tasks for the national assessment should comprise a choice of three prescribed tasks for each task; each task should be designed to give opportunities for systematic assessment of competence in the age range of profile components appropriate to age 7 (paras 101, 103).

A factor that did not appear to figure in the TGAT group's thinking but emerged in a survey of the development of scientific thinking by Driver (1988), was that children's scientific thought does not develop in a sequential order. This could make a nonsense of attempts to profile it in the national assessments and would result in a lack of reliability and validity. The contradiction is one of many to be found when the minds which contrive theory and practice are divorced from the realities of experience. In contrast, in mathematics HMI (1988a) found lower attainers to be greatly motivated by carefully graded sequential steps.

The Task Group refer to children with special needs in the following terms: 'Like all children, those with special educational needs require attainable targets to encourage their development and promote their self esteem. . . . Wherever children with special educational needs are capable of undertaking the national tests, they should be encouraged to do so' (para. 169). They recommend that a special unit within a chosen test-development agency should be set up with the aim of 'producing test materials and devising testing and assessment procedures sufficiently wide ranging and sensitive to respond to the needs of these children' (para. 169).

Working groups in mathematics and science were already set up and reported on the assessments in these subject areas, whilst the Kingman Committee (1988) reported on the subject of their enquiries into the teaching of English language. The Cox Committee was then established to define and set targets for pupil attainment in the area of English. The TGAT report (1988) suggested that the new assessment system should be phased in 'at least five years after the promulgation of the relevant attainment targets' (para. 199).

The National Curriculum may have considerable repercussions in this area: see Appendix 4 below, pages 245–6.

RECORDS OF ACHIEVEMENT: A POSITIVE APPROACH TO ASSESSMENT

According to Burgess and Adams (1985) the organisation of schools is ill-adapted at present to meet the individual learning needs of pupils. They suggest that, to counteract the divisiveness of a system organising pupils into academic groups, age-bands and subject sets, and trying to maintain personal and social needs through a pastoral system, each pupil should have a personal tutor responsible for his or her educational progress through the school. The pupil, they insist, should be helped to compile a record of achievement including in- and out-of-school activities, and they suggest headings for validated programmes as follows:

- creative pursuits
- home/community service
- personal competencies
- courses
- games, sport and recreation

Their book *Records of Achievement at 16* details a system for schools to use to set up records of achievement. This system and their proposals are part of a wider movement on pupil profiling (Broadfoot, 1986) which has been established to broaden the basis for assessment in schools and move it from the narrow, examination-subject-defined basis to the wider, all-round educational perspective. It is a movement which can particularly help those lower attainers in schools who previously had no examination certificates to show what they had been learning. Now they may have their records, their profiles and their school certificates. The issues and problems surrounding this movement, which began in Swindon in the 1960s, are well illustrated in Broadfoot's book, *Profiling and Records of Achievement*. Many projects have been in development since the 1960s but only recently have major and influential LEAs such as ILEA announced their commitment to this more open and participatory form of assessment for all pupils, and this is indeed government policy endorsed by TGAT (1988). There is considerable discussion upon the potential for the profile reports both to recognise attainment across the curriculum and to impose an undesirable level of social control (Baumgart, 1986; Hargreaves, 1984).

However, profile reports are being used to some good effect in a number of schools to motivate and recognise the achievements of pupils with learning difficulties. As a member of two accreditation boards and one who fully supports the records of achievement movement, I have two major concerns. The first is that, in compiling the record, pupils who are poor writers and poor at communicating ideas in writing – the children with learning difficulties – can be placed at a most serious disadvantage if great care is not taken. Only with a teacher who has time, skill and experience can they learn to formulate their records in a positive and constructive fashion that communicates well with an audience. The emphasis is upon the insight and the tutorial skill of the teacher, so that the record is not negative and illiterate – 'I hate games', 'I don't like getting to school on time', 'I'm no good at maths' – or lacking in any concrete evidence to give it credibility: 'I am very honest, likeable and punctual'.

The second concern is that the teachers have found it difficult to give the full tutorial time that is needed to these particular pupils and that they themselves are not necessarily equipped to fill in a profile which requires details of:

- social and leisure pursuits
- skills and competencies

Teachers attending an in-service training course on writing letters of application for jobs had particular difficulty distinguishing between their own skills and competencies and needed some detailed in-service training courses for themselves as well as extra tutorial time in order to cope with their pupils' needs. None of this augurs well for pupils with learning difficulties, for both time and in-service training require money which LEAs and government are not necessarily prepared to give, particularly in the form of increased tutorial time or decreased pupil–teacher ratios. As secondary schools ratios are already down to 12:1 (DES, 1987a), it will no doubt be suggested that it is the schools which should review their management and organisational strategies to provide the time required to meet these tutorial needs. The teachers who are operating the schemes are concerned that the work should be more widespread in the school so that subject-teacher colleagues contribute to the records. As yet, in the particular schools which I have observed, this has not met with support from all the staff. Another desirable objective is that the records should begin for all pupils as soon as they enter schools. Within a twelve-month period many of the problems and difficulties encountered had been resolved, and the documents are being highly valued by the pupils and local employers.

Records of achievement for pupils in primary school would also seem to be a very useful goal, and this is recommended in the report produced by the Task Group on Assessment and Testing (TGAT, 1988). What is most hopeful is that the pupils with learning difficulties in the groups accredited have produced some good records of achievement, especially in relation to out-of-school, but nevertheless important and constructive, activities.

SUMMARY AND CONCLUSIONS

Children with learning difficulties are to be found in all classrooms in ordinary schools. The group includes those who are slower to learn than others of their age and may in addition have reading, writing and spelling problems. Many children with learning difficulties also exhibit behavioural problems and may come from disadvantaging social and environmental backgrounds.

A range of identification techniques are available to teachers to supplement their classroom observations and help them locate these children's particular learning needs. Most of these children's difficulties become apparent only when they enter formal education and the tendency has been for them to be located as 'owners' of the learning problems. There is, however, an alternative view that it is the particular kind of educative experience they are offered that provokes or creates their problems since there are some schools which do not produce a profile of learning failure in their pupils.

The National Curriculum and national assessment proposals are examined with a view to safeguarding the interests of children with learning difficulties and a not entirely unhopeful prospect presents itself if the profession is sure about these needs and can secure appropriate safeguards. Educators, however, are concerned that targets for assessment could lead teachers unwittingly to teach to the tests and to narrow the already limited learning opportunities of some pupils. Teaching methods in these circumstances, with so much content ground to cover, could be reduced to expository, didactic methods which are particularly unsuitable for children with learning difficulties.

These two themes of curriculum and pedagogy will be explored in the next chapter to try to determine whether there is any substance in the claim that it is 'us not them', teachers rather than the children, who own the problems and create the learning difficulties. Ecological models of learning difficulty such as this seek to move away from the within-child model and suggest that problems result from an interaction between the child and the wider environment. In the light of these discussions, and the recommendations in the Fish Report (ILEA, 1985) that all children as far as possible should be taught in the ordinary classroom, the subject of integration will be examined.

Curriculum and pedagogy for children with learning difficulties

INTRODUCTION

The curriculum was considered by Neagley and Evans (1967) to be 'all those planned experiences provided by the school to assist pupils in attaining designated learning outcomes to the best of their abilities'. Hirst (1968) defined it as 'programmes of activities designed so that pupils will attain, so far as possible, educational ends or objectives'. More recently, 'curriculum' has been defined as both the curriculum which is planned, time-tabled and taught, and extra-curricular activities, such as sports, plays, visits, community projects, clubs and so on (HMI, 1981). In addition to the curriculum and extra-curricular activities, the significance of what is called the 'hidden curriculum' has increasingly become a key area for consideration (Dreeben, 1968; Hargreaves, 1978). The hidden curriculum consists of the information, attitudes and experiences indirectly or implicitly transmitted by teachers, the community, the materials, the building and the organisation of space to the learners. It is the hidden curriculum which can be a very powerful and detrimental influence, particularly upon children with learning difficulties. In ordinary schools, these pupils may be put in the 'bottom sets', the 'remedial class', the 'nurture group', and may suffer the denigratory comments of teachers and peers on their abilities, together with the stigma of separate development and inferior accommodation. These all combine to engender feelings of low self-esteem and low self-worth, which can lead to lack of motivation and effort, causing poorer than ever achievement levels. Similar powerful, but unconstructive, 'messages' may be transmitted in relation to gender, class, race and physique.

The Scottish Education Department (SED, 1978) produced an important report on Scottish schools which showed that up to 50 per cent of their children could be expected to suffer learning difficulties at some point in their school careers. It was found that the two major sources of the learning difficulty were an *inappropriate curriculum* and *inadequate pedagogies*. Only 1.5 per cent of these pupils suffered from specific learning difficulties which needed specialist remedial tuition. For the rest, their major difficulties were a lack of higher-order reading and study skills, and a failure to understand specialist concepts and terminology. In other words, schools could be regarded as causing their pupils to have learning difficulties.

The study by Rutter *et al.* (1979) indicated that the examination results of the least able pupils in the secondary schools studied varied markedly between schools. Where there was greater emphasis upon learning subject content in the pursuit of 'academic excellence', few incentives and little opportunity for personal autonomy, the less able pupils did less well. Again a mismatch between pupils' needs and the curriculum offered underlay these findings. Good schools had the capacity for raising the standards of attainment of all their pupils. They offered a particular supporting ethos and learning climate which was facilitatory. The recent survey of primary schools, *School Matters* (Mortimore *et al.*, 1988) has confirmed these findings.

Hegarty (1987) takes up this point and also identifies the school as the source of learning difficulty. He argues that where there is too much subject focus in the curriculum and bodies of knowledge are to be mastered, hierarchies are set up which determine that pupils with learning difficulties will come bottom. This is the situation which Hargreaves (1982) defined as a curriculum determined by 'academic' considerations which emphasised the cognitive–intellectual domain at the expense of other domains. These other domains he identified as the aesthetic–artistic, the affective–emotional, the physical–manual, and the personal–social.

SHOULD THERE BE A SPECIAL CURRICULUM FOR PUPILS WITH LEARNING DIFFICULTIES?

In the field of special needs in education, there is a debate about whether pupils with special needs should be offered a 'special' curriculum or have access to the 'same' curriculum as other pupils. There are dangers which may result from both of these alternatives. In the former, the 'special' nature of the curriculum can exclude pupils from ordinary learning experiences and concerns, give them an unrealistic sense of the world and reinforce segregation. The latter, however, may not lead to full access to the ordinary curriculum but instead to a 'watereddown' version of what is normally offered (Brennan, 1979). Even in the mixed-ability classroom, the 'slow' learners may be given colouring and copying exercises to occupy them whilst the rest engage in more cognitively challenging activities and exercises; they are in effect functionally segregated. One can understand how such situations arise but it ought to be possible to give children with learning difficulties access to the same curriculum as other pupils whilst not watering it down or diminishing its challenge. It is also understandable that some teachers might decide that basic skills are key factors needed by pupils to maintain themselves independently in the adult world and so gear their whole curriculum for the less able towards achievements in these areas, thus lowering their sights with respect to the general educational achievements of these pupils. It should be possible to link achievement in basic skills and competencies in life skills which other curricula have as their overall objectives to the pursuit of access to an ordinary curriculum. These are in fact the expected outcomes of general aims in most ordinary schools' curricula. It is the methods directed towards achieving these aims in ordinary schools which seem to handicap the children with learning difficulties and which will need to be examined more closely.

The argument suggested here is that it is not necessarily the curriculum but the pedagogy which is the barrier to the participation of children with learning difficulties. This is a somewhat different position from that adopted by Brennan (1985), Hanko (1985), Gulliford (1985) and Wolfendale (1987). In the following sections, the aims in education for ordinary schools and, it is suggested, for all pupils will be examined and from these and other sources a theory and practice for teaching and curriculum development will be proposed to help slow learners in mixed-ability and other settings.

AIMS IN THE CURRICULUM

There are global aims set for education, such as 'to educate each pupil to his or her full potential' or, 'to educate the pupils to fit into the modern society and provide them with the necessary skills and capabilities for doing so'. Aims such as these have frequently been criticised as too child-centred and difficult to put into practice in the case of the former, and as social engineering in the case of the latter. Despite such difficulties, which always stem from generalisations, the DES (1981) established a set of aims in the curriculum which they suggested should act as guidelines for teachers in all schools. These they set out as follows:

i)   to help pupils develop lively, enquiring minds, the ability to question and argue rationally and to apply themselves to tasks and physical skills;

ii) to help pupils acquire knowledge and skills relevant to adult life and employment in a fast-changing world;

iii) to help pupils use language and number effectively;

iv) to instil respect for religious and moral values and tolerance of other races, religions and ways of life;

v)   to help pupils understand the world in which they live and the interdependence of individuals, groups and nations;

vi) to help pupils to appreciate human achievement and aspirations.

When teachers on in-service curriculum courses were questioned about the DES aims, they had seldom seen or heard of them but they did espouse the general philosophy. The difference lay mainly between primary teachers, who were more concerned with holistic education and the education of the individual, and secondary teachers, who were more concerned to impart subject knowledge and skills. Taba was complaining about this in 1962: 'Regrettably the major objective in schools is still to "cover" subjects' (p. 179). Unfortunately this is still true according to our researches and those of Hegarty (1987), although the influence of new methodologies associated with GCSE and CPVE could bring about changes in the future. There is often also a mismatch between what teachers state as their aims and what they do in practice. This has been revealed during appraisal research (Montgomery, 1984a), when a content emphasis was found in both primary and secondary teaching.

In an extensive Schools Council review of the curriculum for slow learners in special and ordinary schools, Brennan (1979) found that in approximately 50 per cent of the cases studied there was satisfactory provision, with strong areas of excellence in some patterns of curricula offered. The review found, in addition, a number of unsatisfactory features which needed attention. It found that teachers offered a warmth of relationship and a concern for pupils' welfare which operated to the detriment of scholastic learning, for goals were often set too low so that pupils should be protected from any form of potential failure. There was a concentration upon basic skills to the detriment of other subjects such as humanities and sciences. In the assessment of successful curricula, low status was given to music and the arts and to religious and moral education. The report argued that it *was* possible to meet the *main* special needs of pupils rather than all their individual special needs, for teachers would not have sufficient time to do the latter to any great extent for any individual without others suffering. The report identified that, even in good curriculum settings, there was little attempt to define the outcomes of teaching and learning in relation to knowledge, skills and attitudes, a lack of behavioural objectives derived from the aims and contents, and thus a lack of detail in the diagnostic interventions or the evaluation of progress. This was put down to an insufficiency in the training of teachers and now presumably in their in-service re-education. The report served to find evidence for criticisms which had previously been made of the curriculum for special needs. This could be restated baldly as a tendency to move towards welfare and warmth and away from academic challenge and rigour in order to protect the child from further hurt. In other settings, drills and skills were substituted for academic challenge.

In our research, the typical pattern of provision in ordinary schools by the teacher untrained in special needs work runs as follows. The work is often well prepared, involving first a question-and-answer dialogue between teachers and pupils. The teacher then makes a series of teaching and informational points, the worksheets are given out and the pupils read them or are helped to do so. They must refer to a text or recall what was said and construct answers to fill their sheets. Sometimes these answers may be discussed with partners, most often the pupils do this in any case to ensure they have the 'correct' one. Poor readers, writers and spellers may be encouraged to work together and have worksheets which require less writing by asking them to fill in missing gaps or underline which of several answers is the correct one (multiple-choice). Although typical, this is a wholly inappropriate strategy in most circumstances for educating children with learning difficulties. Those who have difficulty in writing even from copy will be more seriously disadvantaged in this worksheet mode, will more quickly grow disaffected and can become disruptive. They then become 'hard to reach' as well as hard to teach. For them different methods mean first raising their motivation and esteem so that they begin to want to join in. New methods, however, bring new problems and it may well be found that it is necessary to wean learners from old to new methods. The move will at first prove difficult for a pupil who writes clearly and neatly and who can enjoy much praise and feelings of esteem for copying large sections of work quietly; he or she will be reluctant to forgo such reinforcement.

Brennan (1979, 1985) has written two useful texts on the curriculum for slow learners and for special needs which summarise well the current 'state of the art'. He argues for a balanced curriculum and claims that 'no single model or approach is capable of sustaining a full curriculum for children with special needs' (1985, p. 82). He concludes that the *behavioural objectives model* and the instructional approach offer learning efficiency and economy of time. The *process model* linked to expressive objectives is useful for emotional, expressive and cognitive development. The *differential learning approach* ensures a broad-based core curriculum linked closely to the learning needs and learning levels of pupils. Finally, he insists that *situational analysis* directs attention to the wider factors and broader environmental concerns which will guide decisions about curriculum priorities. Whilst one can understand the position where four models are needed to explain the best practice, it is extraordinarily complex. However, from these a matrix model can be formed to assist in curriculum design. A matrix model is perhaps best used as a theoretical tool for curriculum planning teams who are developing distance learning materials and detailed course programmes or for curriculum evaluation projects. What a teacher needs to guide daily practice and decision-making is a model whose general principles are simple enough to apply in an instant on the job. It should also be able to guide decisions in principle on the curriculum and the methodology at not only macro but also micro levels, and be capable of being elaborated to enable detailed planning where necessary.

CURRICULUM MODELLING

It would appear that the curriculum models reviewed by Brennan (1985) are each useful in part and he argues that none can describe the whole. It will be suggested that, to enable pupils with learning difficulties to participate in the ordinary curriculum, we must address ourselves not only to curriculum development but also to pedagogical change.

According to Tyler (1949) there are four important elements in curriculum modelling and these relate to four key questions:

(1) What educational purposes should the school seek to attain (*aims and objectives*)?
(2) What educational experiences can be provided that are likely to attain these purposes (*content*)?
(3) How can these educational experiences be effectively organised (*methods*)?

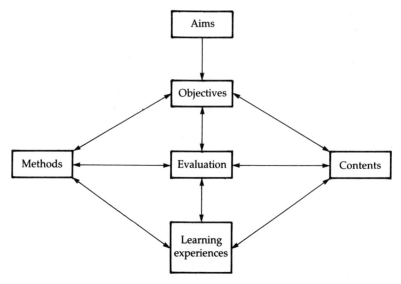

Figure 2.1

(4) How can we determine whether these purposes are being attained (*evaluation*)?

Traditionally it was established that the teacher entered the system at the content and methods stage without ever considering the rationale for inclusion. This was rejected by some and thus, according to Child (1977), the era of curriculum study began.

The curriculum model derived from these considerations might be drawn as shown in Figure 2.1. The aims, which are global and often unattainable, are separated as guiding principles which will enable specific behavioural, cognitive and learning objectives to be identified. These are more closely related to the contents and methods. Tyler's 'educational experiences' have been further subdivided into subject or skill contents and learning experiences such as reading, writing, listening, speaking, acting and so on. The methods refer to the ways in which both contents and learning experiences are organised, and evaluation is linked to all stages of the model rather than to the end products alone.

The development of curricula can benefit greatly, according to Taylor (1968), from the study and application of psychology, and this is borne out in the suggestions which follow for the curriculum for children with learning difficulties. Taylor shows that the psychology of the curriculum has three fundamental uses:

- it structures content or subject matter and provides a rationale for its inclusion;
- it offers empirical methods for studying teaching and curriculum content;
- it provides a set of methodologies for evaluating outcomes.

In addition, the curriculum model for special needs must also guide the teacher in the ways in which the pupils' *main* special needs can be met (Brennan, 1985). It is, of course, always possible to run the risk of oversimplification but, with this reservation in mind, a pedagogical model is proposed in the following pages. It is a cognitive process model with philosophical overtones through which many of the features of Brennan's balanced curriculum, drawing on the best features of each of the four curriculum models, can be realised. It is a model which has been used to guide the practice of teachers and students working with children with learning difficulties in the Kingston Polytechnic Learning Difficulties Research Project over a number of years. The project has now moved to Middlesex Polytechnic. It has the advantage of being a model for neither special schools nor the special curriculum. It was first developed to guide practice in ordinary schools with the large majority of pupils in mixed-ability groups. It was only later elaborated to show how to provide a *developmental* curriculum, particularly for able pupils and then for slow learners.

TOWARDS THE CONSTRUCTION OF THE MODEL

The aims of the school curriculum set out by the DES (1981) include words and phrases such as 'develop', 'acquire', 'use effectively', 'instil respect', 'tolerance', 'understand' and 'appreciate'. Each concerns either individual ends and purposes or those related to the wider human context. If it is the teacher's job to help the pupil towards these goals, then a model of teaching rather than a model of the curriculum might prove more effective. Careful scrutiny of the aims shows that implicit in each are the *same* cognitive objectives directed towards different ends. Implicit and explicit in the aims were a number of ideas which we shall now consider.

If the pupils were to 'develop lively, enquiring minds', they needed to engage in more *open problem-solving* activities in relation to curriculum tasks. They should become *active* rather than passive learners and should not learn by rote rehearsal but by extending their own frontiers of knowledge. They should be encouraged to question and to discuss issues rationally, collecting and reviewing evidence and opinions. These higher-order activities would have to be worked towards and trained for in a deliberate fashion rather than being allowed to develop incidentally as in traditional subject learning. Training the pupils to *learn how to learn* (Thomas and Harri-Augstein, 1984) would be an important part of all this and the emphasis in teachers' minds would need to be changed from a concern with contents to the methods by which those same contents are learned. In other words, the teaching model would also have to have a process emphasis.

Central to this process would be the aim to 'help pupils acquire knowledge and skills relevant to adult life and employment in a fast-changing world'. Associated with this is the third aim of the DES, to 'help pupils use language and number effectively'. It is often said that little of the content of what we learn at school remains with us in adult life, although the skills we learn in reading and number are extremely useful up to about the 10-year-old competency level. What we learn of subject contents has often been received in a passive fashion at a desk and reinforces further the reading, writing and number skills. Recent research has shown that many pupils leave secondary school with the same level of reading skills as they enter (*TES*, April 1987). In the current social and industrial context, according to Stonier (1979), Johnson (1979), and Pym (1980), the skills required are that we should be able to listen to and understand what people tell us; communicate the messages and ideas to others; explain things clearly to other people so that they will understand; and be socially effective and able to deal with difficult situations and people as clients, peers or superiors. The new worker of the technological age needs to be imaginative, thoughtful and flexible in thinking, be able to listen and communicate well, and have good social skills. An MSC survey of 50 major companies' requirements in terms of the knowledge and skills of young employees also reported in these terms. They also needed good 'basic skills', but it was the employers' common view that specific job information could best be taught by the firm when the employee had begun work, in the 'sitting by Nellie' mode or apprenticeship approach. It will be suggested that the methods of acquiring the knowledge and skills, the number and language, could also be through pedagogical methods directed towards problem-solving and other process approaches.

The final DES aims, such as instilling respect and tolerance, increasing understanding of the world and its people, and appreciating past and present attributes and achievements, are all cognitive in orientation but require a wider contextual knowledge and experience than most pupils will ordinarily acquire unless attention is directly focused upon these areas. Although many aspects are beyond the experience and imagination of most young pupils, they can be approached in concrete and direct ways if, it is suggested, the teacher's mind is concentrated upon cognitive process objectives rather than allowing cognitive objectives to be achieved incidentally in a content-orientated curriculum.

A CONSIDERATION OF CURRICULUM CONCEPTS

According to the HMI document on the curriculum of pupils from 5 to 16 (DES, 1987a), there are six desirable characteristics of such curricula. These are breadth, balance, relevance, differentiation, progression and continuity. Pupils with learning difficulties in ordinary and special schools do not, on the whole, have access to such a curriculum (Hegarty *et al.*, 1981; Clunies-Ross and Wimhurst, 1983; Brennan, 1985; HMI, 1986). Not all pupils with learning difficulties, for example, have access to a broad range of curriculum areas and learning opportunities.

Breadth, balance and relevance

The HMI document (DES, 1987a) on the curriculum identifies nine forms and fields of knowledge derived from the analyses of educational philosophers such as Hirst (1968). These are:

- aesthetic and creative
- human and social
- linguistic and literary
- mathematical
- moral
- physical
- scientific
- spiritual
- technological

All pupils should have an opportunity to experience this breadth of curriculum. This need not be in separate units, for there can be clustering of fields such as mathematical, scientific and technical; moral and spiritual; human and social; moral, spiritual, literary and aesthetic; and so on. An educated person looking at a red sunset may, for example, be able to respond to the aesthetic beauty of what is seen, understand how the rich reds and yellows have been created by the dust particles in the atmosphere, appreciate the moral and ethical issues surrounding the subject of pollution, and balance these with the costs of and needs for technological achievement. The development of such an educated person does not arise from teaching factual content in separate subject compartments but from drawing out these issues for note, discussion or consideration by pupils working within a subject field. Hegarty, for example, suggests that cooking can involve 'creative, social, linguistic, mathematical, scientific, and technological learning' (1987, p. 70). If the recipe books of Jane Grigson are examined, then one could also add literary merit to this catalogue of exciting possibilities.

Instead of providing breadth, the courses of study of children with learning difficulties are often limited to a narrower range of options and programmes than those of other pupils. In special schools, the lack of aesthetic experiences and studies is noted (Brennan, 1985). In mainstream schools, slower learners are directed more to art, craft, drama and other practical skills areas than to subjects requiring extensive reading and writing abilities, the traditional 'academic' subjects. These programmes are often supported by classes in 'special English' or 'remedial' work. Most of these pupils also pursue courses in personal and social studies. Such courses can be excellent and, by the use of an imaginative and developmental pedagogy, develop the pupils' cognitive skills to a level of potential not previously thought possible; but they can sometimes be as narrow and limiting as other areas (HMI, 1986). In these latter circumstances, the pedagogy is of the formal 'chalk and talk' kind, often supplemented by extensive colouring and copying activities. Basic skills programmes, 'non-academic' routes and personal competencies curricula do not provide a balanced curriculum for pupils with learning difficulties.

Not surprisingly, many pupils question the relevance of a basic skills programme and perceive it as narrow, different and of low status (Montgomery, 1984). Those who were 'extracted' from their ordinary classes to join 'special' and 'remedial' groups showed shame and hostility to this type of treatment. The pupils told Simmons (1986) that 'the teachers must live in cloud cuckoo land' if they thought that other pupils did not deride them for being in the 'special' group or class. It is not surprising that pupils with learning difficulties in such situations may become disaffected, hostile and aggressive. They have little choice but to try to achieve recognition in other, often antisocial, ways or to opt out of school altogether as soon as possible.

Relevance is considered in ministerial pronouncements to consist of application to job and career prospects and is related mainly to vocational skills. This is too narrow a concept of relevance.

Differentiation

> The setting of different tasks at different levels of difficulty – these must be suitable for different levels of achievement or it allows us to set common tasks that can be answered in a positive way by all pupils (GCSE Guidelines, 1988).

Differentiation in the curriculum advocated by HMI allows for individual differences in pupils' abilities and situations to be catered for. Whilst in primary schools considerable efforts are made to do this, it is less likely to happen in secondary schools. The reasons for this are numerous. The primary teacher most often is the class teacher who is with the pupils all day and has extensive opportunities to get to know the pupils' needs and abilities and so tailor the task to meet those needs. The teaching groups are of mixed ability – although for maths and language they are most often set within the class by ability (Bennett, 1986) – and the teacher is well aware of the need to cater for the whole range. During a day there is time to work alongside each individual to monitor and evaluate progress and the responses to the tasks set. When teaching across the range of curriculum areas, it is possible to identify different patterns of strengths and weakness and make opportunities for pupils to achieve success in some area. This is important so that they do not feel they have failed the teacher. The orientation of primary schools is towards ensuring the developmental progress of pupils from one learning stage to the next in all curriculum areas. In secondary schools, on the other hand, the overriding emphasis is less upon the individual's progress than upon progressing through subject content towards a syllabus end. In the brief meetings it is less easy to get to know pupils' individual differences and to cater for them.

The extremes of these positions are the child-centred versus the subject-centred forms of education. There is, however, a third perspective in which the best features of both can be married: the *learning-orientated curriculum*. The individual's needs are matched to the demands of progression through the curriculum by the selection of an appropriate pedagogy. In this pedagogy, teaching methods, strategies and tactics will be geared to meeting the needs of groups and individuals in their pursuit of learning subject content and skills. There are many different perspectives on differentiation, each of which can apply to mainstream or special schooling and which a teacher needs to consider. It is common practice to teach to the middle of a mixed-ability group. It is assumed that by means of this strategy two-thirds of the children are reached. Most teachers then give 'the less able' extra attention to help them over any difficulties (Hegarty *et al.*, 1981). The able pupils in this scheme receive little or no attention at all.

An alternative to this approach is for the teacher, usually a primary teacher, to provide different levels of work in the different subject areas for groups of children in the same class. This is often on a rotating basis where the pupils move during the day through language, maths, creative studies and topic work. Introducing new material into the 'wheel' can prove tedious for the pupils and disadvantaging to the pupil with attentional, memory, language and thinking difficulties. He or she has unfortunately to wait for a series of different subject introductions to the work before starting. Some teachers avoid this problem by withdrawing groups to introduce new material, but this can prove distracting to those reading or engaged on worksheets who half-listen to the teacher. On some occasions an input given in the early part of the morning is not acted upon by a particular group until late in the day. Moreover, the groups working at different levels or tasks within the same subject area quickly develop a pecking order and know who is doing the easy work. In some classrooms this can provoke hostility and derision towards the group moving more slowly through the work, and of course is demotivating for them.

It is therefore understandable that for children with special needs an individually planned and developed programme for each pupil is advocated: 'Every child is on an individually tailored programme to suit his or her needs'. This is a claim most proudly made by many special needs teachers and is often much recommended in special needs texts. If, however, the pupils are observed on their individual programmes, it will be noted that much is rote activity under the guise of practice to fill time until the next input. It is often insufficiently cognitively engaging, although the pupils may be quietly absorbed. Individual programmes cut down upon legitimate social interaction and conversation about work problems. It is this aspect which, it will be argued, pupils with learning difficulties most need and which an individual programme denies them. Bennett's survey (1986) showed that pupils doing individual work in organised 'groups' engaged in little 'on-task' talk and when they did it was of a low order. Similar results are derived in individual programmes: talk is 'off-task' and social. On-task talk is geared to requests for loan of materials and factual information. Pupils in groups may also be perceived to have developed their own task strategies. Quite often one motivated pupil does the work whilst the others chat and then they copy down the answers. Other groups organise the more able or knowledgeable pupil to do the work and the rest copy the answers. As can be seen, educational goals are ignored or not understood by the pupils and they have evolved their own simple and 'person-effective' strategies for getting the correct answer and producing the completed page. Quiet classroom observation can reveal many such patterns and organisations.

The problems of differentiation were well articulated by Brennan (1979) as follows:

> If the curriculum is to be differentiated in order to meet the special needs of the slow learners, then at what point (if any) does the differentiation become a separatist device, in that it 'cuts off' the slow learner from the common aspects of the curriculum which contribute to cultural and social cohesion in our society?

Differentiation by group, task and level can be a separatist device, as can differentiation in the curriculum as a whole. Differentiation can create social stigma and deny pupils equal access to the same curriculum as other pupils. As such it presents a major equal opportunities issue. Separatism also carries with it economic and political implications. Leaving things as they are, however, and teaching to the middle is equally unsatisfactory. Both must be replaced if we are to help children with learning difficulties. *Differentiation in which all pupils can share in the same task and gain positively from it* is to be preferred, and this theme will be pursued in the next chapter.

Progression and continuity

Progression and continuity are also thought to be desirable characteristics of the curriculum for pupils from 5 to 16. They are sometimes difficult to achieve when pupils move from primary to secondary or from special to mainstream school unless there has been good liaison between the relevant schools and curriculum planning for transfer. Continuity is not always achieved even within an individual school, and it is not uncommon for a pupil with special needs to study an interest topic such as football every year throughout middle school (Surrey Inspectorate, 1983) because teachers have not liaised with each other on the curriculum and ensured that they have progression and continuity for all the pupils.

The document, *The National Curriculum 5–16* (DES, 1987a) sets out as one of its aims the rationalisation of provisions regarding continuity. Under its provision it is claimed that pupils would be able to move from one school to another both locally and on a national scale without hindrance or curriculum disadvantage.

The TGAT report (1988) elaborates on the notion of attainment targets and sets out ten levels in a range of subject areas through which pupils will be expected to progress during their years of compulsory schooling. The working parties established in the core subjects have been asked to determine the subject-specific targets and levels and will define an assumed normal rate of progression from one to the other. It is to be regretted that there was no special needs representation or expertise on these various committees, an omission which is both a political and an economic statement in itself. This is surprising when some 20 to 50 per cent of the school population (DES, 1978; SED, 1978; respectively) may be regarded as having special educational needs and when an increase in disruption in schools led the Government to set up a committee of inquiry in 1988 under Professor Elton.

Knowledge, concepts, skills and attitudes

The HMI document (HMI, 1981) identifies four elements which are also acquired: knowledge, concepts, skills and attitudes. Here there could be some dispute. It is difficult to distinguish knowledge from concepts. Knowledge means 'to know and understand', but this understanding is based upon our development of conceptual structures and hierarchies. Thus we might 'know' that the object we are sitting on is called a chair but, at the same time, we have abstracted a set of critical features (Farnham-Diggory, 1978) for 'chairness', in other words formed a concept by which we might identify other similar things. At first, we might put stools in this set because they are also sat upon, but we soon learn that they do not contain all the features required for chairness – they are not proto-typical (Anderson, 1980) – with back, seat and sometimes legs/plinths to raise the person off the ground. A concept, then, is an hypothesised mental structure by which we define, know and structure our world. Learning processes are thought to be the means by which we develop these concepts. They are called 'schemata' by Piaget (1952) and 'coding systems' by Bruner (1972). They are a higher form of knowledge. Knowledge of subject facts, however, may be passively absorbed or memorised and can remain inert, unable to be used or incorporated into any new or old conceptual framework.

Facts are lower-order cognitions than concepts. There are various types and levels of concept, for example:

- *chair* is both the name and an *object* concept;
- to *chair* a meeting represents an *event* concept;
- *chairs, tables and settee* belong to a group called *furniture* which is a *category* concept.

These three are all examples of *concrete concepts* and can be pointed to in the real world. This distinguishes them from *abstract concepts*, such as love, justice and equality, which can be defined only by giving complex, comparative, conceptual exemplars or by further verbal redefinition.

Constructs are developed from complex hierarchies of concepts and are used to view and define our world (Kelly, 1955). Attitudes form part of this construct hierarchy and determine ways of perceiving, understanding, and responding emotionally and behaviourally to the environment (Krech *et al.*, 1962; Bindra and Stewart, 1966).

Skills areas can be subdivided into perceptuo-motor routines – which may be subject-specific, such as titration in science and somersaulting in PE – and *cognitive skills*. These latter are extremely important in learning and teaching but are given scant attention in any report. Cognitive skills are the means by which we *manipulate* incoming information, facts and concepts in order to learn new information and develop new concepts, skills and understandings. It will be suggested in the subsequent sections that the development of concepts and cognitive skills are the crucial focus for concern if we are to help pupils with learning difficulties achieve anywhere near their true potential. In order to do this it will be necessary to examine teaching methodologies which facilitate such pupil learning.

Focusing upon subject content and how it should be delivered becomes secondary to determining which cognitive skill is going to be identified to cause the pupil to learn the particular content. It does not, however, ignore content for method: both are required. In the past it seems that cognitive development has been allowed to occur incidentally to subject learning. It is suggested here and elsewhere, on the basis of extensive work by the author with teachers and pupils in schools (Montgomery,

1982, 1983, 1984a, 1985), that only when we redirect our attention from subject teaching to pupils' learning can the aims in education be achieved. This requires a concentration upon a pedagogy which engages cognitive processes and skills so that pupils with learning difficulties can enjoy the full curriculum offered by ordinary and special schools.

The development of a teaching theory from grounded research

Over a period of many years, helping students in initial training and teachers on in-service courses plan lessons for pupils with and without special needs in ordinary schools, it has become apparent that there are two key approaches to helping learning take place. These are:

- offering learning experiences which 'engage brain' and so are geared at a suitable level for each individual;
- providing opportunities which require the pupils to talk as they are learning and so to direct and explain their own learning to themselves and others.

These experiences always prove to be more absorbing than more typical, content-based approaches, and the pupils often continue with them long after the lesson has ended.

In projects on 'homes', pupils were given details of climate and shown slides of terrain, tools and vegetation. They were then set to design the most suitable form of home for themselves to live in, given that for three months of the year there were monsoons. Pupils were set to discuss the problem in small groups of three and four and then to draft a design of the most suitable form of home for these conditions. They of course eventually proposed houseboats and homes on stilts. The relative merits of the two designs were discussed and decided upon. This problem-resolving style of learning proved to be much more involving and motivating for all the learners and, in contrast to Bennett's observations (1986), it caused genuine on-task discussion to take place in which pupils had to formulate ideas, ask questions and use extended language. It was learner-directed and learner-orientated so that individual differences were taken into account. This style of teaching contrasts favourably with the more traditional, expository (content) approach in which the topic is given as 'Homes on Stilts' and the pupil's task is to find out more about the dwellings and the lives of their inhabitants (food, tools, climate, etc.). The essential, intrinsic motivation – the resolution of a perceived problem – is missing in this second model. The pupils can and often do question why they are learning about such matters when such a content approach is used. After all, what is the relevance of homes on stilts to their own daily lives? After the initial novelty of looking at pictures there may be little genuine interest left. It is only by the curious, and those who are intrinsically motivated, that learning is pursued in such circumstances, the rest need some outside pressure, some extrinsic motivation, to maintain their interest or attention to the task. It has already been suggested that many children with learning difficulties lack this curiosity and intrinsic motivation to learn. This statement can be modified to suggest that children with learning difficulties do not find didactic methods helpful and have little interest in learning undigested and apparently irrelevant material. They could be right; they could point us in the direction of better teaching.

Evaluating pedagogical success – 'good' teaching

The successful match between the learner's needs and the curriculum offered can be said to be achieved *when the teacher has difficulty stopping the learning activity* rather than when he or she has difficulty maintaining it. This is a very hard test. Many teachers would argue that their pupils would learn nothing at all unless they were watched, reminded and *made* to learn. For pupils with special needs it is particularly important to try to apply this criterion: if they have to be 'made to work' then the content and/or method do not match the need. In many circumstances it may be perfectly clear that the content is appropriate; if the pupils still have to be made to attend to the work it can then be concluded that it is the method which is unsuitable or mismatched. In other circumstances the method is appropriate but the content is unsuitable. It is, of course, not only pupils with special needs for whom there is this failure to match to individual needs (HMI, 1981, 1983).

The transition from 'made to learn' to 'want to learn' is not easy. It is not achievable in an instant; it takes time to develop the new strategies to replace traditional activities and to apply the evaluative criterion. Two lesson-plan outlines follow which illustrate again the essential differences between the product or traditional expository style and the cognitive process, learner-orientated method. The pupils are 6–7 years old.

Traditional-style lesson (minimal version of product-orientated approach)

Lesson objective   To introduce standard units of measurement

Introduction (10 minutes)   Question-and-answer discussion with children on how to measure length and why we should use units that are all the same. Notion of standard unit introduced, rulers discussed.

Practical work (40 minutes) Children using, e.g. hand spans and rulers to measure and record various lengths, e.g. desk, books and cupboards.

Conclusion (10 minutes) Tidying up and checking results.

This would constitute a very poor lesson: telling information predominates and able pupils and those with previous experience are at a distinct advantage. The practical work is too loosely structured and of a rote kind. Pupils can do as much or as little as they please and no attempt is made to ask them to *estimate* first before measuring in order to try to develop the concept of length. The learning objectives need to be made more explicit to the learner.

Process-style lesson (cognitive process method)

Lesson objective To introduce standard units of measurement

Introduction: Practical (5 minutes) Pupils are requested to find out without using a single word or noise who has the largest and the smallest hands in the class.

Stage 1: Q/A (10 minutes) Results and how they were achieved are discussed. Children talk about direct experiences with the teacher and perhaps suggest more efficient ways of solving the problem on a future or similar occasion.

Stage 2: Rôle play (15 minutes) Two pupils with the smallest hands selected 'to serve in the imaginary shop' and three pupils with the largest hands to buy from them. The buyers are told that they will not find things in the shop satisfactory and that they should ask if they can have all their lengths of cloth measured in their own hand- or arm-spans. The sellers are quietly told to sell only in their arm- and hand-span measures. Other pupils should be watching. The 'play' is stopped when enough is achieved to establish the understanding of what is at issue.

Stage 3: Q/A (5 minutes) Pupils and teacher discuss what the real problem was between buyer and seller. The teacher asks how it could be resolved . . . standard units. Current standard units of measurement, e.g. centimetre, are introduced and their origin explained.

Stage 4: Practical (20 minutes) Strips of card and a 1 cm square

are given to each pupil. They are asked to design and make their own centimetre ruler. They may make it of any length: this will provide a useful teaching point next lesson.

Conclusion (5 minutes) Rulers are checked with each other to see if they are standard across the class, then any new problems are discussed and resolved. It is explained that the next session will involve pupils using their standard rulers.

Although the first lesson is very limited in cognitive content and would not be that advised by a mathematician, approaches of this nature are nevertheless commonly seen in classrooms. Major improvements could be made which would first involve using hand and foot spans to measure desks and classroom before introducing the concept of the standard unit. In the practical work, teachers could be advised to introduce estimation before measuring, but the children rarely grasp why and usually cheat. These two improvements are commonly made when students are trained to teach this aspect of the subject. Even so many of the pupils become so absorbed in the practical activity that they lose sight of the general purposes which measurement by spans and estimations seeks to achieve. In this expanded traditional or product-orientated approach, using spans and estimation would take up the first lesson, leaving the measurement with standard units to begin at about the same time as in the second example, the process approach. Thus it can be seen that the process approach does not require more time than most extended product-orientated methods. The minimal versions may be found in more formal school settings and where 'covering the syllabus' is an overriding objective.

If the learner's experiences in the two approaches are examined, further contrasts can be noted. In the first approach, mental processes in relation to the establishment of concepts about measurement and units are taking place at a somewhat abstract level by verbal connections, a level quite unsuitable for most pupils with learning difficulties. It is easy for the able pupils to cope and by the end of the session most average pupils will have understood the message if it has been repeated several times. These inequalities in access to the daily curriculum can be seen to present insuperable barriers to many of our pupils. These increase over time, make later tasks inaccessible, and cause pupils to fail to learn and fall further behind. We could argue that they are *made to fail* and are doubly discriminated against by teachers' use of inappropriate teaching methods.

In the process model the pupils all begin the task with the

same experience. There is no reliance on able pupils having answers which they tell to the rest. The problems, the clues and the answers are all present in the direct and immediate experience of all the learners; they do not need past remembered experience to fall back on. If more time was needed for the concept to be deduced, discussion groups could be introduced after the rôle play to arrive at group solutions to present to the rest. This strategy could be useful when the whole group has learning difficulties.

When concepts are established in this fashion they become part of the pupils' construct system. They are accommodated to the pupils' own scheme of things. This is what is meant by Piaget (1952) when he discusses meaningful learning. Too often the expository methods by which we choose to teach pupils with learning difficulties are unsuitable and the content is a watered-down version of that used with able pupils. What is required is a method which is learner-orientated but suitable for all pupils, and enables mixed-ability teaching to become a reality.

The process lesson just described really did take place and all the learners in the mixed-ability group enjoyed the experience and grasped the essential points. In the class were four slow 6–7-year-old learners and one who was wholly unable to read, for, as he announced proudly, he was 'dyslexic'. Each of them could identify with the learning experience and the peer tutors. Each of them could take out of the learning experience what they needed to help them understand the concept. The able pupils most probably enjoyed the interpersonal variances even more and learned other things as well, but for those for whom the concept of the standard unit was essential all the evidence was there and immediate within their experiences. The teacher could point to it as a concrete example and use it as discussion material. It was not presented at the usual abstract, discursive level. When a teacher omitted the rôle play in the shop but did all the rest, simply explaining the need for standard units, all except the able pupils failed to grasp the essential concept. They were then asked 'Why are you guessing your length first?' and 'Why do we need rulers?' Their answer: 'Because Miss D said so'.

It is this and many similar experiences which have led to the synthesis of a teaching theory concerned with particular kinds of cognitive process in relation to the developmental needs and levels of the learner. The model is drawn in iconic representation in Figure 2.2, and principles and practices in relation to special needs teaching and learning are derived from it (Montgomery,

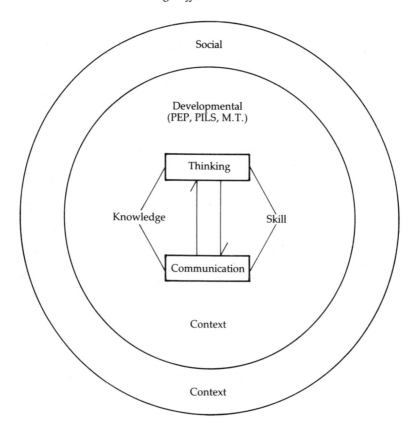

Figure 2.2 *A model of modern teaching (Montgomery, 1981a)*

1981a, 1982). It is used to underpin the design and development of teaching materials and learning resources for able and gifted pupils, for slow learners, and for mixed-ability groups, all in ordinary settings (Montgomery, 1985). It is a model that can facilitate differentiation in which all pupils can participate in the task in a positive fashion.

In this model it is argued that the two central objectives in teaching across the ability and subject range are:

- to enable the pupils to think efficiently;
- to enable them to communicate those thoughts succinctly, whatever mode of communication is desired – verbal, sign-ing, body posture, graphic, artistic, numerical and so on.

Thinking processes

Telling children information is regarded as a product-orientated approach in which known information is associated with new information by verbal connections. Teaching, it is argued, should be a process-orientated approach which causes new information to be incorporated into old knowledge structures and either reinforces what is known (assimilation) or causes it to change or be restructured to encompass the new (accommodation) (Piaget, 1952). This seems to occur best when the learner is allowed to operate on the material to be learned in an action-orientated fashion and when he or she is placed in a state of 'active uncertainty' by having a problem to resolve. In this way the new information, selectively used, can create some form of satisfying closure.

Incorporated into the general theoretical framework linking subject knowledge and skills with the overall cognitive process emphasis are principles and practices derived from Bloom's taxonomy of educational objectives (1956). A description of the major categories in Bloom's cognitive domain are set out in Table 2.1.

Table 2.1 *Descriptions of the major categories in the cognitive domain (Bloom et al., 1956)*

(1) **Knowledge** Knowledge is defined as the remembering of previously learned material. This may involve the recall of a wide range of material, from specific facts to complete theories, but all that is required is the bringing to mind of the appropriate information. Knowledge represents the lowest level of learning outcomes in the cognitive domain.

(2) **Comprehension** Comprehension is defined as the ability to grasp the meaning of material. This may be shown by translating material from one form to another (words or numbers), by interpreting material (explaining or summarising) and by estimating future trends (predicting consequences or effects). These learning outcomes go one step beyond the simple remembering of material and represent the lowest level of understanding.

(3) **Application** Application refers to the ability to use learned material in new and concrete situations. This may include the application of such things as rules, methods, concepts, principles, laws and theories. Learning outcomes in this area require a higher level of understanding than those under comprehension.

(4) **Analysis** Analysis refers to the ability to break down material into its component parts so that its organisational structure may be understood. This may include the identification of the parts, analysis of the relations between parts and recognition of the organisational principles involved. Learning outcomes here represent a higher intellectual level than comprehension and application because they require an understanding of both the content and the structural form of the material.

Table 2.1 *continued*

(5) Synthesis Synthesis refers to the ability to put parts together to form a new whole. This may involve the production of a unique communication (theme or speech), a plan of operations (research proposal) or set of abstract relations (scheme for classifying information). Learning outcomes in this area stress creative behaviours with major emphasis on the formulation of new patterns or structures.

(6) Evaluation Evaluation is concerned with the ability to judge the value of material (statement, novel, poem, research report) for a given purpose. The judgements are to be based on definite criteria. These may be internal criteria (organisation) or external criteria (relevance to the purpose) and the student may determine the criteria or be given them. Learning outcomes in this area are highest in the cognitive hierarchy because they contain elements of all of the other categories, plus conscious value judgements based on clearly defined criteria.

One way of using this set of descriptions is to apply them to the construction of syllabuses and to the development of teaching and learning objectives in relation to those syllabuses, as in BTEC courses. This has led in some cases to an overemphasis on the hierarchical nature of Bloom's categories and an attempt to structure syllabuses in a similar taxonomic fashion. Students thus enter at the lower levels of knowledge, comprehension and application and are perceived as competent to operate only at the higher levels of synthesis and evaluation after many years of schooling. This has been an approach adopted in a number of North American courses (Clarke, 1984). It heavily reinforces, of course, the content approach to the curriculum. What we have found when taking process methods into local schools is that if the situation is well prepared we can enable many 5- and 6-year-olds to move through all of Bloom's levels in the course of their learning. We have many instances of mixed-ability classes in the 5–13+ range where all learners have operated at each of Bloom's levels in turn, often astounding their peers and their teachers.

Evaluating curriculum materials and methods

When applying Bloom's criteria for the evaluation of curriculum materials, it will be found that there needs to be a close and careful examination of precisely what he means by each category. For example, the analysis of a word into component phonemes, b–e–d, and its resynthesis as be–d, b–ed or b–e–d for spelling, does not comply with Bloom's criteria for analysis. His analysis involves splitting into component parts and determining the rules governing the relationships between the parts. A pupil sounding out a word is operating to a prescribed format for splitting words, a serial process to give clues to meaning. Other clues gained from the sentence structure or an adjacent picture may enable the word to be predicted accurately from these context clues, together with the sounding-out process. This form of analysis would approximate to the comprehension level in Bloom's taxonomy. This does not mean to say that some forms of analysis of words for spelling might not approach the analytic level, for example learning to spell 'separate' correctly may involve noting the prefix *se* and its meaning, finding the Latin root 'pare', noting that to *part* or *pare* reflects the meaning of the whole word, and recombining root and suffix se–pare. This procedure can fix the correct spelling in the mind and has proved a very successful strategy for remediating student misspellings. It is one of the twelve cognitive strategies for remediating misspellings which will be described in Chapter 5. The writing of imaginative stories can present a similar problem in relation to synthesis. Story-writing for most pupils, unfortunately, can consist of the recombination of old ideas and experiences in sequential order, a transformational activity reaching applications level only rather than synthesis. Similarly, the words 'judge' and 'evaluate' are used in relation to objectives set for pupils in curriculum activities but what is observed most often is the pupils giving an opinion, sometimes supported by evidence. An example of evaluating would be where a set of criteria for the judgement of essays were established from A down to E on a 12-point literal scale. Each part of the scale would have a set of describers showing the level and quality of work to be assigned that grade (Montgomery, 1983a).

In summary, in the cognitive process-orientated approach, the attention of the teacher must refocus on the learner and how he or she can most successfully and pleasurably learn. The curriculum content becomes subordinate to this end and the learner is able to be more autonomous, working for personal internal and externally directed goals. This is moving towards the rational–logical teaching model advocated by the philosopher Hirst (1968).

There are four main types of approach suggested to teachers to achieve these ends:

- the problem-solving and problem-orientated approach to the curriculum, incorporating Bloom's cognitive objectives;
- the cognitive study skills approach, including DARTS – Directed Activities Related to Texts (Schools Council, 1980);

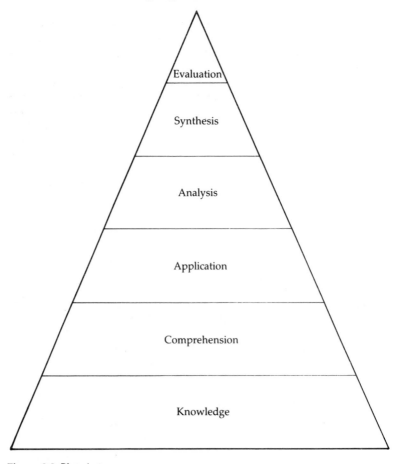

Figure 2.3 *Bloom's taxonomy*

- the language experience mediation approach (Bowers and Wells, 1985);
- games and simulations.

In the next section we shall look at the first three of these in turn.

SOME APPLICATIONS OF COGNITIVE PROCESS METHODOLOGY

Problem-solving approaches

When most curriculum materials, and even enrichment projects for able pupils at infant, junior and secondary stages (e.g. the

Essex Materials or the Middle Ages Project by Nene College), are closely examined (Montgomery, 1985), it will be found that few reach beyond Bloom's third level, that of application. If the teacher intervenes and questions pupils on the materials, higher levels can sometimes be achieved, especially with the question 'Why?' But the materials are intended to be used by pupils independently and so evaluation and synthesis are rarely achieved. In planning cognitive process curriculum activities, situations need to be set up in which pupils *are given some information* but then asked to use it in different ways, to transform it, to apply rules and criteria, and to develop new and different products and processes on the basis of their operations and activities. This is best demonstrated in examples from our own and other projects.

The work began with the development of enrichment materials for able children in mixed-ability classrooms, but it was quickly found that all the pupils could use and benefit from them. This was particularly so when instead of leaving them to their own devices the teacher played a full part in the teaching and learning, just as in the general problem-solving approaches with which we began. The children with learning difficulties also had the opportunity to enjoy the activities and to shine amongst their peers.

A good example of materials where pupils are required to operate at all the levels in the hierarchy is illustrated by the Motorway Project produced by the Maidenhead Group of Teachers (1985) and published by LDA (Learning Development Aids). The materials were intended as an enrichment pack for able pupils in the upper-junior and middle school. When the teacher works with the pupils, helping them read the materials and organising the groups, all the pupils in a mixed-ability class can participate. Similar results are found with the Newspaper Project from the Kingston Polytechnic Learning Difficulties Project. The example, 'Mediaeval Castle Building' (Figure 2.4) derives from the *National Association for Curriculum Extension and Enrichment Newsletter* (Mordecai and Lloyd, 1988).

History lessons on castles and monasteries more typically used to take the form of making notes about castles, answering questions upon them and drawing or tracing pictures to put in folders. This NACE problem-solving approach proves very exciting and motivating to all learners when a little more structure and support is available if needed to get pupils started.

PROBLEM RESOLVING STRATEGY

MEDIAEVAL CASTLE BUILDING

PROBLEM:—

" It is 1280. You are King
Edward I's master mason
and you have been told to
design and organise the
building of a new castle
at David in North Wales"

INFORMATION GIVEN:
- Labour force details
- Materials, equipment, payments
ISSUES:
- Defence,   ● site of Gatehouse,
- round or square towers, ● number
  of crenellations ⌐⊓⌐, ● windows
- doors etc.   Cost of slits & doors.

Figure 2.4 *Problem-resolving strategy: 'Mediaeval Castle Building'*

Cognitive study skills and process method

Study skills are a form of self-directed learning. When a chapter in a book is read in order *to use* the information obtained, then study skills of some kind are being used to extract the relevant information. This is termed *reflective* reading in the DARTs project (Schools Council, 1980). When reading a novel for pleasure, or a newspaper to pass the time, the text is easier and as our eyes flow over it we extract meaning simultaneously without pausing. This is termed *receptive* reading. Neisser (1967) has called such receptive or fluent reading 'externally guided thinking'. If, however, we try to apply this strategy to school texts, comprehension will begin to fail, for these materials are more dense and difficult, with several concepts and constructs to each sentence. In order to understand, according to the Schools Council researchers (1980), pupils would have to stop and reflect upon what they were reading. They would engage in the 'broken read', which the DARTs programme is designed to induce.

Information skills

Information skills are *forms of study skills* and can be called *search skills*. Many examples are described in the University of Lancaster project (CERD, 1980). The skills involve learning to use a dictionary, indexes, directories and so on. In other words they are the skills for locating information. Cognitive study skills involve not only locating but also extracting the relevant information, concepts and principles from amongst competing sets of data and using them in relation to a specific purpose.

Different types and levels of study skill are needed for different tasks and can be applied to verbal, written, diagrammatic and filmed material, to events, simulations and rôle play. They are *not* restricted to textual material, although the following examples do refer to text.

Survey, Question, Read, Recite, Review: SQ3R (Johnson, 1964; after Robinson, 1962)

This is often claimed to be a higher-level study skill but it is really only an *organised memorising method* for tests and examinations. It is extremely tedious to pursue and few pupils with learning difficulties have sufficient motivation in the first place to persevere. It is to be avoided as a method of learning. If it is required it demonstrates that earlier teaching has been unsuccessful. In other words material has not been accommodated and product rather than process methods of teaching have been used.

S = Survey:	Glance over headings in, e.g., a chapter and note points which are to be developed.
Q = Question:	Turn each heading into a question to direct the following.
3R = Read, Recite, Review:	Reading in order to answer your questions, turn away from the book and try to recite the answers to your questions. When chapter is complete, review the notes made in the survey.

Robinson in his research advised that the technique is not easy to master and gave detailed instructions for practice. For most school and college purposes SQ3R is not really necessary if the pupils have successfully accommodated what is in the material presented. Half-hearted attempts at SQ3R in practice often result in pupils committing large chunks of text to memory which they then relate parrot-fashion with little understanding in examinations.

Cognitive study skills

The activities in which pupils might engage to use some cognitive skills are:

- reading for the main point (or studying visual material for its main point);
- outlining main, subordinate, co-ordinate and irrelevent points;
- constructing a mnemonic from the main points;
- summarising;
- flowcharting;
- mapping – writing down the main idea in the centre of the page and then attaching strings of ideas and connections to it;
- diagramming;
- modelling;
- evaluating;
- engaging in critical comprehension activities;
- classifying;
- sequencing;
- restoring concepts and ideas which have been deleted to reconstruct the meaning of material;
- tabulating;
- rôle playing and simulating.

Two examples follow; others may be found in Royce-Adams (1977), Schools Council (1980) and Montgomery (1983a).

Reading for the main point

> *Discuss in pairs.*
> With a food surplus, the Pueblos were able to turn their attention to other activities besides locating or growing food. In one particular area – pottery making – the Pueblos developed a high degree of artistry. Potters became artists and developed individualised techniques, painting fine-lined geometric designs as well as reproductions of life forms on their vessels. Paints were improved and pottery has been found that contains three or four different colours.
> From *Columbus to Aquarius* (Dryden Press, 1975)

Answer: *'With a food surplus'*.

Reorder to give the correct sequence

> *Renumber after discussion in pairs.*
> Lighting the Bunsen burner:
> (1)   Light taper
> (2)   Open air-hole
> (3)   Stand burner on asbestos mat
> (4)   Close air-hole
> (5)   Turn on gas
> (6)   Light gas

Answer: *(3), (4), (1), (5), (6), (2)*.

The careful reading and discussion required to do these tasks and persuade others to agree with you means that in the process both the main ideas and many of the details have been learnt. Successful learning can be determined by asking the pupil to explain the answer to others so that they can also understand it.

Analytic procedures can be applied to other curriculum content areas as well as to skills acquisition and are particularly useful in relation to *cognitive scripts* (Anderson, 1980), such as story schema.

Script analysis

It is usual for teachers to explain to pupils that they must make their stories 'have a beginning, middle and end', without defining with the pupils exactly what this might mean in the particular context. We have found it helpful to apply 'script analysis techniques' to such activities and use these to help the pupils to write their stories and to plan their experiments and topic work. Teachers find the most surprisingly good results can in this way be achieved by children with learning difficulties and low motivation. For the first time, they have a structure which helps them formulate and fully express their ideas.

Using the schema notion of stories having a beginning, middle and end, beginnings (first lines and paragraphs) of some of the pupils' favourite stories can be copied for them to study and to decide in pairs whether they are time, place, atmosphere, person, climate or event beginnings. They might also try to work out which book they came from and then what the middle and end sections of the story were about. Pairs or individuals can then prepare different story schema beginnings for the same title to practise their newfound knowledge. In discussion with a partner, they can then develop one of the best of these for a story-writing session. When this is complete (the writing down or word processing can be shared or done by the more fluent scribe), the process can be repeated for the middle section of the story. Again, a series of extracts or readings from short story middles can be discussed, this time with the teacher as they are more detailed and complex. Middles selected need to illustrate introduction of character(s) and participants, plot (and, with older pupils, sub-plot) event sequence, atmosphere, place change and so on. Similar exercises can be given with respect to endings and pupils can try to decide what the plot was and who the characters were or how it all began. Research on such strategies and their effectiveness is just becoming available (Simon, 1986).

It is extremely important that teachers study story schemas and practise outlining them so that story-writing skills can be taught to their pupils. Able pupils and those who read widely acquire implicit knowledge of schemas which they incorporate into their stories; other pupils benefit greatly from being directly taught. Serendipity and incidental learning must not be the ways in which we leave pupils to uncover these things for themselves, for some of them may give up long before they do so.

Script analysis underlies many of the activities undertaken in practical science and mathematics. Experimental procedures with 'apparatus, method, results and conclusions' can be used as scripts for both undertaking and recalling what was done. Historical texts can be explored using script analysis of events in the past, and at a more complex level can be drawn up from the positions of opposing sides. Evolutionary and geographical scripts can also be defined and then the expansions of the scripts researched and written in. These activities resemble the cognitive approaches to study skills already outlined.

Problem-orientated approaches and cognitive study skills offer many opportunities for the pupils to engage in both thinking and communication activities, either in pairs or organised as small-group work. The communication skills are first developed orally and will involve the use of extended utterances rather than one-word answers to teachers' questions. Negotiation and social skills are also required to resolve any differences between pairs and the larger group. Although in the early stages pupils will need help to handle the presentation and reception of the ideas of others, they very quickly learn to listen and give each other time. Too often schools have been criticised by HMI for their lack of attention to developing oral language. These techniques can enable teachers to undertake more oral work whilst they provide a means for overcoming the problem of having only one teacher to listen to 30 or so individuals who all need to be encouraged to express their ideas in an extended fashion (Kerry, 1979). More traditional group work, when carefully observed, is found to consist of individuals sitting in groups engaged on identical tasks and *making social chat*, seldom about the work in progress (Bennett, 1986).

Language experience mediation methods

The third cognitive process method, the language experience mediation approach, is much used in the management of disruptive behaviours (Bowers and Wells, 1985; Rawlings, 1989). The strategies involve listening skills, developing a co-operative working environment, and negotiation and problem-solving related to specific learning contents and to social and personal issues (e.g. 'What are our rights?', 'Coffee-bar incident', 'Broken eggs, broken squares' (see Appendix 3, pages 243–4), 'Co-operative monsters'). Language experience methods are frequently content-free. The pupils supply contents from their own experiences *or* discuss their responses to tasks they were set. For example they might be told the story of Little Red Riding Hood from the Wolf's angle. The purpose of this is to get them to think about things that happen from other people's points of view. This can lead to imaginative reconstruction of common playground events and other famous stories with new perspectives. Inducing reflective thinking is part of helping them understand others and be more tolerant towards them. This process of reflection helps them tap into their metacognitions about feelings, attitudes and intentions.

Working in this fashion can produce the most surprising results. Slow learners turn out to be not at all as slow as they were perceived, hidden talents are revealed, and the potential and motivation for learning suddenly increase and seem unlimited. The pupils' self-confidence, articulateness and understanding grow beyond recognition. School becomes an enjoyable place to be. Pupils in one 'remedial' class of 11-year-olds reported, when their process method teacher left, 'We don't come to school on Fridays no more'.

Teachers themselves change when they have these experiences of pupils' achievements. They cease to have such low expectations of them and the new pupils they meet. They too rise to the challenge and try to find new ways to unlock a particular individual's potential. Student teachers in training who are enabled to have even a few of these learning experiences with pupils become much more capable of matching work to individual needs; they become more sensitive to them and determined to recreate that exciting experience again for both themselves and their pupils.

KNOWLEDGE AND SKILLS IN THE PROCESS MODEL

The emphasis on learning processes and learner-directed experience may suggest to some that the pursuit of these is at the expense of knowledge and skills. This is not so. Subject knowledge and subject skills have in the past occupied a central rôle in teaching theory. This theory was not so much explicit as implicit and used to guide teachers in their preparation of *what* pupils must learn to *cover* the syllabus. It has held sway for most of this century and is most prominent in the way parents and the public at large describe education. Process methods are *not* content-free. They use precisely the same contents and skills as the substrate of the children's learning experiences, for no one can think in a vacuum. It is the emphasis which has changed and thus knowledge and skills are not represented as the central objectives in the model (see page 64) but are essential to and subordinate to them.

DEVELOPMENTAL CONTEXT

The central objectives of the process model are embedded in the developmental context. This means that whatever is being planned for teaching must take account of the different developmental needs of individuals. The developmental perspectives include individual, perceptual, emotional, physical, personality, intellectual, linguistic and social developmental levels and needs. Each child will have his or her own pattern of developmental levels in each of these areas and so learner groups need to be carefully matched by the teacher to either complement or encourage individual differences. Even in groups which are 'streamed' or 'setted', and particularly those which are age-matched, there will be large developmental differences. Many of these differences, for example in emotional and social needs, can more effectively be catered for in process methods of teaching and learning (Brennan, 1979) than in product-orientated approaches, for there is a considerable emphasis on self-expression. Similarly, intellectual and linguistic developmental levels can be more easily matched. Knowledge of intellectual levels of development according to Piaget (1952) can provide useful guidelines for planning the presentation of material but it will be found that if the right learning opportunities are provided, pupils normally responding in pre-operational mode can give much more sophisticated responses. They are not stuck rigidly at a particular level as stage theory would predict.

THE SOCIAL CONTEXT

The cognitive and developmental aspects of the model are further embedded in the social context, particularly that of the new industrial revolution in which there are changes of great importance in the knowledge-based industries (Pym, 1980). Now knowledge can be accessed by computers on a large and increasing scale such that, according to Stonier (1981), many jobs in which keepers of information sell their knowledge to others are under threat. This has serious implications in the future for professions such as law, medicine and teaching if all they do is purvey information. Clients may well prefer to tap their cases into the terminals and receive advisory print-out sheets. If all teachers do is 'tell' information then in the future it may be more efficient for pupils to sit at home with interactive video and 'learn' this information, and only come to school for social events. Stonier (1981) developed a number of such scenarios in which product-orientated teachers are shown to be under considerable threat. What he and such others in his field as Pym (1981) and Johnson (1982) find is that industry itself requires major changes in its workforce to meet these industrial needs. For example, whilst companies in many instances require basic literary skills, they urgently need people who are able to listen to instructions and explain them to someone else. They need people who are more thoughtful and who have flexibility in their thinking. They need more creative employees and people who have good social and communication skills. Our secondary schools, they maintain, have not been noted for their ability to produce such skills in the majority of their pupils. It is here too that the process approach can provide a better match between the needs of the society in which we live and the skills of its workforce.

The experientially based method described seeks to free pupils from the limitations of their immediate social circumstances, to demonstrate that good teachers can make a difference (Hegarty *et al.*, 1981; Swann, 1987), that education can compensate for society, in contrast to Bernstein's early findings (1970), and that children with learning difficulties can have access to the ordinary curriculum and participate fully in it.

THE HIDDEN CURRICULUM FOR CHILDREN WITH LEARNING DIFFICULTIES IN PRODUCT-ORIENTATED CLASSROOMS

The hidden curriculum for pupils with learning difficulties is to instruct them that they are not able to cope and that they are too stupid to understand what their peers understand of the daily content of lessons. They therefore feel failures, become failures, grow disheartened and cease to make an effort (Dreeben, 1968; Hargreaves, 1978). Because of this failure their peers and teachers perceive them as dull and incompetent. The pupils may respond by becoming alienated and disruptive, thus gaining esteem from peers in another way. Sympathetic teachers give these pupils extra individual time or work of a simpler level to help them over difficulties. Others may provide an individualised and differentiated curriculum (Hegarty *et al.*, 1981). This hidden curriculum discriminates against pupils with learning difficulties for other pupils again see these differences in treatment and can regard the recipients as inferior. This argument will be developed further in the next chapter; it too needs further expansion for it is not a popular view.

Unhelpful attitudes to children with learning difficulties may be reinforced further by teachers who refer to the 'slow table' or the 'red table' in primary school and the 'thickos', the 'non-academic', the 'slow' and 'remedial' groups in secondary school. Although most teachers do not use insulting labels to refer to pupils, some may show a negative attitude to learning difficulty by becoming angry when asked to repeat information or sarcastic when points have not been understood or remembered. The hidden interpersonal message in all this is that these pupils are *not important* although they have the greatest needs. Such inequalities in treatment and thereby of opportunity are rife in education at all levels (Barton and Tomlinson, 1984). The principles which seem to operate are 'to those who have shall be given', or 'most approval and support should be given to those who already are the most advantaged'. This is something teacher educators must tackle. These positive attitudes by teachers to able pupils but not to others are not surprising, for when a pupil learns what the teacher has attempted to teach it is reinforcing and supportive to the teacher. Failure to learn presents negative information to the teacher, who is then much more likely to seek to support and interact with those who give positive information in interpersonal encounters (Good and Brophy, 1972). There may thus be a withdrawal of support for children who are failing and a distancing from them by some teachers. The issue of the hidden curriculum, of teachers who are discriminatory in either a sympathetic or a negative way, cannot be adequately resolved until a complete revision of teaching theory and method for all pupils has taken place. Although many surveys of good practice have now been undertaken, and more are promised with the aid of further research, what seems instead to be needed is a series of carefully controlled experimental studies to evaluate different theories and practices in teaching.

SUMMARY AND CONCLUSIONS

In order to help all pupils to learn and fulfil more of their potential, it is proposed that teachers and teacher trainers direct their attention to two central objectives in teaching all curriculum subjects: to help the pupils think efficiently and then to help them communicate those thoughts succinctly. These practices form the central thrust of the cognitive process model and are guided by a cognitive and humanistic psychology in which in recent years a large number of advances have taken place in knowledge of how children learn.

Nothing is new, of course, and many earlier researchers such as Taba (1962), Taylor (1970) and Gray (1970) have argued for a cognitive approach to the curriculum, whilst philosophers such as Hirst (1966) have emphasised that we *are* our concepts and that education should seek to produce rational–autonomous beings. Looking even further back, one finds in Rousseau the following recommendations about the education of Émile and other young people which coincidentally epitomise the style of education suggested in the foregoing:

- real needs rather than artificial ones should be satisfied;
- quality of learning is more important than quantity;
- direct experience is preferable to book learning and research and discovery preferable to formal instructions (the pupils learn more when the teacher talks less);
- pupils should study only what they can understand and perceive to be useful (teachers need to show pupils the relevance and purposes of what they are doing very much more);
- when they cannot be shown the value of an activity it should be deferred unless present necessity requires it;
- they should *wish to do what they do* rather than what they wish (it is an essential part of the teacher's rôle to motivate pupils to want to learn).

A general guideline for evaluating the effectiveness of teaching has been suggested – the extent to which pupils *want* to learn as opposed to having to be *made* to learn – and this too is embodied in Rousseau's principles. It is not, however, being suggested that pupils will be doing exactly as they please and learning in a random fashion. What seems to have happened with Émile was a shortfall between the principles established for his education and the practices at the hands of an untrained tutor. It has also to be remembered that what can be undertaken in a one-to-one tutorial setting is different from school teaching. The setting in which most teachers find themselves is the large group or class of 30–40 pupils. Here methods need to be different although principles can remain the same.

The selection of an appropriate pedagogy to match the needs of pupils with learning difficulties is an equal opportunities issue. Certain types of curriculum provision have been reviewed to show their underlying content emphasis and relation to expository modes of teaching, and it has been argued that such techniques do not allow children with learning difficulties to participate as fully as they should in classroom learning. Instead a cognitive process pedagogy has been developed to show how any curriculum material can be presented so that all pupils may participate in the same task in a positive fashion and achieve the learning goals. This form of differentiation is recommended rather than that which places too heavy an emphasis upon individually tailored programmes in which all the learning outcomes are defined by the teacher. There is a place for individualised programmes but they need to be set within the much broader context of learning if a pupil is to have access to the same full curriculum as others.

This text is mainly concerned with the ways in which the classroom teacher can provide for the needs of pupils with learning difficulties. Reference will be made to systems approaches and the ways in which patterns of provision are made, but for a more comprehensive survey of delivery systems and patterns of provision the reader should refer to Booth *et al.* (1988); Wolfendale (1987); Hegarty (1987); Hodgson *et al.* (1984); Clunies-Ross and Wimhurst (1983) and Hegarty *et al.* (1981).

There has been some discussion in this chapter on general principles, practices and methods in special needs teaching with the suggestion of a framework for guidance to teachers. In the next chapter some research evidence which seeks to validate the claims made for the cognitive process approach will be presented, together with an evaluation of some current practices in schools.

A discussion of some practices and research on helping children with learning difficulties

INTRODUCTION

It has been proposed in Chapter 2 that a cognitive process approach to teaching pupils with learning difficulties would be appropriate to cater for their main special needs. This proposal needs to be set against current developments and practices in the educational field to give some feeling of the context in which we are working.

The cognitive process pedagogy requires that the teacher should specify, for the lesson plan and for the pupil, the key concepts and skills which the learner is intended to acquire. Methods of teaching should then be drawn up into a tactical lesson plan with clearly defined *learner* activity changes throughout the timed sequence, e.g.

Listening → Talking → Recording → Reading → Reporting → Practical → Recording → Discussing.

In this sequence, talking, reporting and discussing would be slightly different modes of interaction using speech:

- When *talking,* children would perhaps be assembling their ideas and trying them out on each other.
- *Reporting* would involve presenting the ideas to the rest of the group in a coherent form.
- *Discussing* would include explanation, questioning and answering in dialogue with the group.

The activities should have the direct purpose of helping to form the concepts and acquire the skills which have been determined. The teacher is then able to diagnose the success or otherwise of the teaching method by observing the learner's performance on the various tasks and by direct questioning during the lesson.

If some pupils fail to acquire the concepts or skills then the teaching–learning strategy can be revised to match the learning need.

This type of approach is sometimes referred to as the 'assessment through teaching model' (Pearson and Lindsay, 1986). It involves a curriculum-based diagnosis of learning difficulties, with further teaching to complete the cycle of assessment and teaching. There are, however, variants of this model to be found within the field: for example between the 'skills versus abilities' training models (Stephens, 1976) and the behavioural objectives model (Ainscow and Tweddle, 1979) on the one hand (see Chapter 5), and cognitive and learning objectives emphases (Chapter 2) on the other. It should be noted that what is proposed is an *emphasis* on cognitive and learning objectives in the school curriculum, not that behavioural objectives should be avoided. Definition of, and teaching to, behavioural objectives can prove very useful within a narrower context and with individuals in ordinary schools who have learning blocks and learning failure, particularly in basic skills in reading, writing, spelling and number. Teaching to behavioural objectives has also proved effective in the area of basic social skills and adaptive competence, particularly with children with severe learning difficulties (Mittler and Mittler, 1982), although criticisms have been raised about the narrowness and the educational merits of this as a curriculum approach (Wood and Shears, 1986).

SURVEY RESEARCH ON THE PEDAGOGICAL ASPECTS OF PROVIDING FOR PUPILS WITH LEARNING DIFFICULTIES IN ORDINARY SCHOOLS

Hegarty *et al.* (1981) investigated the implementation of the curriculum for pupils with special needs in the ordinary school by mainstream rather than specialist teachers. They first pointed to the relative scarcity of information about techniques for educating such pupils and then went on to analyse the responses of teachers to a questionnaire which asked:

'Have you had to modify your teaching approach in any way (because of the presence of pupils with special needs)?' The majority of respondents, 49 per cent, replied 'Yes' to this. 29 per cent left this question unanswered because many of them did not teach pupils with special needs. Teachers indicated a range of ways in which they had modified their teaching approach, but most common were the two following approaches:

- give more individual attention, make more time, both personal and academic;
- simplify teaching, give instructions slowly and clearly, break content matter down to its components, work more slowly, set shorter objectives.

My general view of what these researchers reported is that some of the teachers evolved useful pedagogical strategies to include children with learning difficulties. In particular, the woodwork teacher's paired learning approach and the science teacher's group work and structured practical seem particularly important and successful strategies. It has been suggested that this type of collaborative learning is an important way of achieving many learning and teaching objectives. This approach has also been advocated for pupils who exhibit behavioural and emotional problems, to help them towards social integration (Kingston Friends Workshop, 1985; Masheder, 1986; Rawlings, 1989).

Teachers reporting difficulty in coping with pupils with learning difficulties are recorded as spending too much time on writing activities (HMI, 1986), on basic skills (Wilson, 1981) and on teacher-directed tasks which require individual attention from the teacher if the pupil is unsuccessful. Here the teachers complain of lack of sufficient time to attend to individual pupils' needs. This is understandable when the teacher has 30 other pupils who also need some attention. Consider the problems of competing attention when the whole class is working on individualised programmes. In these circumstances the children with learning difficulties and those who misbehave, often because they cannot cope with the work, absorb most of the teacher's time. The rest must get on as best they can. Practice activities and rest from work are often overextended to fill the time until the teacher can return. Questions need to be raised about whether all individual 'programmes' are equally effective and can be considered as examples of good pedagogy. Defining good teaching is not easy as recent studies of teacher appraisal have shown (Montgomery, 1984a, 1988; Graham, 1985; AMMA, 1986; Marland, 1986). It is not surprising therefore that researchers who are most often not teachers confine themselves to surveys of existing teaching practices, whether good or not. What is required is a number of controlled analytic studies of the relative effectiveness of different methods and models of teaching. Before this can be undertaken detailed descriptions of good teaching need to be assembled and their theory and practice analysed. Of recent note in this respect are descriptions of teaching children with special needs by Booth *et al*. (1987) and Hope (1986).

TEACHING STRATEGIES: EXPERIMENTS AND ACTION RESEARCH

Two central cognitive objectives in teaching were proposed in Chapter 2. In the section which follows, a teacher, Rene Judd, tries to test the validity of these objectives in her classroom, and Carole Cattermole tries out a pyramiding, teaching learning strategy.

An evaluation of the extent to which teaching to cognitive process objectives can help children with learning difficulties

The study arose because the head teacher of the school for children with moderate learning difficulties, having obtained a computer, wanted the pupils taught how to program it. This seemed to us to be a very tall order. . . . The pupils' experiences of computers extended to the usual skill games but none had a computer of their own at home. As a result of this period of observation and diagnosis, it was reluctantly concluded that the head's objectives were inconsistent with the needs and abilities of the children. If the pupils were to learn to program, it would need to be established as a long term objective whilst, in the short term, each one needed to learn to sequence their own thoughts and actions in daily life and in school tasks. Each one was assessed as being very much in the Piagetian stage of pre-operational thinking, i.e. were egocentric, impulsive, making motor responses to questions, and at an intuitive level of mental operation where they had difficulty explaining their ideas or actions in any logical order. It was decided that, as a first step, it would be necessary specifically to teach the thinking strategy of sequencing so that they learned to pre-program and order their own actions and ideas before expressing them. They would also need to have the relevance of this made explicit. Each learning experience would need to be direct and concrete so that the learner could 'be and do' these things and perhaps be enabled to learn. The emphasis of the lessons was directly upon teaching a thinking skill rather than a specific content but, of course, the lessons were not content free (based on Judd, 1982).

The subsidiary aim of the study was to extend and develop the group's expressive communication skills. This, it was thought, would be facilitated by providing extensive opportunities for the pupils to talk through what they were doing as they were doing it and then to spend time explaining and summarising what had happened after each event. By these means, it was hoped to develop expansion skills (de Bono, 1976) which would transfer to open-ended writing.

The design set-up was a pre and post test with a group of eight matched controls. The controlled design is particularly useful in research but can be extremely difficult for teacher-researchers to carry through. The eight children in the experimental group from the school for moderate learning difficulties were the whole class of 10–13-year-old boys. The control group of eight boys was randomly drawn from a local school in the same surburban area, from a mixed-ability class of 6–7-year-olds who had previously been taught by Rene. IQ data were not available for the control group to convert to mental age but the pupils seemed to be a homogeneous group of about average ability for their age. As can be seen, an attempt was made to match for area, sex, and cognitive ability expressed as mental age. As a result chronological age is invariably higher in the experimental group (see Table 3.1).

Table 3.1 *Mean chronological and mental ages*

	Children with learning difficulties	Control group
Mean chronological age	11 years 10 months	7 years 2 months
Mean mental age	7.4 years	7.2 years
	(IQ range 46–89)	Assumed mean

At the outset of the experiment, the pupils in the experimental group were asked about football and if they played it at home and school, or watched it on television. This was to check that they all had some practical working knowledge of the game. They were asked to imagine that ET (an extraterrestrial being) had come to visit them and wanted to know how to play. They were asked to write him a list of instructions to follow.

It had originally been planned that both control and experimental groups should describe playing a game such as snakes and ladders in the pre and post tests. It was found, however, that not all the experimental group knew how to play it and that the control group had already been doing some writing on football in the previous week. A compromise had to be made which spoiled the research design but which is typical of what can happen in field research. The pre and post test of the experimental group was on the game of football and the control group's was on snakes and ladders. Although they do not compare in complexity in the first instance, the instructions could be marked at a simple level for sequential order of ideas presented. The number of words used, words per sentence and total number of sentences were calculated to examine the capacity for expansion by the two groups and compared with Myklebust's 1965 norms for similar groups.

At the end of a period of eleven 1½-hour teaching sessions spread over 1½ terms, both groups were asked to describe again how to play football and play snakes and ladders, to discover if there had been any increase in the experimental group's abilities to write such instructions after training in sequencing skills and discussion about them. No teaching intervention was made with the control group, members of which were tested at the outset and at the end of the experiment. It was assumed that on the pre test their ability to do the task would be somewhat better and less haphazard than the experimental group's and would as a result of increasing maturation show some developmental improvement in skill over the intervening period. The control group's teacher was not given any information to suggest the nature of the investigation and her children's role in it.

Of note was the wide range of IQs found in the experimental group (49, 51, 56, 62, 72, 73, 89). This spread is not untypical of such groups; the more able pupils find themselves in the sheltered setting of the special school for a number of complex social and educational reasons.

Programme of teaching (examples)

Week 1 Pre test. Followed by groups of three to design a game and state rules of play. Hear results and discuss.

Week 2 Memory-span digit game. Play tape of noises; pupils note down what they are. Discuss with groups and note on board. Pupils to try to write a horror story using the noises to sequence it. Read out extracts to rest.

Week 3 Cards of child running a race distributed randomly. Pupils have to try to get themselves in the correct sequence. Discuss.

Banda sheets with picture of boy kicking a ball through a window. Pupils try to write down what is happening in each picture. Discuss their writing and stress pictures in sequence. Aim to expand descriptions orally. Pairs compose a story about the boy to tell to the police from a witness's point of view. Write down their story. Class debate as a jury to decide which tale is correct and what will happen to the boy.

Week 6   Children shown items of clothing. Clothing then put out of view. Order in which clothes to be put on is given orally. Children take turns to carry out the sequence.

Analysis of rumour – two children leave the room temporarily. The rest listen to an adapted comic strip story. One child enters the room, the group tell him the story. He then tells the story to the next child who was outside the room. Discuss how the story has changed, talk about rumours. Discuss the need for sequencing and expansion in story. Tell a rumour then ask pupils at random to expand and distort the tale.

Week 8   Children listen to a repeat sequence of clapped rhythms.

Ask children to make a small man from plasticine. Explain he is going on a journey round the classroom and that he has not been in the classroom before. Children are to explain what might happen to him and the hazards he has to negotiate. Then allow them to move their men round the room to see what happens to them, return and write a story of their adventures. Read out the points from all the children's work.

Week 9   More clapping rhythms shared. Children write briefly how to strike a match. Allow each in turn to call out their instructions and another child to perform. Discuss results! Explain that in 100 years' time people may have no need for matches.

Children write about the match and how to strike it to inform people. Like the 'Smash' advert.

Ask all the children to follow their own instructions in front of the group.

Week 11   Post test.

Some of the ideas in these lesson outlines were drawn from the *Early Language Programme*, written by Ainley and Clarke (1980) to help children in their school for children with learning difficulties develop improved language skills. As can be imagined, the pupils in this study had a very enjoyable time. The results of two typical subjects' work in the pre and post tests, Neil (experimental group) and Jake (control group), are shown in Figure 3.1(a) and (b).

The results showed a highly significant difference before and after training in the total number of words used by the pupils in the experimental group, who almost doubled their scores. There was a marked increase in the total number of sentences

(2)

Task 1   Pre-Test.

1 you get your bortes
2 and you and kickrhe
   ball ✓
3 you takell your ar
   aponant.
4 you get kick [n the leg
   Good work neil. it must hurt to get
   kicked in the leg!

(3)

Neil J

Monday February 15th
                    Post-Test.

How to play Football
1) Get chaged from your
   school clothes
2) cet in to your Football
   clothes -
3) put on your football
   socks
4) Then you put on you
   football boots on.
5) you warm up and kick
   the football.
6) the rerer tells the
   plairs to put the ball
   in the mibble.
7) The game brgins.
8) To beat the other side
9) you hat to skor a goal

Figure 3.1 *(a) Example of pre- and post-test data for experimental group*

Jake.   Pre - Test

first you put your counters on
the board. and then you throw
the dice. and you hafto get a Six
then you can Stert, and if you land
on a ladder you ...go up the ladder.
and if you land __on a Snake
you go down. and if you get a Six
you can have a nother go.

Jake   Post-Test

first you get the board out then
you get the Counters then you get the
dice and the Shaker. and you
Work your way to 100 from the
Stait. ~~We~~ When you get to a Snake
you go down.

Figure 3.1 *(b) Example of pre- and post-test data for control group*

used and in the number of words per sentence, although these did not reach statistical significance with such small numbers of items and subjects. The control group scores on pre and post tests declined slightly on each type of item on the post test, although this did not reach statistically significant levels. This is not an uncommon finding when using repeated measures in classrooms (Montgomery, 1979). The control group's motivation probably diminished somewhat on the second test, for they were doing the same task as before and it had lost both its novelty and interest as nothing had happened as a result of it in the interim.

When the sequencing abilities were analysed, there were no significant differences between the control group's pre and post test work but there was a highly significant improvement in the experimental group's work. This group's post test writing in the opinion of the researcher showed an improvement in ability to write down ideas in a logical order. In analysing these data, however, there was more judgement required on the part of the tester and so the results have to be treated with greater caution than the purely quantitative data used to assess expansion. What of course was incapable of assessment in any quantitative way was the general, all-round improvement noted in the pupils' confidence, self-esteem, ability to organise their approaches to other tasks and general raised level of motivation and interest. How much better it would have been, though, if the sequencing and expansion tasks could have been incorporated into the general programme of classroom learning rather than being 'bolted on' in this fashion in a piece of research.

This small-scale study is encouraging, suggesting that defining cognitive objectives for pupils with learning difficulties to achieve through experiential learning can enhance their academic achievements. If this were to be reinforced in all the curriculum areas, the pupils could be helped substantially to achieve far more than they have been previously allowed or encouraged to do. Rene Judd, in fact, goes on to describe later teaching sessions in cookery, science and computer games where sequencing and expansion were reinforced (Judd, 1982).

What can also be drawn from this study is the power of defining and teaching to *key* objectives. The emphasis here is upon the word 'key': rather than structuring a learning session by defining a hierarchy of behaviours which, if entered into, will enable the goal to be achieved, one gives the learner some autonomy and control over his or her own destiny but within a structure. It is less mechanistic than a formal behavioural approach and is perhaps more suitable to achieve the wider ends and purposes in education. It assumes neither that the learner proceeds in an entirely orderly fashion (Driver, 1988), nor that the teacher can and must specify all the sub-stages and steps towards achieving an objective.

Using pyramiding as a language and learning strategy

Carole Cattermole, a teacher in a comprehensive school, tried pyramiding with a second-year class which had already been identified within the school as a 'low-ability' group and was estimated to be in the bottom 10 per cent of the general ability range. Pyramiding has been found to be successful as a method of promoting thinking and language work through discussion, group co-operation and negotiation for both slow and able learner groups (Montgomery, 1985).

The class were first asked to work alone and write down in their rough books an answer to the question: 'Look at the signs on this page. Write down where you might expect to see each one of them: [e.g. NO SMOKING, FIRE ALARM, PUSH BAR TO OPEN, etc. (see Groves *et al.*, 1983, p. 41)]'. After about five minutes they were paired up to compare ideas and decide upon one answer for each. It was stressed that they needed to discuss any differences and to reach a mutually acceptable answer. All the pupils participated well at this stage. Pairs were made up into groups of four and then fours into eights. At this stage one of the girls commented, 'It's like building a pyramid', and was delighted when told that she was very clever to think so as the process was called 'pyramiding'.

Discussions became a little heated at the fours stage and again the need for giving reasons for answers reached was stressed. It was pointed out that *listening* to others' ideas was a very important part of the exercise. Despite some cries of 'Oh, no! Have we got to do it all again?' when moving into groups of eight, most entered into the discussions willingly and several commented that it was fun. Only one girl was reluctant to co-operate with the other seven in her group because they disagreed with her over one sign. This was not altogether surprising since she tends to consider herself superior to several of her classmates and does not like to be proved wrong. She had co-operated well up to this stage and this was likely to prove a good experience for her.

Finally the class was called together and a spokesperson from each of the two groups of eight put forward their group's ideas. They gave reasons for their decisions where different opinions were held and a list was made on the board of their final decisions. Some adjudication was required as each group were convinced they were right!

The teacher concluded that this was a very successful exercise as for once *all* the pupils had been able to contribute fully. She records:

> The groups had co-operated well and there was a lot of discussion. As the discussions progressed the locations became more precise and it was interesting to see who emerged as discussion leader/ organiser as the groups became larger. The class did enjoy it and there were many requests of, 'Can we do it again?' They were delighted when I congratulated them on their success in handling a 'sophisticated' process, which I had thought they were not able enough to cope with so sensibly. They are usually very difficult to cope with when trying to do class discussions. Most have something to say but *few are willing to listen* to others and are only too ready to interrupt and shout each other down.

Developmental Positive Cognitive Intervention (Developmental PCI)

Apart from direct cognitive process strategies used in teaching subject contents and skills through which a range of attitudes and values are imparted, teachers use many other cognitive strategies. One major but more indirect teaching strategy is Developmental PCI, in which the teacher focuses upon whatever content the child is working on and seeks to move the task into the cognitive realm or along towards a higher cognitive level. This is achieved through positively supporting and encouraging the current activity and then moving the pupils towards the next. A good example of this is illustrated below (Foster, 1971).

The teacher was working with a class of 11-year-olds within which were a number of slower learners. This group of pupils read hesitantly and were only just coming to terms with computational skills. Foster describes the situation familiar to many teachers where three of the boys were cutting card for stock and had trimmed up some coloured paper which had been used for display. They had enjoyed this routine, mundane activity:

> They had reached the stage when they were playfully shredding the waste material and this was obviously unproductive. The teacher went over to them. Her approach was totally positive. She did not reprimand them for the paper-shredding, but thanked them for their earlier efforts and suggested the following activities.
>
> 1. Divide the coloured paper into small, medium and large. Label the piles.

2. Take any odd-shaped pieces and cut them into squares and rectangles of a given dimension which they would decide after seeing the paper which was available. Label these sheets and give the dimensions.

3. Count the cards, sort them for size and label these, giving dimensions where there were sufficient of one size to warrant this.

What the teacher had done was to intervene in an unfruitful activity, build on another useful one, and provide a task which involved some of the mathematical skills in which they needed practice. The teacher was aware of the need for skills practice, and allied this to the other, more isolated activity (Foster, 1971, p. 4).

The teacher was able to incorporate an isolated individual learning experience into a planned sequence of learning, redirecting the pupils' motivation and interest into a more constructive educational activity. The pupils could see the relevance between the two.

It is often this more unobtrusive method of teaching which makes one teacher a success and another who does not engage in it prone to failure with difficult classes. The technique can help pupils perceive the relevance of the ordinary curriculum and convert potential misbehaviours into constructive activities. It is these activities which add to the complexities of lessons which untrained observers do not always know how to record. They are nevertheless a major contributor to effective teaching, as observed in our appraisal research (Montgomery, 1984a; Montgomery and Hadfield, 1989).

LOWER ATTAINING PUPILS' PROGRAMME (LAPP); SURVEY FINDINGS FROM THE FIRST TWO YEARS (DES, 1986)

Recent HMI inspections have contributed substantially to our knowledge and understanding of what takes place in schools and the needs of the pupils in them. In particular, their reports have shown that, although efforts have been made both before and since the raising of the school leaving age in 1973 to help low attainers, progress has been slow in this field. Two major HMI reports, *Aspects of Secondary Education* (HMI, 1979) and *Slow Learning and Less Successful Pupils in Secondary Schools* (HMI, 1984), served only to confirm this view. They reported that the curriculum for these pupils was most often narrow, undemanding and seldom pitched at a level and in a form which demanded worthwhile achievements whilst retaining interest.

Purposes and pathways were unclear and expectations of staff and pupils were set at the lowest levels. Educational objectives were often underemphasised or substituted for maintaining goodwill and pastoral welfare. This could be viewed as a containment strategy for dealing with problems and is moving towards the situation described by Brennan (1985) in which he finds special schools providing warmth and refuge from the learning failures the pupils had previously experienced.

It was in this context that the then Secretary of State announced his concern for the 'bottom 40 per cent' and, in September 1983, provided £2 million per year to fund development programmes for which all LEAs were invited to make proposals. Twelve projects were set up in 1983 with the purpose of improving the educational attainments of pupils mainly in the fourth and fifth years of secondary school. These were pupils who it was deemed were not fully benefiting from school and for whom the existing examination structures at 16+ were not designed. The improvement was to be achieved by: 'shifting their education away from narrowly conceived or inappropriate curricular provision and teaching styles to approaches more suited to their needs and by giving a practical slant to much of what is taught; to prepare them better for the satisfactions and obligations of adult life and the world of work; and to improve their self respect and motivation' (HMI, 1986, p. 3).

Because not all the issues were understood and there was no measure of agreement about how to achieve these ends, developmental projects rather than a national programme were funded. The new examination system, the General Certificate of Secondary Education (GCSE), could not be included in the survey, for the courses were not yet being designed in the project schools.

The 'lower-attaining pupils' in the programme included those with lower abilities than the norm, those with specific learning difficulties, those who were poorly motivated and therefore low in achievement, and those whose achievements were low as a result of poor attendance and visual difficulties or other handicaps. Each LEA devised its own criteria and selected its preferred groups so that a range of provision was seen. One school deemed all its pupils low attainers, others could not include all they had identified, some were pupils from the renamed remedial groups, and others ran mixed-ability groups in their project. The HMI survey criticised both the selection and evaluation procedures of the institutions as insufficiently detailed to be capable of differentiating accurately individual needs and responses.

The general curricular programmes which resulted from the investment were similar to those offered to other pupils, but overall there was a neglect of aesthetic education, in particular in music, drama and art. Practical activities were defined in a narrow, manipulative sense and HMI concluded the curriculum lacked balance and breadth. This is similar to the criticisms made by Brennan (1985), reporting on his survey of the curriculum for special schools.

The general criticisms made by HMI (1986) concern the failure to improve the quality of thinking of the pupils in the programme. Although this was often a central objective, they concluded that 'there was still some way to go in changing teaching methods to achieve this' (p. 12). Other extracts from the HMI survey are also of interest in relation to the proposed pedagogical changes for children with learning difficulties. Despite the fact that special funding was directed to improve the pupils' attainments, self-respect and motivation the HMI results showed that these aims were not always met:

> Many pupils had seen much of their school work in the past as pointless and it proved difficult to change this view. One approach to overcome this problem was to discuss a given task in more depth with individual pupils and to draw attention explicitly to the reason for it and its present value to the pupils . . . (p. 20)
> A girl, well known to teachers as 'difficult', showed a similarly impressive degree of motivation in her response to organising the school's snack bar . . . (p. 22)
> Pupils responded well to what they regarded as 'useful' knowledge and skills, if these were taught in an interesting fashion. Pupils and staff did not always share the same view of relevance . . . (p. 23)
> In many cases teachers . . . seized too readily on whatever seemed to interest and occupy the pupils instead of selecting what would enable them to achieve a precise curriculum objective . . . (p. 24)

Talking with pupils so that they grasped relationships proved effective. On a one-to-one basis with the teacher this can prove time consuming, whereas pyramiding, a different pedagogical strategy, does not and can effect the same results. Talking with pupils as individuals and offering them responsibility in a practical way increased their motivation and showed teachers a different and capable side of them. This indicated that there was great untapped potential in pupils. Although teacher training tries to impart this knowledge and these values about pedagogy and pupils' potential, it seems to become lost when teachers try to put it into practice. Nevertheless during appraisal interviews they frequently cite cognitive process objectives which in practice they fail to meet because of poor class management and ineffective pedagogy.

The LAPP project specified that teaching styles should be more suited to the lower attainer's needs, but HMI found:

> There was still an almost automatic tendency to require a written response after discussion even though the pupils clearly experienced difficulty in committing to paper the ideas they expressed orally . . . (p. 12)
>
> Where this [oral work] was good, pupils were encouraged to develop their skills of observation, think more systematically and communicate more clearly . . . (p. 23)

What was needed was a description of the nature of this oral work to show how it achieved the objectives set. Instead we are told that:

> The difference in attitude and achievement shown in those few lessons observed where pupils were encouraged to discuss, put forward their own ideas and participate actively in practical work compared with those spent in copying worksheets and with minimal practical involvement, was quite striking (p. 27).

The same criticisms apply to the science and mathematics reports: instances of good practice are noted but not analysed. Many teachers set out to encourage discussion and problem-solving only to find that the pupils become rowdy and uncontrollable or cannot muster their ideas and articulate them coherently. On science, 'There were some examples of excellent practice. Though rare . . . ' (p. 26). On mathematics:

> Some enterprising individual teachers used the curriculum development opportunities of the programme to extend the thinking skills of the pupils through exploration of the elementary applications of mathematics. Unfortunately too often such work was the exception rather than the rule, and for a significant number of pupils mathematics continues as a dreary path through the 'basics' (p. 26).

The conclusions which may be drawn from this survey confirm that it is teacher attitude and pedagogy that need to be changed. Where there was an increase in language experience work, an attempt to involve and engage the learners in the curriculum, and to link it with their perceptions and levels of understanding of meaningful situations and events, then motivation and successful accomplishments were achieved. The cognitive process style pedagogy was found to be the more successful route to motivation and learning for the low achievers. In a later section, 'Defining Educational Objectives' (para. 149), it was reported that consideration was beginning to be given to 'whether there are essential differences between the programmes and teaching and learning methods provided for lower attainers and those for the rest of the peer group', and whether experiences, contexts and approaches should be common. It would be my argument that the cognitive process method which was suitable for able learners was essential for slow learners and that average pupils too could profit from it. This HMI survey provides confirmatory support for this form of pedagogy and its effectiveness with slow learners, but points also to its suitability for mixed-ability teaching.

USING NEW TECHNOLOGY TO FURTHER COGNITIVE PROCESS OBJECTIVES

Many teachers are finding considerable advantages in using modern technology in the classroom with all pupils, but it can be argued that it has particular value in helping pupils with learning difficulties (Hope, 1986). Initially the microcomputer seems to have been adopted in remedial settings to give *drill and practice*, being used as a resource to occupy pupils profitably whilst the teacher directed attention to others. The children's main response to computer-assisted learning of this kind, where for example phonic drills and skills are reinforced, is one of relief. Relief, for the computer will repeat instructions endlessly, without question or annoyance. The pupil is not made to feel he or she has failed or has gone down in teacher's estimation by not answering correctly or first time round. Disks which contain programs of this kind demonstrate technology which adopts the instructional paradigm. Two other important paradigms identified are the *revelatory*, or problem-solving mode, and the *conjectural*, which involves hypothesising, model-building and exploring. The links between these and cognitive process pedagogy are apparent. However, the potential benefits of computer-assisted learning all tend to hinge upon the dedication, persistence and ability of good teachers. As will be seen in the examples, it is the perceptive use of software by teachers which is the key to its success for children with learning difficulties.

A second major development in this area has been the introduction of word-processor facilities. It has enabled DARTs (Directed Activities Related to Texts; Schools Council, 1980) to be presented and children's narratives to be printed out and displayed or kept in work books and files. It has also enabled a major breakthrough in story writing to occur, using such programs as PROMPT and FOLIO.

Peters and Smith (1986) described children coming into comprehensive school unable to read or write. They argued that 'six years of phonics, simple reading books, and activity work books had had no effect on their reading. What none of them want or need is more of the same' (p. 162). They explained that there had never been the same pressure on their writing as upon reading, for the teacher had always given the pupils the words they needed, corrected their mistakes, warned about correcting spelling and created learned helplessness. The authors described a system where Dean, for example, who had just transferred to mainstream from special school, was offered a volunteer scribe to write his stories. Over time Dean was transformed from an over-anxious poor reader and writer into an enthusiastic, confident story writer. What was important was first to separate story composition from writing skills until the latter were developed enough to cope. His compositions gave him relevant and meaningful material which he was encouraged to read, expand and research.

The use of the word processor also allows this distinction to be made between composing and transcribing, helping children:

> to reflect on their writing, to redraft not just surface structure, improving their secretarial skills, but encouraging the cognitive skills of drafting and redrafting at deep structure level to take place. The children, in rehearsing to themselves what they have written, take on the role of reader/reflector (Peters and Smith, 1986, p. 169).

The Bullock Report (DES, 1975) drew attention to this particular problem with the observation that, in much of the considerable quantity of writing which takes place in school, the pupils' first attempt is expected to be the finished article: 'There is not enough encouragement of the idea of the first draft to be followed by a second, more refined production' (p. 167, para. 11.10).

The act of writing requires both the mental aspects of composing text and the physical aspects of producing and editing it. What is even more apparent is the deterioration in a pupil's work, whose skills in handwriting and spelling are poor, when asked to compose and write, rather than copy, a story. For some pupils, the act of handwriting requires so much concentration that the mind is completely absorbed by it so that poor spelling becomes worse and creative input is negligible (Cotterell, 1974; Alston, 1983). It is only on re-reading that spelling and content can be upgraded, and it is for this reason that redrafting is essential for almost all pupils in the early years and especially those with learning difficulties. But it is understandable that teachers are loath to ask a pupil who has just taken 45 minutes of total concentration to write three lines to redraft the story. Thus resorting to the use of scribes and now word processors is an important part of the work in imaginative writing in many schools (Smith, 1985). Straightforward redrafting has in itself assumed prominence as a consequence of results from the DARTs and Study Skills programmes. When word processors were used as an aid to composition, it was found that all students modified the organisation of their texts even though they rarely reorganised handwritten texts.

Typical of the type of learning régime which we wish to move away from is that illustrated in the following extract. It describes the learning programme for a group of slow learners withdrawn three times per week for 'remedial' work.

> I found that the children, because each worked on an individual programme, experienced very little group work. Each time I observed them it was the same thing, they read words learned, read a few pages of their books and carried on with the set work. They either spent some time receiving individual attention, perhaps reading to the teacher, or sat at their desks following the teacher's instructions as best they could. If a child kept asking the teacher for help then it meant less individual time for one of the other children. Because their abilities had not developed as well as other children of the same age, they appeared to be restricted to essential but repetitive and sometimes boring work . . . It did not occur to them to ask for help of each other (Dobinson, 1987, p. 69).

This observation is not untypical of the type of work found in many so-called 'remedial' environments, and in basic skills and extra language classes for pupils with learning difficulties (Wilson, 1981). The purpose of this text is to argue that this is not the way forward, that, in particular, children with learning difficulties are no different from others in their learning needs but are *made* different by the nature and style in which the curriculum, in ordinary schools especially, is delivered. Pupils with learning difficulties will benefit more from a collaborative language experience and oral problem-solving approach which is built into a basic skills programme than from non-conversational, desk-based routines, however well structured and interspersed with games activities. A greater emphasis has already been advocated in HMI reports (1979, 1983, 1986) on oral work for all pupils, but particularly for children with learning difficulties, given their main problems in the area of language and thinking. Successful approaches in the area of spoken language are reported by Dyke (1986) from the Manchester Special Education Resource Centre.

Adventure programs which involve problem-solving activities are particularly suitable for children with learning difficulties. A popular program of this type is 'Granny's Garden' (by 4 MAT ED Resources). 'Granny's Garden' consists of two programs in four parts and the teaching objectives are: problem-solving, decision-taking, logical reasoning, prediction, group co-operation, reading, language and communication. The program involves finding a magic tree which leads to the Kingdom of the Mountains. Once there, the pupils have to rescue the King and Queen's six children, whilst exploring various settings with the assistance of a magic blue raven, a talking toadstool and so on. An extract follows from action research by Dobinson (1987), using the program with the pupils described earlier. Their passive, dependent and unenthusiastic behaviour in the 'remedial' setting is contrasted with their progress in the computer-based learning situations.

Session 1
The second group of children consists of Ross, June and Dean. June positions herself in the centre chair, directly in front of the computer, Ross sits to her left and Dean to her right. Following the same process as with Group A, I explain what we were going to do.
    When I ask these three children if they have used the computer, June mumbles that she has one at home. Although June sits in the middle she makes no attempt to type. This is left to Ross, who appears to have no trouble typing . . .

Session 3
The children all remember the password needed to take them into the Giant's garden. Ross and Dean have begun to talk a little louder but June is still very quiet. She does however talk a little to me telling me that she has an Atari at home . . .

Session 7
Wayne [who has replaced Ross, who has moved away] is absent from today's session but June and Dean are present and are so eager that they practically run into the room. To save time I have

already run the program through to where the children were, previous to the session with Wayne.

June has relaxed to such an extent that she now sits with her feet tucked under her and is more than willing to reach over when she wants to type in a word. She is contributing far more than in previous sessions and is now willing to try to work out a word she doesn't know. If the word is in the context of a sentence then she normally manages to get it right.

At the end of the program when all the children had been found, June asked if they now had to free the King and Queen. I replied that their task had been to find and rescue the children. June was most concerned, she said that at the beginning of the program it had said that the King and Queen had been locked up by the wicked witch and that they had not released them. June was adamant about this but Dean was not too sure, so we went back to the beginning of the program to see if June was right. June had obviously listened, understood, and remembered the beginning of the story. She was the only one, out of all the children, to remark on this point. Perhaps with a little more foresight the writer of the program could have ensured that the King and Queen were released and reunited with their rescued children!

Summary of sessions
Although in the first session I felt Dean and June would not be able to complete the program without a great deal of support by the end of the sessions my feelings were that they had enough understanding of the context of the text, to enable them to complete the program with the minimum of assistance.

The text used in this program required the children using it to read, think, understand and then to reason about what they had read . . . Mrs R says she is surprised at June's chattiness. June's ability to converse with adults has definitely shown improvement.

The following shows the work of Mary Yates of St Philips School, Chessington, another teacher dedicated to achieving learning objectives for her pupils, and demonstrates her sensitive and responsive interventions as the children are working. It concerns the first imaginative story composed and written by two 8-year-old boys in a special school (for children with moderate learning difficulties) using the program PROMPT on BBC computer.

Tony and Chris were very similar in lots of ways – eight-year-olds who did not find learning easy: both had experienced 'failures' within normal main stream schooling before being transferred to St Philips, and both consequently had very low self-esteem. They were in the process of discovering that they were far more capable than either believed but were by then achieving at perhaps 'middle-infant' level.

Although Tony and Chris had fairly good manual control, they still seemed to regard any form of creative writing as a tedious chore. When attempting to write about their experiences, they were usually too easily satisfied with the minimum – heaving sighs of relief when their efforts were accepted as finished. They were however able to compose and write simple sentences and were coming to understand the different forms of language required for written recording . . .

The class had recently been introduced to PROMPT, with its advantage over typing of being able to delete errors immediately, and to get a 'print-out' when satisfied with a piece of work.

'The old man' was the first imaginative story these boys attempted together using PROMPT 2 [MEP Blue File].

The two boys sat in front of the computer and I asked them to decide on a title for their story. They decided on the 'The old man', and I typed the title in for them, asking them to insert their names. At this stage they had no idea of the content of the story.

I told them to start by writing down what he looked like . . .

When they had agreed on his 'raggy clothes' (with spelling help needed for both these words), I asked, 'What did he do?'

One replied that he 'robbed a bank' and the other said he 'went to the shops', so I asked them which he did first and why he went to the shop and again left them to decide while I attended to the rest of the class.

Each time I returned to them, I helped them to form sentences verbally (being careful to use their own language structures), then said, 'Write it down, then!'

To the question, 'How did he rob the bank?' one said, 'He had a gun'. I pointed out that merely having a gun was not enough, so they discussed exactly how he went about it.

By the time they had answered questions like, 'How did he do that?' and, 'What happened then?' to the point that the old man had counted the money (the end of the first page), they were very impressed with what they had achieved and we printed their work out. We stopped for playtime.

After play they were not so keen to go on – probably feeling that they had already done more than their fair share, but when they were settled again Tony suddenly exclaimed, 'Cor, this is easy!' Presumably from watching television, this was a topic with which they felt familiar.

During the after-play session they appeared to be getting the idea and needed less verbal help beyond questions like 'Then what happened?' and 'How?'

This whole morning's concentration on one topic was quite new to both boys, as was the animated discussion that went on between them each time I put another question.

Their success impressed the rest of the class so much that other

The Old Man
by Chris and Tony

The old man had some raggy clothes.
He went to the shop and he bought a
paper then he robbed some money
from the bank. He had a gun. He said
lay down or you will get shot. So
they lay down then he pinched the
money.
Then he ran home then he counted the
money.

The police went to the bank. They
asked the people in the bank what did
he look like. The people said he had
white hair and raggy clothes.
The police looked for the man.
They looked in Kingston and they
looked in Surbiton. They found the
old man in Chessington.
The old man said if you come closer
you will get shot. The police shot
the old man.

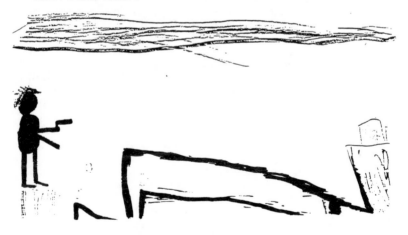

Figure 3.2 *'The old man' by Chris and Tony*

children got together during playtimes to decide on stories they wanted to write – the motivation was that the best ideas gained priority for a turn on the computer . . .

Later, we printed unedited pieces of work, corrected errors on the printed sheet; the corrected version was then copied into books in 'best writing' and then re-copied on to PROMPT and reprinted. There was very little persuasion needed to revise a piece of work in this way, and reading fluency and comprehension skills improved as a result!

Many similar examples to these, showing improvements in self-esteem and motivation, language skills, basic skills, number skills, problem-solving and interpersonal skills in children with learning difficulties, may be found in Hope (1986).

CURRICULUM-BASED ASSESSMENT AND TEACHING

A general view of assessment is that it is the process of collecting data about individuals for the purpose of making decisions about them. These decisions may involve referral, classification and selection, evaluation of progress and evaluation of instructional programmes or curriculum interventions. When pupils have been categorised and subjected to different forms of instruction, according to Ysseldyke (1987) they have not, with the exception of those with sensory handicaps, profited from them. A number of researchers have argued that the practice of classifying students is irrelevant in guiding decisions about instruction. This is not surprising since, although tests might tell us *what* to teach, the decisions about *how* to teach require us to determine which methods and strategies will be effective in ensuring that the learner learns. Thus knowing one's subject may be of less importance than taking a prescribed content from a text and enabling the learners to learn it. This last part, *enabling*, would be easy if all had good reading abilities, study skills, concentration spans, motivation, persistence and keen interest, but they do not, and therefore teaching becomes a more complex task than 'telling' or learning by reading.

Even using tests to tell us what to teach can become fraught with difficulties and ambiguity. For example, a test of early reading skills might contain an item thus (see Figure 3.3): 'Point to the picture which begins in the same way as *cat*. Say the words as you point to the picture.'

Figure 3.3 *Example of so-called auditory discrimination test item*

The pupil may well be able to name the picture and know the hard sound of 'c' (k), or have sound-to-symbol correspondence, and yet may not be able to identify *cup* as the key word to match *cat*. Usually the pupil knows neither that 'c' is said (k) nor that *cup* begins with (k). The constructor of this particular item informs the teacher/tester that this shows the child has poor *auditory discrimination* skills, but the problem is one of *phoneme segmentation* not auditory discrimination. The teacher using this test to diagnose weaknesses might then spend many wasted hours on auditory discrimination activities instead of phoneme segmentation because the test label and theory of construction had been misleading.

Tests of complex abilities, such as those for reading, spelling, writing, concept formation, thinking and intelligence, are extremely difficult to construct with high levels of validity, for our understanding of their nature is as yet limited. Thus it can be seen that, unless tests are of purely factual material, defining what to teach from them may be misguided and haphazard, so that even if the appropriate pedagogy was selected it would lead to a nil return. This may well be the case with many of the examples which Ysseldyke has been exploring. Recently the focus has moved from diagnostic–prescriptive teaching (Lerner, 1971) and what might be called the 'psychological classroom' to *curriculum-based assessment*. This is a procedure for determining the instructional needs of a student based upon the student's performance within existing course content, and is the procedure recommended here for teaching. It deals with variables and procedures that teachers can control and so is likely to enable them to be more effective. They need, however, to record systematically and evaluate progress, and to be capable of selecting the appropriate methodology to effect learning; in other words, the *how*, or pedagogy, becomes even more important. Curriculum-based assessment has several different interpretations, but most frequently it is found with reference to 'task analysis'.

Task analysis

Task analysis was introduced into the educational field from industrial psychology and the field of programmed learning. Programmed learning was based upon *behaviour control* principles (Nuttall and Snook, 1973). This label was applied because 'underlying its concepts is the notion of teaching as a method of controlling the behaviour of students and the conditions of learning' (p. 54). Each task is analysed and broken down into small, manageable units or steps and the learner proceeds from step to step up through the task gradient with each small success being positively reinforced. If there is a failure at any point, the problem area is immediately identifiable, reteaching can occur and the programme rolls forward again. Linear and then branching programmes were developed to teach numerous mathematical and scientific skills and contents. Gagné (1973, 1977) did much to promote these techniques in the broader context of task/skills analysis in the classroom, demonstrating the value of breaking down complex tasks into the shorter teaching units with regard to his 'hierarchy of learning' and 'conditions of learning', linking both behaviourist and cognitivist approaches.

Descriptions of learning outcomes (Gagné, 1969, 1973) or the end products of learning (Grönlund, 1970) are often called 'behavioural' or 'performance' objectives and sometimes 'teaching' or 'instructional' objectives. In essence, they describe what the pupil should be able to do after learning has occurred and should be quantifiable and measurable. For example, at the end of the session 'the pupil shall be able to identify the "sh" digraph in beginning and end positions in words and find it with 95% accuracy in any piece of text at own reading level'. This type of behavioural objective conforms to Vargus's conditions (1972, 1973). It contains three components:

- a verb which describes an observable behaviour from the pupil;
- a description of conditions for the performance;
- a description of the criterion to be achieved.

The objective, 'to learn five new sight words from the reading scheme by the end of one week to a 90 per cent criterion', is another example of this type of behavioural objective, and most examples given derive from the basic skills areas of reading, spelling and arithmetic, which seem to lend themselves to such programming and are a feature of the technique called 'precision teaching' first developed by Lindsay in the 1960s (Formentin and Csapo, 1980). Precision teaching is more a method of record-ing the pupil's responses in a systematic way – counting using golf counters (ref. 'clickers' of Wheldall and Merritt, 1984b), recording rate of response, time to completion, time sampling or time-ruled checklists, checklists for criterion-referenced quality of performance, graphing cumulative results and testing – than a method of teaching.

Unfortunately rote learning under teacher scrutiny is often the only required pupil response and so where pupils have severe *specific* learning difficulties, the value of learning five words without the property of generalising to other words may in the end prove negligible. The time could have been better spent on a structured and coherent programme which was theoretically sound and empirically tested. Our studies have also shown that such pupils often prove incapable of learning even two sight words by these techniques, however encouraging the teacher, and however precisely the objectives are framed. What seems to be important in precision teaching is to find out what the pupil's mind is doing whilst he or she stares at the five new words. Some suggestions on this will be discussed in the final chapter under the subject of *metacognition* and ways will be outlined in which these learning processes might be fostered to help pupils overcome the barriers presented by print and by teachers' methods. Of significance in motivation is the autonomy often afforded by precision teaching to the pupils in being allowed to monitor and record their own daily progress on the assessment and recording charts.

Coventry LEA psychological services personnel (Ainscow and Muncey, 1983, 1984) produced the SNAP – Special Needs Action Programme – incorporating precision teaching. The programme is marketed widely and used by other LEAs and training insti-tutions on special needs courses. In contrast to the DISTAR materials developed in the American Headstart programme, SNAP is flexible and not prescriptive about content, and it can also be applied to any teaching style or method. It has been widely acclaimed as a useful tool in teaching and was, like most teaching to objectives systems, based on methods developed by psychologists with teachers in special schools where the pupil ratios were smaller and the staff support greater.

DATAPAC (Daily Teaching and Assessment for Primary Age Children) was produced by a group of psychologists (Ackerman *et al.*, 1983) as an assessment-through-teaching package for indi-vidual pupils. The materials consist of assessment tools, teaching sheets and teaching instructions in the areas of reading, hand-writing, spelling and mathematics. In other words DATAPAC, like DISTAR, had defined teaching programmes. DISTAR has been criticised by teachers in this country for taking the teaching out of their hands: they become the 'pencil and sheet monitors'. Swann (1985) criticises Direct Instructional (DI) approaches such as these for their lack of relevance to the children's experience outside schools and their narrowness of contents.

More recently, task analysis has been introduced on a wide scale into ordinary classrooms to help pupils with special needs, and very useful texts have been produced on the subject to help teachers and in-service trainers: for example, Ainscow and Tweddle (1979), Solity and Bull (1987).

In a recent ILEA survey of teaching in primary schools (Mortimore *et al.*, 1988) the effectiveness of task analysis and objectives-based approaches to the curriculum are underlined. The survey drew attention to the complexity of the role of the teacher and isolated a number of variables which appeared to contribute to this form of effective teaching. Good teaching was exemplified by positive school and classroom climates for learning, structured sessions, intellectually challenging teaching, a work-centred environment, a limited focus in lessons, good communication, good record keeping and parental involvement. These also contribute to effective cognitive process methods.

Apart from the narrowness of many task analysis activities, there are more fundamental problems. Although it may be stated that task analysis has been undertaken, questions should be asked: Has the task been suitably described and defined? Has the task been suitably analysed or broken down into relevant units? The answer to these questions is often 'No', especially with regard to the complex area of reading, writing and spelling skills. Hierarchies of *relevant* skills have not been defined and taught, so that programmes can occupy a pupil's time interestingly but with little profit. Pupils can also work through some of the programmes without having established the concepts, learning the correct response through repetition.

The first significant endorsement of the curriculum defined in terms of the objectives-based model appeared in the Warnock Report (DES, 1978). It required for pupils with special needs the presence of 'well-defined' guidelines for each area of the curriculum, and 'programmes . . . planned for individual children with clearly defined short term goals within the general plan' (11.5). The 1981 Education Act endorsed these practices by defining assessment procedures for statementing in terms of the categorical distinctions made in the objectives-based/skills analysis approach to the curriculum (Wood and Shears, 1986). The National Curriculum, with its criterion-referenced assessments

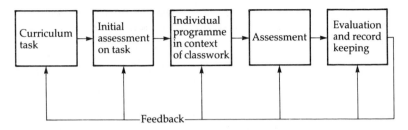

Figure 3.4 *The process of assessment through teaching*

and subjects defined in terms of ten levels and targets, seems one more step towards a closed curriculum and a dependent learner. Is it that the alternative model, the process model proposed by Stenhouse (1975), is insufficiently understood by those who observe education and by many practitioners because of its often indefinable outcomes and the dangerous autonomy which it offers to the learner?

Matching pupils' needs and the task can significantly reduce attention-seeking and the time off-task which can be used in disruption. In assessment through teaching, the curriculum task is used to determine what the pupil can and cannot do. Hospital teachers, for example, have to become particularly adept at this when they meet patients for the first time and need to continue these pupils' educational studies. By presenting text to read or a subject to write about, the teacher can make a rapid assessment of the level of reading and writing skills and find a better match of reading and writing materials and subjects. Diagnostic questioning about a subject can reveal the previous knowledge-base from which the teacher can work. Decisions about teaching method and resources can be made and then records of progress can be compiled.

This procedure, formalised by psychologists in the objectives-based approaches, accords with the processes which many teachers naturally undertook in their effective teaching programmes. Two examples follow. The first illustrates the sterility of the diagnostic–prescriptive classroom, especially when it narrows down to a mainly basic skills curriculum with all children on their individual programmes. The sessions nevertheless appear well structured and are achieving certain objectives. The second example consists of a more open evaluation of a lesson taught by a final-year student who has tried a cognitive process pedagogy, and demonstrates her curriculum diagnosis capabilities.

Report on a typical day in the life of a class of children at a school for moderate learning difficulties (John Shannon, teacher-researcher, 1987)

The children normally arrive between 9.05 and 9.15 a.m. depending upon where their coach or other form of transport has to come from. On arrival they immediately get out their own work without any initial teacher input or direction and begin the relevant exercise or activity on their own. This generally consists of a page from the 'Sound Sense' series, the 'Ginn 360' workbooks, or the 'Introductory English Workbook' set. The children work at their own level on an individualised programme.

If this exercise is finished before assembly the children know that they must get out their reading book and read quietly to themselves. This school, and indeed this class, has a large variety of reading schemes which do not appear to have been graded to any recognised system of classification such as Moon's Individual Reading Scheme. Rather, each pupil selects a book that he or she thinks they will be able to read and which appeals to them. Ms X then either agrees to let them use it or refers them to a book which she thinks is nearer their own ability. The main schemes used within this class alone include the 'Ginn 369' series, the 'Wide Range Readers', and the 'Griffin Readers'.

Throughout the first session of the day, i.e. before and after assembly, Ms X's role is one of consultant and adviser. Whole-class input is almost nil as she expects the children to know what they are required to do and to be increasingly responsible for their own learning. This policy of increasing the children's organisational and educational autonomy has been one of the most noticeably effective pedagogical changes since Ms X joined the school . . . After break the upper-junior section of the school divides into three reading sets grouped according to reading age and disperses to different classrooms. Ms X has eight children in her group of which four are from her own class and four are from the other two classes within the age-range. During this lesson Ms X normally begins with a class input, such as initial vowel digraphs, and discusses these with all the children using the blackboard. An associated exercise is then usually set during which Ms X and her teaching assistant circulate amongst the group offering advice and help as required. In my experience it is most unusual that this exercise should last more than ten to fifteen minutes. For the remainder of the lesson therefore the children are allowed to choose whether they wish to play a language game or continue with some individual learning by way of, for example, the 'Stile Language Laboratory'.

Ms X has established a good rapport with the pupils and helped them achieve independence and a certain amount of autonomy. The tasks set show clear evidence of teaching to carefully defined and achievable objectives with short, structured periods of activity. To all intents and purposes it might be thought to be an example of good teaching, but questions need to be raised about both the curriculum and its pedagogy if these children's main learning needs are to be met. The timetable and observation showed that this day's pattern was typical, week-in and week-out. Brennan's research (1985) and that of Wilson (1981) showed the narrowness of such basic skills curricula so often offered to pupils with learning difficulties. Recently, Booth *et al*. have written: 'This raises the question of basic skills work within the individual curriculum. The danger is that for some pupils, particularly those requiring long term remedial support, programmes can become overloaded in this direction, often with a disproportionate phonic content' (1987, p. 136).

These difficulties and limitations would seem to arise from the lack of differentiation between the needs of children with learning difficulties and those with specific learning difficulties, and the resultant different curriculum provision and pedagogy which is suitable in each case. In the previous example it would seem that children with learning difficulties are being provided with an extended remedial rather than a developmental curriculum, something which is inappropriate to their learning needs. Children with learning difficulties need classrooms in which there is collaborative learning, negotiation, oral problem-solving and discussion between pupils. The individualised programme and the remedial tutorial are generally unsuitable as a *main* teaching vehicle for them, for they limit the communication channels which are open for learning at the pupils' own levels and throw them back on their own limited cognitive resources. The classroom communication networks, however, need to be opened up so that children can use each other as well as the teacher as a resource.

The types of network which need to be established in addition to the formal ones involving teacher-directed class and individual activities are indicated in Figure 3.5.

In the formal setting the teacher directs and leads the class, allowing only single channels between herself and individual pupils to be open at any one time. If during this time they talked to each other as well, no one would be able to hear anyone else. The teacher is the 'star' and receives all communications. To avoid overload she can attend to only one message at a time and this places severe constraints upon the communication opportunities of all the other pupils.

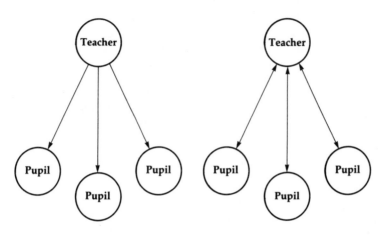

Informational lecture mode

Teacher questioning/class discussion
mode – individual programmes mode

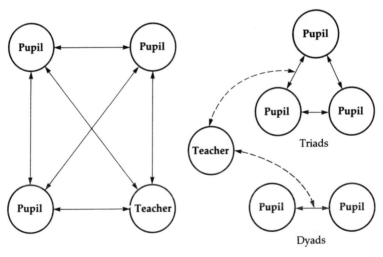

Group discussion – seminar mode
Teacher as partner – collaborative mode

Teacher as resource –
collaborative mode

Figure 3.5 *(a) Formal communication networks (based on Leavitt, 1951)*
(b) Informal communication networks

Lesson evaluations by Elaine Bassett, a third-year student in teacher training at Kingston Polytechnic, 1987

This was the seventh week of teaching practice in an ordinary school with two more to go. The lessons have involved the use of some cognitive process and 'engage brain' methodology, and demonstrate some curriculum-based assessment. The children in this half of the term were engaged in a project on 'The Sea' and the groups were named Whales, Stingrays, etc. accordingly. The situation was open-plan with 24 7–8-year-olds working an integrated day. Two mathematics, language and art groups were in progress at any one time and were rotated during the day and week. The following evaluations for some of the work on Monday, 15 June appeared in the student's file:

Lesson Evaluation – Mathematics   15 June 1987
Stingrays were re-doing and completing an activity on measurement with metre sticks. On Friday, 12 June 1987, this group did not show any grasp of the tasks involved, and showed signs of confusion. They were recording results for problems such as for writing down the length of an object to the nearest whole or half metre for the length of their arm, and so on. I also noticed that, despite my constant requests, they were mostly 'guessing' *after* they had measured, and writing their guesses the same as their actual 'measurements' (even though these were completely inaccurate!) – I decided to re-do this activity, and resolved to give clearer, more precise and simple instructions, as I thought that it was possibly for this reason that they were confused.

However, I have concluded that this group do not have a clear concept of the length of a metre. They particularly seem to find measurements that do not even measure a whole metre very difficult, for example, in measuring Tracey's arm, as a demonstration to the whole group, I asked them to tell me how long her arm was, in metres. All of them replied '1 and a bit'. I pointed out that Tracey's arm was not even as long as 1 metre, let alone longer! I asked them to try again, and this time they replied '1½ metres'. I showed them how long 1½ metres was, with 2 sticks, and asked them if Tracey's arms were this long. They laughed and said 'Of course not!' – They obviously have the concept of longer than/ shorter than, but have difficulty in specifying how long/short.

After several minutes discussion, I decided to take the group on a trip around the classroom. Together, we all measured, compared and specified lengths of classroom objects to the nearest whole or half metre, saying 'about 2 metres', 'nearly 1 metre', etc. After doing this for about 10 minutes, I took the children back to their work, and showed them what they had recorded earlier. They seemed a little surprised, and could each point out their mistakes to me. Jamie and Michael, in particular, were quick to correct their mistakes, and eager to get on and measure some more things.

Lesson Evaluation – Language 15 June 1987
The discussion of types and uses of boats recalled a lot of information and ideas previously discussed following the trip to the River Thames.

At the start of the following session, 'Seahorses' gave a description of the use of one of their types of boats, and the rest of the class guessed its name. The children enjoyed this immensely, and also showed they had retained a lot from earlier discussion. It also demonstrated to the children the importance of accurate descriptions – otherwise the possibilities could be endless!

Of particular note in these examples is the clear expression of the lesson objectives for each session and each group, with the student carefully observing the children's performance on-task. From their response the diagnosis of their learning needs is made and then implemented.

'Seahorses' giving their one-minute talks and untitled descriptions are an example of the type of cognitive target-setting suggested in the de Bono programme (1983) and our earlier examples of study skills activities. This is often an excellent way of getting children to concentrate when they are reading and making notes about any topic. It prevents topics and research work from becoming copying exercises done whilst pupils chat and which do not cause them to think about what they are writing. These 7-year-olds, having researched their subjects, then have to tell the other children about it. The subject is not named, in order to provide extra motivation for the rest of the class to listen and also to think about what is being said. As was reported, children enjoy this sort of cognitive challenge immensely, and 5- and 6-year-olds as well as older pupils, slow learners and able pupils can all gain from these learning opportunities.

INSTRUMENTAL ENRICHMENT

Instrumental enrichment (IE) is a method developed by Professor Reuven Feuerstein (1980), an Israeli psychologist, to help children whose families had been destroyed. Many of these children demonstrated intellectual performance which was so low on psychological tests that they were classified as children with moderate or even severe learning difficulties. It was his belief that these pupils were 'low achievers' because of cultural breakdown, rather than as a result of 'genetic impairment'.

Feuerstein described intelligence as the ability to learn from experience and argued that, when there is cultural breakdown as after the Holocaust, parents and grandparents are unable to pass on the basic thinking skills which enable the children to make sense of their world. He suggests that this breakdown is common among immigrant groups moving from underdeveloped to highly sophisticated, technological societies, and where such groups and cultures are fragmented by poverty and war, or social and geographical upheaval. As can be seen, this could include vast areas and many peoples of the world, for there have been more than two hundred wars recorded since 1945, some approaching their second decade. There have also been vast famines, earthquakes and translocations of people from one country to another. One might also include in this equation not only the social and cultural problems of battle, famine and earthquake, but also emotional shock, which can bring with it severe emotional trauma as a barrier to learning (Herbert, 1975).

In Israel, some 40,000 children are reported to receive instrumental enrichment in state schools; in Canada, the prison system has claimed success with its use; and Venezuela has incorporated it into state education just as it did de Bono's (1976) CoRT thinking skills programme. In Britain the system has had a mixed reception, but trials at three Somerset comprehensive schools are nearing completion. Blagg (1987a), who carried out this study, reports that the results are good and confirm the predictions of Feuerstein.

The instrumental enrichment programme is made up of over five hundred pages of paper-and-pencil exercises, divided into twenty instruments. Each instrument purports to focus upon a specific cognitive deficiency, but also enables other prerequisites of learning to be acquired as well. Fourteen of the instruments are regularly used in any classroom implementation and provide material for a one-hour lesson on 3–5 days per week for a period of two years. When using the materials in a diagnostic–prescriptive remedial programme, the 'instruments' are selected to match the pupil's need.

As Blagg has noted in the Somerset study, there are drawbacks. Instrumental enrichment requires a high degree of theoretical understanding of how flaws may develop in children's thinking and how these can be corrected. It also requires 200–300 hours' teaching for two years, and many schools are unwilling to give up so much time for seemingly abstract thinking skills work.

One factor which may have influenced the Feuerstein class's success was that they were on a 'special' programme and so thereby saw themselves as special, deriving more meaning and significance from the process than they ordinarily might. The programme, even at its simpler perceptual-skills level, involves some *acquisition of vocabulary, concepts and operations*. The pupil labels not only the figures but also the operations and the strategies used to construct them, and these can transfer to other subject areas. They tend to talk themselves into a problem, for example 'Now, what do we do when we are given a problem? First we have to find out what the problem is . . . '. Nevertheless the encouragement of verbalisation in IE transferred to the wider context and provided structure, organisation and system for tackling other tasks.

This is very valuable learning but we might suggest that this is what good teachers do anyway, and it is what all should do: teach pupils to organise their responses to problems and to learn how to learn. Perhaps it is a good programme for those who do not know how to teach or for those who are unable to move beyond rote approaches to subject contents, but it seems a very roundabout and time-consuming method of achieving cognitive and learning objectives. It assumes transfer will take place from the abstract to the educational contexts, but this is not assured. Able children are likely to benefit most, for they will transfer their learning more easily. Slower children will find this much more difficult, for transfer of learning from one situation to another is what they have difficulty doing (Green *et al.*, 1982). Lower attainers and children with learning blocks could well profit from a structured and systematically rewarding approach to help them overcome their difficulties. IE is probably one of the best examples we have at the moment of the psychological classroom: individuals work on their own learning programmes defined by their performance upon psychological tests, their behaviour directed towards goals defined by psychological theory. This proceeds in parallel with normal school curriculum and positive transfer to it is expected.

CoRT PROGRAMME

The Cognitive Objectives Research Trust was set up by de Bono and serves to promote this thinking skills programme (1976). The programme has six sections, each of which consists of ten lessons of about 35 minutes each. The lessons are given at about the rate of one per week and the full course lasts about two schools years. It is aimed primarily at the 11–12-year age-range. The aspects of thinking covered in the programme are:

- breadth

- organisation
- interaction
- creativity
- information and feeling
- action

The programme teaches and trains a set of skills which are assumed to be key tools in thinking.

As with Feuerstein's work so with de Bono's, cognitive skills are trained in lessons parallel to the normal curriculum and again this presents the problem of transferability, especially for slow learners. There are, however, many differences between the two approaches, with de Bono's being more intimately related to typical British classroom activities which involve both individual and group work and problem-solving. The lesson plans which de Bono sets out could easily be incorporated into a language or English curriculum, for there are many useful ideas and techniques. What one would want to see is the strategies and skills which he outlines being incorporated into *all* subjects in the curriculum, so that the teaching strategy is converted to a process methodology. Although a number of schools in this country have used the CoRT programme, again no extensive controlled research studies appear to have been made since the development programme reported by de Bono (1983).

Personal reports by teachers who have used the programme suggest that, like study skills programmes (Meek and Thompson, 1987), unless the techniques are incorporated into the normal curriculum, the pupils fail to perceive the significance of what they are learning, and cannot transfer it to content lessons, for different requirements are made of them. This can lead to dissatisfaction and disaffection so that the normal competition for timetable space causes the closure of the course.

PRIMARY SCHOOLS: SOME ASPECTS OF GOOD PRACTICE

A booklet with this title was produced by DES (1987b) to illustrate what was considered good practice by HMI, based upon the criteria laid down in their recent publications and surveys. These criteria have already been subject to some criticism, particularly their notions of knowledge and concepts and their lack of attention to cognitive skills. The following extracts taken from this latest booklet illustrate the apparent confusion which exists even in the minds of experienced inspectors about what constitutes a good lesson. These extracts will be looked at from the pedagogical point of view and 'good' and 'poor' examples of cognitive process pedagogy will be identified. It must be noted that all the examples are put forward by DES as 'good' practice. The first extract concerns a science lesson.

> The good practice described and commented on in this document is characterised by the pupils showing a lively interest in the challenges presented to them and by the teachers having clear aims and intentions about what the children are to learn.
>
> Three six-year-old children, two boys and a girl, are testing various objects to see whether they will conduct electricity. They are using a simple circuit board, two electrical cells and a bulb from a hand bench.

> | Boy | 'Miss, look, look at this tin lid'. |
> | Girl | 'When we put the wires on this side it lights up.' |
> | Boy | 'But it doesn't work on the other side Miss, look.' |
> | Teacher | 'Do it again. Show me again, please. Make sure you make the contacts firm.' |

> The activity is repeated. The results are the same. They test the set of lids and their results are consistent.

> | Teacher | 'What's happening do you think? You carry on, try testing some other tin lids.' |

> More testing is carried out on different parts of the lid and on other tin lids. The teacher returns to the group.

> | Teacher | 'How are you getting on? Let's look at all these lids. What's usually on the top of the lids but not underneath?' |
> | Girl | 'Colours.' |
> | Teacher | 'What do you mean by colours?' |
> | Boy | 'She means the paint, Miss.' |
> | Teacher | 'That's right, you've noticed what I think might be the cause.' |
> | Boy | 'The paint, Miss?' |
> | Teacher | 'Well, you try all those tin lids which have paint on one side and not on the other and see what happens.' |
> | Girl | 'It's right Miss, it is the paint that's doing it.' |
> | Teacher | 'That's what I think. I think the paint protects the metal. It insulates the metal.' |
> | Boy | 'Insulates, Miss?' |
> | Teacher | 'Yes, let's talk about it a bit more this afternoon when we can tell the other children what you've found.' |

> The lunch break intervenes (DES, 1987, p. 1).

The inquiry proceeds well until the key point arrives:

> | Teacher | 'How are you getting on? Let's look at all these lids. |

What's usually on the top of the lids but not underneath?'

The leading question which elicits the one-word answer:

Girl   'Colours.'

The next key point arrives:

Teacher   'That's right, you've noticed what *I think might be the cause.*'

The children now simply have to check out the answer. Do they even wonder if the teacher thinks wrongly? Are they encouraged truly to think, observe, question and formulate an hypothesis by this means? I think the answer is no. This extract is an example of traditional didactic pedagogy within a practical setting.

What the teacher concerned with cognitive process pedagogy might have said is:

Teacher   'How are you getting on? Now let's count these lids, it looks as though you have a good sample. [They count.] OK, I think you have got the answer there somewhere. Just spend two minutes talking it through to see if you can come up with some hypotheses. I'll come back then.'

This would encourage the pupils to check the lids and in conversation order their ideas, determine the reason, and then be able to explain it coherently to the teacher on her return. Proceeding in this fashion helps the pupils develop more of a sense of responsibility for their learning; they do not have to wait to be told the answers. They will after this form of training know the routine and will discuss their hypotheses to tell the teacher on her arrival at the group. This conversational, problem-posing approach to learning would particularly help the girl with her choice of vocabulary, and she would not have to be corrected by the boy in front of the teacher.

The following extract from later in the DES booklet is from a natural science lesson.

As part of a project on 'Myself' being undertaken by a class of seven and eight-year-old children the pupils were asked to draw and write about themselves.

This led them to compare their own eye colour, hair colour and skin colour with those of other pupils and to seek explanations for the differences and similarities. Some explanations were provided by the teacher and further information was found from simple reference materials available in the classroom. By enabling pupils to draw upon the personal characteristics their interest had been aroused about a complex biological issue and they had made scientific observations. This work quite naturally led into other curriculum areas such as mathematics, as graphs were made of the various pupil characteristics, and geography, as different physical characteristics were traced to different geographical regions. Throughout the whole project the teacher encouraged the pupils to discuss rationally and accept the normality of the differences and similarities between different ethnic groups.

A characteristic of the studies was the way in which the teachers maintained the pace of the work and timed their expository teaching to match the children's practical experience. Given this kind of practical experience that is informed by clear and effective teaching it is apparent that primary school children can grasp quite sophisticated ideas and relate them to new situations but for this to happen they need time to explore and order their thinking through discussions with their teachers, other children and informed adults. These discussions enable ideas to be made explicit to the children so that facts and observed phenomena relate to unifying concepts such as growth and change over time (DES, 1987b, pp. 6–7).

In this example there is insufficient detail in the account to show whether or not it is an example of good practice. We have only the inspector's word for it. A clue to its real didactic nature is found in the second paragraph, 'timed their expository teaching [telling-lecturette] to match the children's practical experience'. 'Given this kind of practical experience that is informed by *clear and effective* teaching it is apparent that primary school children can grasp quite sophisticated ideas and relate them to new situations . . . they need time to explore and order their thinking through discussions with their teachers, other children . . . enable ideas to be *made explicit to the children*' – again the 'telling' mode predominates in the inspectorial mind. What is not evidenced is how all the children responded and what conceptual level of understanding was achieved. Any experienced observer of classrooms has the problem of distinguishing between what appears to be absolutely clear and understandable to the adult mind and seemingly suitable for children, and what the child understands and draws from the experience which can be deduced from listening to them and observing them in action. The final product, a wall display or a project file, has little real value as an indicator of quality. This so-called 'guided discovery' learning (Bruner, 1972) is typical of most scientific practical work undertaken in the many hundreds of lessons observed. 'Guided discovery' in operation is a pseudo-cognitive approach, although I am sure Bruner never intended it to be degraded in this way.

The other examples in the DES booklet describe some enterprising and interesting curriculum activities. These are, however, described in such global terms that the processes by which the activities have been developed and the outcomes achieved are not available for analysis. We cannot therefore infer that these are good or poor examples of teaching. The two extracts presented at the outset would be classified as minimally competent but low-grade pedagogy in relation to cognitive process objectives.

SUMMARY AND CONCLUSIONS

A pattern within the field of learning difficulties seems to be emerging, and it is one which is problematic for teachers and teacher training. As teachers become more knowledgeable about the special educational needs of pupils and try to engage in mixed-ability teaching, they search for appropriate techniques and strategies. The baseline stragegy seems to be for subject teachers to give the pupils with learning difficulties more teacher time and easier levels of work. More time for one takes time away from others, and different and lower levels of work can make the pupil feel of lower status. This makes access to the ordinary curriculum for all a prime consideration, and an equal opportunities issue. A second pattern of responses which may be found is that the teacher adopts the remedial perspective in which, normally, one or two pupils are withdrawn for intensive remediation of substandard reading, spelling and writing skills. In the classroom for pupils with learning difficulties, this can mean classes of 12 to 30, all undertaking untutored worksheet drills in basic skills areas for a large proportion of each day.

It is contended that neither of these patterns is suitable for children with learning difficulties. Teaching is not just a matter of giving extra time or selecting suitable worksheets. It is a dynamic process involving learners both individually and in groups with the teacher in the pursuit of broad and specific educational aims and objectives. It is suggested that the achievement of these educational aims (HMI, 1981) can best be accomplished by a movement for radical pedagogical change throughout all schools. Courses of training for teaching should have as the major focus, with both explicit and implicit programmes, the subject of pedagogy. These are necessary to transform teaching from the content-based, expository approaches to which pupils have been subjected, to cognitive process methodology suitable for pupils' learning.

This move will remain problematic and unlikely to occur whilst there is an absence of hard research evidence, although across the country there are vast numbers of incidences of good practice. The examples in this chapter are illustrative of the style of some of these advances. They seek to show that teaching and learning is about the pursuit of rational–logical objectives, personal autonomy, and intrinsic motivation within the ordinary curriculum through individual, group and class activities.

The most positive help that can be given to teachers and intending teachers to enable them to help pupils with learning difficulties in ordinary classrooms is to train them to *teach* and reduce the actual size of their classes to fifteen so that the effects of that teaching can have the maximum benefit for all the children.

—4—
Managing the behaviour of children with learning difficulties

INTRODUCTION

Managing the behaviour of children in classrooms is not always the easiest of tasks, even for the most experienced teachers. Young children, used to individual attention on demand from their parents or child-minders and to roving in and out of doors in an independent manner, may cause problems. Teachers need pupils to be responsive, listen, co-operate and conform to the requirements and social mores of the classroom. These expectations are not always met by young children or pupils of any age-group and the teacher has to engage in strategies which inculcate the children into 'appropriate' school behaviour. To some extent the classroom is a strange and unnatural place to confine young people and it is not surprising that individual motives, needs and expectations conflict with those of others and of the teacher who is attempting to pursue educational goals.

> The prospect of occupying thirty children productively for one whole day would fill most adults particularly non-teachers with horror. Add to that the injunction that the children are to be confined to one room, and are to remain seated, and for many the task would be beyond belief (Booth, 1982).

Booth (1982) suggested that the very structure of our society demands that some children must be regarded as failures. This term 'failure' is applied after the child's performance has been compared to that of peers or to standards of achievement built into various forms of assessment. It would seem unreasonable that all children should be expected to attain these standards in lock step (Hemming, 1988). Significant researches have shown that failure in school may be related to social position. Thus children from overcrowded homes, large families, low-income groups and 'working-class' backgrounds may have many disadvantages to overcome (Douglas, 1964; Davie *et al.*, 1972; Willis, 1977; Leach and Raybould, 1977; Wedge and Prosser, 1979; Galloway *et al.*, 1982). These disadvantages may prove insuperable in some school settings (Rutter *et al.*, 1979; Hargreaves, 1984; Galloway and Goodwin, 1987). Inequality of opportunity to benefit from the education offered may place many pupils at risk from learning failure and predispose them to exhibit emotional and behavioural difficulties (Chazan, 1964; Stott, 1981). In these circumstances Becker (1963) suggested that the children who fail lack the protection of the system and may bring into force their own defence mechanisms, resulting in under- or over-reactive behaviour. This makes it even more difficult for them to fit in with established school expectations. Anna Freud warned that disruption is not the only problem behaviour that should concern us:

> individual children who as late as the ages of fourteen, fifteen or sixteen show no such outer evidence of inner unrest [are] perhaps more than any others, in need of therapeutic help to remove the inner restrictions and clear the path for normal development however 'upsetting' the latter may prove to be (Freud, 1958, pp. 255, 278).

According to Holt (1967) and Donaldson (1978) most children initially do well at school. At this early stage the pupils seem eager, lively and happy (Donaldson, 1978), but by the time they reach adolescence their early promise frequently remains unfulfilled. She blames teachers and teaching methods in secondary schools. Others hold similar views (Sharp and Green, 1975), but although the problem is most often manifested at secondary age it can be seen that the seeds of disruption are often sown much earlier. This is to some extent because younger children are viewed more tolerantly (Chazan and Jackson, 1971) and because the pressures in primary schools until now have been less traumatic. Attitudes to minor infringements of school and classroom rules appear to play a significant rôle in the subsequent development or cessation of disruptive behaviours.

HMI (1979) defined disruptive behaviour as 'Any behaviour which prevents other pupils from learning and causes undue stress to the teacher'.

When children do not respond quickly to the teacher's requests, the teacher may wait for attention, ignore the behaviour, switch to something more attractive, or decide to intervene or comment. How such interventions and comments are made can greatly affect the pupils. This was investigated by Kounin

(1970) who studied group management in a Detroit kindergarten, and many of his findings are relevant today. He classified teacher 'desists', telling children to stop doing something, along three dimensions: firmness, clarity and roughness.

Firmness described the degree to which the message that the teacher meant what was said and that it was to be done *now* carried over to the children. It involved following up the instruction and ensuring that it was done, watching the child, walking towards him or her and speaking emphatically rather than questioningly or quaveringly. Other children also responded to the instruction and stopped misbehaving: the 'ripple' effect.

Clarity conveyed who was to stop, what was to be stopped, and what should be done instead. This is in contrast with generalised admonitions to a class to 'keep the noise down' or 'be quiet' (Scott MacDonald, 1971).

Roughness concerned the teacher's expression of anger or frustration by look or tone and threats, or even physical punishment. Kounin confirmed Scott MacDonald and his co-workers finding (1971) that 'rough desists' were less effective than clear ones and also caused more disruptive reactions. Scott MacDonald found that 'desist' behaviours of the teacher more often led to off-task and disruptive behaviours of pupils within three seconds of the desist and were the least effectively used as control mechanisms by teachers. On the whole, desists created no significant improvement in behaviour, they merely served to stop some of them temporarily.

What is socially acceptable or desirable behaviour according to one teacher may not be quite as acceptable to another. Behaviours which may be tolerated in one school or area would not be so tolerated in another. Managing these behaviours in groups of thirty or more seems to require somewhat different skills from managing individuals and small groups. These managerial skills also seem more difficult to acquire and in some instances need specifically to be taught. Teachers are thus in the position of having to learn not only teaching of curriculum subjects but also class management strategies. Engaging in both at the same time is a complex process not easily mastered. An attempt to unravel some of these complexities is made in subsequent sections under three separate headings: *class*, *behaviour* and *task* management.

SOME TYPICAL PATTERNS OF BEHAVIOUR PROBLEMS

The most frequent and unwanted classroom behaviours reported by teachers in many hundreds of schools in our studies were, in order of frequency, as follows:

(1)	attention-seeking	included by most
(2)	disruption	teachers (90+%)
(3)	short concentration span	referred to by about
(4)	aggression	40% of teachers
(5)	negativism – refusal to work or co-operate	referred to by a few teachers (10%)
(6)	lack of motivation and lack of interest	

These behaviours correspond to the findings of Wheldall and Merritt (1984b) who recorded 'talking out of turn' (TOOT) and 'hampering other children' (HOC) as the most frequent unwanted classroom behaviours reported by teachers in their researches. Other problem behaviours such as lying, stealing, truancy, fighting, fire-setting and vandalism were mentioned infrequently and were of less concern to teachers, for they took place more often outside the classroom and so seldom disrupted the work of the class. It is the six classroom problem behaviours listed and their management upon which we will focus in this chapter.

The behaviours which prevent the teacher from teaching are generally *attention-seeking* and *disruption*. *Lack of motivation* and *boredom* are major problems from the pupil's point of view. They are probably due to the fear of failure (Holt, 1962) and can lead to various displacement activities including disruption and attention-seeking, the *acting-out* dimension or *withdrawal*. Children who are withdrawn receive much less teacher attention and concern, but may be the ones who, as Freud (1958) has pointed out, need the most help in the long term if they are not to develop more severe and even chronic emotional problems. Behaviour problems need also to be regarded as on continua from mild to severe and profound. A pupil asked to settle down to work may do so immediately, may mutter and mumble under her breath and slowly but eventually start work, or at the other extreme she may explode in a torrent of abuse, hitting the teacher as she walks towards her. There is usually a history of minor infringements and indiscipline leading to such outbursts, coupled with a number of instances of mismanagement.

Teachers often refer to their pupils as 'problem children', as though they were a separate group; in fact their differences are more of degree. But where there is an overemphasis by the school upon academic goals and a neglect of personal needs, more children seem predisposed to fail and become 'problem pupils' in the school's eyes (Rutter *et al.*, 1979; Laslett, 1982; Hargreaves, 1984). Galloway and Goodwin conclude as follows:

> Moreover these differences cannot readily be attributed to the catchment areas which the schools serve. The implication is that the number of pupils regarded as having special educational needs on the basis of their difficult behaviour depends more on the school they happen to be attending than on the pupils themselves, or their families (1987, p. 151).

Croll and Moses identified what they called a 'slow learner behaviour pattern', characterised by 'lower levels of engagement in work, particularly work directly on a curriculum task, high levels of fidgeting and much more time than other children spent on their own distracted from work' (1985, p. 133). They also found that teachers spent more time with these pupils but that this still did not bring their work up to an average standard. The children with behaviour problems shared most of the characteristics of the learning difficulties group, and half of them were also in that group, but the teacher was less likely to work with them and they distracted other pupils more. Although these are described as patterns of behaviour associated with particular learning or behaviour difficulties, the same patterns can be observed in any group of children or adults when the work given is too difficult for them or not sufficiently motivating and engaging.

Some children with learning difficulties tend to be more sub-dued in the classroom than their peers. They may be less responsive and less curious than other pupils and tend to adopt a passive rôle. This may well be a learned phenomenon resulting from past unsuccessful learning experiences so that they have ceased to listen and to try. Other children, some 25 per cent according to HMI (1979), who are not the most difficult in terms of behaviour often leave school at the minimum age with modest or no tangible achievements. These pupils are often patient but passive, lacking motivation and stimulus. Such pupils were labelled RHINOs (Really Here in Name Only) by a recent Grampian regional working party, and are regarded by Lawrence *et al.* (1977) as too apathetic to protest.

Despite the current concern about disruption in schools, which has culminated in the setting up of a committee of inquiry under Professor Elton, the majority of classrooms are relatively quiet and orderly places in which good teaching can be observed. Talking still accounts for almost all the misbehaviour observed and is still the most chronic form of misbehaviour (Davie *et al.*, 1972; Wheldall and Merritt, 1984b; DES, 1989). Steed (1985) has suggested that we should not expect pupils to pass through secondary education in particular without protest; they should not be schooled so easily. It has been suggested that children perceive the game element in classroom time in a way we as adults tend to forget. This game element often makes up for the 15,000 hours spent compulsorily in schools, making it less boring and almost endurable. Anyone who has undertaken any number of 'shadowing' day-long duties as a consultant to a school or LEA will know of the interminable tedium of much of the school day, relieved only by social interaction and the thrill of 'the game'.

Pupils' strategies to conceal learning difficulties include:

- withdrawal
- avoidance
- evasion
- distraction
- digression
- disruption
- daydreaming
- clowning

One of the unsurprising findings in relation to pupils manifesting behaviour problems is that they suffer from:

- a low self-esteem;
- a much diminished sense of self-worth (Wilson and Evans, 1980).

The more severe their problems, the lower seems to be their self-esteem. The connections seem to be that 'since I am useless and perceived by others to be useless and hateful, then I might as well behave as I like and live up to that image'. It is difficult for anyone for whom no one has respect to develop self-esteem or learn to have respect for others. It is this vicious circle that the teacher must systematically set out to break down, and the strategies and techniques which follow later try to explain how to do this.

CHILDREN AT RISK

Behaviour problems manifested in school seem often to be the outcome of extra-school influences combined with the impact of the school's curriculum, especially the 'hidden curriculum'.

Head teachers of schools commonly report that their pupils with learning difficulties more frequently come from homes where the social conditions are disadvantaging, often both socially and educationally disadvantaging. There is also a similar pattern according to West (1982) in relation to the backgrounds of children with behaviour problems. This is, however, not the whole picture: it could be suggested that children from more advantaged circumstances are less likely to be perceived by teachers as prone to learning difficulties and behaviour problems. The home circumstances may, for instance, provide a set of social and linguistic skills and strategies which may keep the child out of deeper conflict in the classroom. In any case, home background can be seen as providing an 'at-risk' factor by failing to supply the appropriate social techniques for fitting into a larger group, or it may fail to provide basic emotional support which the child then seeks to satisfy in various and often inappropriate ways in school.

Where families are under duress and there is discord and quarrelling, break-up and divorce, illness and hospitalisation, children again become vulnerable and may suffer anxiety and distress (Herbert, 1975). Where family stress leads to lack of affection and support for a particular child, or to positive rejection and even abuse (Kempe and Kempe, 1978), the child suffers emotionally and behaviour and schoolwork can deteriorate. These consistent factors underlying disruptive behaviours have been found by many researchers in long-term studies from Robins (1922; reported in Robins, 1966) to West (1982). The disruptive behaviours emerge under stress or at crisis points in a child's life. Once they occur, they may go on the school record and a reputation is established with peers and teachers from which it is difficult to escape (Mongon *et al.*, 1989). Families which predispose their children to be at risk in schools have been found to be those with particular types of disciplining technique (Robins, 1966; Hewitt and Jenkins, 1946; Jenkins, 1968; Mitchell and Rosa, 1981; West, 1982). These are summarised as follows:

- excessive physical punishment;
- gross laxity in disciplining;
- inconsistent use of disciplining techniques, which becomes

serious when associated with neglect, and very serious when associated with rejection (leading to aggression and violence);

- excessively overprotective methods;
- excessively controlling in emotional terms, using withdrawal of love as a major strategy – more serious when coupled with too high standards set for the child.

The child behaviours most highly associated with later criminality according to Mitchell and Rosa (1981) were:

- stealing
- destructiveness
- wandering from home
- lying

Excessive worrying and food fads were shown by these researchers to have a negative correlation.

Families whose children were least prone to become attention-seekers, disruptive or deviant were those where:

- the family was strongly approving of the child, her/his activities and friends;
- there were harmonious relationships within the family;
- the home routine was regular but not rigid;
- the demands made upon the child were consistent and supportive, and leniency prevailed over severity;
- standards of behaviour and procedures were open to discussion;
- the child appeared to develop strong positive feelings towards the parents which later transferred to others (Peck and Havighurst, 1960).

When children under family stress or under duress because of fear of failure come to a school where rigid and punitive disciplining techniques are used, for a time in the younger years unwanted behaviours may be suppressed and produce a false sense of conformity and control. When these constraints are released, such as out of school or at lunchtimes, pupils release their tensions and frustrations to the extent that bullying and scapegoating increase. Art lessons and sports sessions often also provide release valves for this suppressed energy. Any teachers in such a situation who try to act informally can release for themselves unparalleled behaviour problems. In these circumstances an inexperienced teacher is advised to wean towards freedom and openness rather than expect pupils to be able immediately to cope with it.

Pringle (1973) showed that a heavy and inflexible use of school rules was actually linked with bad behaviour, whilst vandalism was shown elsewhere to increase in settings where there was lack of mutual respect between pupils and staff or lack of feelings of responsibility for the pupils' own learning and to the school.

The incidence of seriously disruptive behaviour, according to Lowenstein (1976), was 4 per cent, working out at about one or two pupils in any classroom. He found that 10 per cent of pupils were occasionally disruptive. However, where pupils were clustered in low-ability or disadvantaged groups, then the problems were more common (West and Farrington, 1973; Laslett, 1977a). Teachers in these circumstances who report that 'all my class are behaviour problems' can find that working with them for long periods of time is extremely stressful, especially when they are given little support.

Disruption has also been found to be more common in secondary than primary schools, amongst boys than girls, and in urban rather than rural areas. Although teachers report that problems are on the increase in all these groups, there are still many schools and classrooms where there is no disruption. Some schools seem to succeed in reducing pupils' delinquency rates whilst a few seem to produce higher rates, according to Galloway and Goodwin (1987). Pringle (1973) linked violent and disruptive behaviour with a curriculum which placed too little emphasis on individual, non-academic achievement and too much on competition. In such a setting, Hargreaves (1976) maintained that pupils were unable to achieve academic success and so turned to disruption and bullying to gain attention and status. He argued that streaming merely aggravated this problem.

Pupils who come from difficult or distressing home circumstances, with or without a learning difficulty, are more at risk in a school system where little care and attention is given to the individual and his or her needs and concerns. Secondary schools, with their large numbers of pupils and continually changing timetable of rooms, teachers and subjects, can increase these pupils' vulnerability, for it is easy to begin to feel alienated and lose identity and identification with the school and its purposes in these circumstances. This is not to say that secondary schools and large institutions cannot overcome these problems where the staff and pupils share common ideals and purposes. Primary schools, because of their small size and continuity of staff contact with pupils, can more easily prevent the 'at-risk' children from suffering further stress and alienation, but even this is not a necessary contingency since much depends upon the people in these schools and the *quality of the relationship* which they offer to the pupils in their care.

To counteract disruptive behaviour in schools, Lawrence *et al.* (1984), in their review of research, proposed an 'X' factor. They advocated strong controls in school but advised that these must be characterised by *warmth, friendliness* and *participation.* Their research in two comprehensive secondary schools, one co-educational (1,200) and one boys' school (800), concentrated on teachers' strategies for dealing with trouble once it had arisen, rather than finding out how to prevent it from arising. Teachers were asked to keep notes of every disruptive incident, how they dealt with it and what the outcome was, to build up a file of successful interventions. Although this is useful, it is insufficient to help establish a theory and practice for prevention.

During one week, staff in one of the schools reported 77 incidents, including fighting in class, insolence, talking, whistling and eating sandwiches in lessons. As a result of their incident analysis, Lawrence *et al.* offered teachers the following advice:

- nip the incident in the bud – if a problem is brewing try warning the pupil off or order her/him to switch seats (what happens when they will not?);
- take account of group dynamics in class – look for leaders, find ways of changing the group layout, stand in a different place;
- do not accuse groups of theft when only two are involved;
- talk to individual troublemakers outside lesson time, especially when a pupil is becoming a persistent nuisance over several lesson periods;
- give children the benefit of the doubt if they make excuses which cannot be checked, such as stomach-ache;
- defuse a potentially dangerous situation by cracking a joke;
- think carefully before getting too angry about pupils eating in class;
- avoid becoming personally involved, be alert to your own feelings and state of mind and be careful not to over-react if you are in a bad mood;
- if you do decide to have a confrontation, do it on your own ground and on your own terms, and know what you are going to say.

The authors advised that schools themselves can cut down on disruptive behaviour by changing their timetables, curricula or internal organisation. They can space out periods with the same class and cut down time a particular group of pupils spend together. They could find more efficient means of changeover between lessons and avoid over-rigid structures or sanctions for misbehaving.

Now, whilst this list contains some useful advice, it also conveys an attitude of teacher style and action that is negative and austere. It is a *policing* policy they have recorded, not their positive, supportive 'X factor'. In teaching, one needs to work for harmony and involvement in the task, not aim to preside over suppressed resentment by the use of control devices and policing. It is an approach to disruption which is symptom-orientated, treating the pupils as troublemakers and most often in the wrong. If, however, one is aware of the social and psychological context and content of pupils' behaviour, it can be seen that it is often the teacher who perhaps should change in attitude and approach to lesson planning and teaching in order to engage and involve all the pupils. Containment strategies are uneducative and pupils can come to reject schooling as a hateful, unedifying chore. They become alienated rather than educated young people eager to seek further development.

One further factor which needs to be considered is the inter-

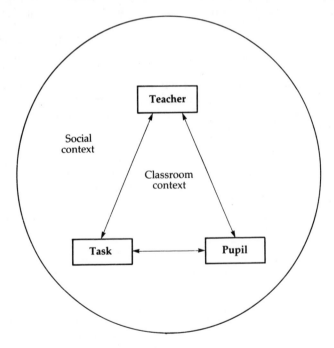

Figure 4.1 *The interacting forces in the learning environment*

action between the pupil and the curriculum and pedagogy, the cognitive dimension. Research by Kerry (1979), for example, showed that boredom and dead time caused pupils to switch to clowning, social interaction and other off-task behaviours considered by teachers to be a nuisance or disruptive. Associated with this is the fact that, if the curriculum itself is not very exciting, the learner may turn his or her attention to misbehaving under the eyes of the teacher for the sheer excitement that this engenders. The inexperienced teacher may often over-react to this, or inadvertently encourage it by inappropriate control strategies. Unsuitable peers may also be a contributory factor. How these behaviour problems can be prevented from occurring, or managed if they do occur, will be examined in the following sections.

CLASSROOM MANAGEMENT

Over recent years more serious attention has been given than previously to the organisation and management of classroom resources (Montgomery and Rawlings, 1986), classroom layout and positioning of desks (Wheldall and Merritt, 1984b), density problems (McGrew, 1972), and determining classroom rules and social agendas (Wragg and Kerry, 1979). These concerns have all proved important in helping gain and maintain the attention of the children in the class. They become essential when children have to be taught what others pick up incidentally in the course of lessons. This difficulty with incidental learning is a characteristic of children with learning difficulties (Green *et al.*, 1982). If teachers can pinpoint organisational features to teach these pupils, many muddles and much noise and confusion can be prevented.

Organisation of the setting

Most primary classrooms and some secondary ones are laid out on a group plan, with pupils seated in fours, fives and sixes round tables rather than in rows. The purpose of table groupings is to facilitate social and linguistic interaction between the pupils whilst working on group activities. What most often occurs is that the task given is an individual one which does not require interaction, and thus talk is more about requests for rubbers and pencils, or is irrelevant social chit-chat (Bennett, 1986). This table grouping can increase opportunities for children with learning difficulties to spend time off-task, avoiding or evading cognitive activity. Research by Wheldall and Merritt (1984a) showed that pupils spent more time concentrating on-task and producing more work when they were organised in rows. They were also found to be easier to control when at single tables. When working in difficult settings, it is most helpful to organise the layout which best suits the task until a routine of getting on with work is established and then it will not matter much what layout is used. If pupils are highly distractible, placing them in a quiet area can be helpful, perhaps facing the wall where there are no pictures to catch the eye. Work at study carrels or individual work stations, which can easily be constructed (Montgomery and Rawlings, 1986), can also help these children. Opportunities to use tape recorders and headphones in the work stations can be an additional means of focusing concentration on the task in hand. Where collaborative learning is in progress, tables for pairs work or larger groups can be arranged. Flexibility in attitude is needed towards the arrangement of the room and furniture.

Teaching position

The work of Wragg and Kerry (1979) stresses the importance of not teaching from the same position in the classroom all the time. For example, it is possible even in a fixed-bench laboratory to teach from the side benches and from the back of the room whilst directing pupils' attention to the board or screen. Diagrams and pictures pinned up on side walls also provide different focuses for their attention.

Wherever the teacher stands to teach, there is a 'cone zone', subtending a 30–45° angle and extending about 4–5 metres, in which pupils (about one-third of the class) receive most teacher attention. Children with learning difficulties and those with behaviour problems learn to sit outside this searchlight zone and can avoid having to answer many questions or receiving a great deal of teacher notice when they are off-task. The cone zone will be deflected to the right or left of the teacher depending on his or her hand preference. Placing children by the teacher's desk at the front of the class, or to one side of the room where there may be fewer distractions, can act against the interests of the pupils when they need to attend to what is being said. Thus children at study carrels need to be brought back into the centre of things during class activities and discussions. Because pupils with learning difficulties and behaviour problems give teachers less reinforcement by answering fewer questions and by inattention, teachers tend to give attention to those who do offer it (Good and Brophy, 1972) and to give more extended information and support to their attentive and responsive pupils. Pupils who receive less teacher attention and support will tend in turn to give less attention and interest themselves and so they make less learning progress than they might. Those pupils who are overdemanding of attention can frustrate the teacher's intentions to spread individual tuition, or can prevent the teacher from doing other intended tasks, and hostility and frustration can grow. Placing these pupils in the cone zone and using cueing strategies and training devices to help them learn to pause and think, wait, or obtain help from another source can help release these tensions and deflect potential disruptive outbursts.

Quality of the learning environment

It has frequently been recorded (Galloway and Goodwin, 1987) that problem classes and low-status learner groups, which include those with learning difficulties, are often given the lowest-status teachers and the least pleasant environments in which to work. The quality of the architectural aspects of the learning environment, as has already been noted, is part of the hidden curriculum which suggests the worth, or otherwise, of its inhabitants. It is, therefore, essential that the classrooms and resource centres for children with learning difficulties and behaviour problems are maintained to the highest quality and standard. At the least, they should be no poorer in quality than any other room the pupil might enter. Children who are distressed, irascible, explosive, distractible or noisy need an environment which is quiet and calming. The first essential is a carpet or carpet tiles and quiet, cool colours for the décor. Carpeting has the most surprising calming and quieting effect on previously noisy classrooms, it cuts down chair and table noise and pupils do not have to speak louder to overcome the background hubbub. This has a particularly relaxing effect for all concerned. If the tables and chairs are also of good quality, the correct size and not pitted, marked and scribbled over, this is also beneficial. Where graffiti appear regularly, this indicates pupils' lack of involvement in the work presented and their alienation and dissociation from the institution. It becomes essential to take positive action and erase graffiti before these become a tool of abuse.

Resource organisation

Pupils with learning difficulties have more problems than others in reading labels and instructions and in remembering where things are placed or locating them in space. It is therefore essential to devise equipment routines for getting things out and putting them back. The simple activity of tidying up after themselves is an important routine for them to learn so that it eventually occurs automatically. Although the introduction of monitors and duty rotas can give needed responsibility to some children, it can also be an undesirable device for absolving the rest from any responsibility for their own work and work space. The general goal should be to enable the pupils to become self-organised and self-generating, and they will not be if they are attended to by monitors.

Difficulties with reading can be overcome by, for example, colour coding and naming areas containing different apparatus, for example red for language, blue for mathematics, and so on. Most disturbances occur when books, pencils and apparatus are being distributed as this is a good opportunity for socialising, causing a disturbance and releasing tension. Much of this can be avoided by establishing the equipment routines early on. These routines should not be arbitrarily imposed but discussed with and explained to the pupils so that they know why things are thus. The rules can be changed when better ones are evolved by the pupils or new ones can be devised by them as needs occur. Their rules can be recorded and posted on the wall as a reminder to all. What is particularly important is that just the right amount of time is given for the routines to be completed, without some spinning out the time and others rushing and not doing things properly. Proper completion of tidying up, for example, can then allow a resumption of seats and some quiet for a few moments so that the pupils can leave the room in a calm and orderly manner and frame of mind.

Size of rooms and furniture

Where there are difficult classes or disruptive pupils, it is particularly important to have a large room or fewer pupils in it, so that furniture can be spaced out and individual study areas made. The space allows for ease of movement between tables with less opportunity for pushing others and knocking their work off the table top. The teacher may also move quickly to areas of noise and disruption and be seen moving to them.

Proximity and movement towards pupils is often sufficient to cut down or stop unwanted behaviour.

Every class needs a home-base and pupils need a place to put their personal belongings and school books. The personal space may be a place at a table but this reduces flexibility of movement about the class for different tasks. It may be a personal filing drawer in a chest of such drawers at the side of the room. Most classroom fights of young pupils begin in defence of territory or defence of property. With older pupils, fights and disruption more often arise from gratuitous verbal insults of one kind or another.

If the room is smaller than desired, then judicious choice of furniture and tall storage cupboards can give maximum flexibility and space.

Setting the classroom rules

On first meeting a class, it is not usual for a teacher to dictate a set of rules, the social agenda, for the classroom. However, each teacher has a set of implicit rules and guidelines which, over a period of time, are made explicit to the pupils. According to Wragg (1981), observing 313 different lessons, these rules centred mainly upon:

- no talking whilst the teacher was talking in a public situation;
- no disruptive noise;
- no interfering with others;
- various rules for entering and leaving the room.

Each of these rules is more likely to gain compliance from the pupils if the reason for it is explained to them. Thus, whilst a sharp 'Don't talk whilst I am!' may temporarily stop the undesirable muttering, the quieter but more positive 'Sarah, listen please so that you will know what to do' will be likely to gain a better and more long-lived attentional response from the pupil (Scott MacDonald, 1971).

Ideally, one wants pupils to enter the classroom quietly, to be welcomed, smiled at, encouraged and listened to, whilst all the rest settle to tasks left uncompleted or prepare themselves for the next session. To achieve this a long period of training may have been necessary. This training towards autonomy may have been easy where pupils, as in nursery and reception classes, arrive a few at a time over a longer period and settle to activities of their choice, which have already been set out by the teacher or nursery or classroom assistants. In other settings, most of the pupils arrive at once and have to wait until all are assembled and registered before teaching begins, a period of dead time such as noted by Kerry (Wragg and Kerry, 1979). Entering the room can be the source of disruption which spreads throughout the lesson and so it is important to manage this period rather than quell the disruption once it has arisen. To induce calm and quiet, it is useful in such circumstances to line the pupils up outside the classroom and calm the queue down before it enters the room. The teacher can then stand by the doorway and send away noisy entrants to the back of the queue as they try to enter. It is usual practice to be very firm on first meetings about this and send the pupils out again and again until they enter quietly. This usually only takes two returns. It may seem a trivial point but carries to each one an important message that the teacher really does mean what he or she says. This is what Kounin (1970) would consider both the clarity and firmness of the message which the effective teachers demonstrated. When sending the pupils out and quietening the queue, it is essential that Kounin's third principle, not shouting or acting 'roughly', is upheld. It is much more effective when quietening to do so quietly but firmly, and encourages pupils also to lower their voices. Shouting teachers induce shouting and noise in their pupils. Once the pupils learn to assemble and enter quietly, they can then be moved to the next stage, which is to enter as soon as they arrive and sit or stand waiting to begin, or start work immediately, whatever routine the teacher has established with them.

The more formal the setting, the less opportunity there is for flexibility and personal autonomy for the pupils. These formal settings are thus less suitable for pupils with learning difficulties, who particularly need to learn how to become independent and autonomous young people and for whom each smallest opportunity to achieve personal control is very important. One of the problems with a routine such as lining up before entering the classroom is that, once successfully established, it becomes an end in itself and is not seen by the teacher as a stage towards something more appropriate.

Room management (RM)

Some useful examples of effective room management come from the EDY (Education of the Developmental Young) staff training programme at the Hester Adrian Research Centre, Manchester University, and have been evaluated by McBrien and Weightman (1980) and Farrell (1985). Behavioural principles underpin the programme and these have been taught to some four thousand staff from schools for pupils with severe learning difficulty. The techniques involve allotting specific rôles to staff in the special classroom during activity periods. There is the *individual helper* who works with individual pupils for short periods of time, the *activity manager* who looks after the rest of the pupils during this time, and the *mover* who protects the other two from the disturbances of toileting, fetching materials, sharpening pencils and disruptions. Thomas (1985) studied the effectiveness of RM techniques in a primary school, using the parents and an ancillary helper with some success.

Similar organisations can be seen in embryo in nursery classes, where the teacher acts as activity manager and assigns the nursery assistant as mover and a parent helper or ancillary to engage in language work with individuals. If more training could be given to teachers to promote ways of facilitating language work after the style of Chazan (1974) and Blank and Solomon (1969), considerable help might be forthcoming for many children in ordinary classrooms. These researches concerned the exploration of questioning and conversational techniques for promoting language and cognition in the early years, tasks in which Tizard (1987) has found parents more effective than nursery schooling. Ordinary school teachers could then learn to organise and train their helpers more specifically to facilitate language using RM principles.

In primary and secondary settings (Booth, 1982; Hart, 1986) where ancillaries, peripatetic remedial and support teachers work alongside individuals, giving structured intensive help during ordinary lessons, the RM techniques could be said to be working in a diluted form.

The term 'room management', in fact, does not seem to be entirely the best description of what is being undertaken when translated to the ordinary setting. It is more rôle and task management which is under consideration in most circumstances. A number of schools which operate such support schemes were reviewed by Hodgson *et al.* in a recent NFER survey (1984). More recently, the numbers of primary schools developing and evaluating parent-involvement projects, particularly in reading, has rapidly multiplied (Wolfendale and Topping, 1985; Kirklees LEA, 1986; Topping, 1986).

Whilst assistance from other professionals, support teachers and parents can be extremely helpful to both teacher and pupil, the majority of classroom teachers do not have such help. One of the purposes of this text is to try to show the lone classroom teacher that it is possible to maintain class control and task involvement whilst, at the same time, undertaking group and individual teaching in task context.

Wolfendale (1987) lists the pedagogic advantages of having extra personnel who would corporately bring about learning gains by:

- giving immediate feedback;
- swiftly applying correction procedures to error;
- promptly reiterating instructions;
- facilitating self-monitoring by pupils;
- ensuring that short-term sessional or daily goals are met;
- redirecting pupils to alternative or related tasks;
- flexibly matching materials and resources to child;
- anticipating and dealing with behaviour;
- maintaining motivation and on-task behaviour by frequent attention, interest, encouragement and support.

She argues that an RM type of approach within primary classrooms, where each child receives some structured, intensive teaching and support during a school day, would be advantageous, and sets out nine learning gains which could accrue from this.

The use of human resources to improve learning can clearly be seen as valuable when listed in this way, but in practice all the contributors do not always pull in the same direction. Parents, aides and ancillaries can have different educational aims, goals and purposes for the children, concerning truth and factual correctness. They often do not value fantasy play or see the purpose of many of the teacher's goals and intents, and why should they? They have not received a professional training.

Where support teachers are involved, they can often engage in a programme of work in the classroom quite divorced from the mainstream work or even alien to it, and bring their segregated provision into mainstream as task segregation. The teachers in primary classrooms often do not have the chance to share plans and purposes with each other because no time can be set aside for such discussion.

It can be extremely useful to have a *mover* in the classroom to help a pupil with severe emotional and behavioural difficulties, but even then the pupil may decide to monopolise the mover totally and provision finally results in that child having a personal tutor to manipulate in the ordinary classroom. In such a situation, the teacher might well have been able to cope if there had been a reduction in class size. In order to support pupils with learning difficulties and special learning needs, it is perhaps this factor above all, the one of class size, which needs to be addressed in ordinary schools.

Class size

A teacher with 36 lively pupils cannot provide adequately for all their individual learning needs and yet engage fully in mixed-ability teaching. If there is one pupil in that group with behaviour problems as well, then the extra time needed to be devoted to him or her means that all the rest of the pupils will suffer some neglect.

Class size and organisation have been a focus of several recent studies. In the ORACLE project (Observational Research and Classroom Learning Evaluation), the researchers (Galton *et al.*, 1980a) concluded that the purpose and organisation of group work needed a lot more attention. They found that children supposedly in working groups were in fact doing individual parallel work on their own rather than co-operatively and that there was little small-group collaboration. Galton *et al.* believe that the maximum class size for a British primary school should be twenty, in order that effective mixed-ability teaching can take place and co-operative learning be promoted. However, it is not class size which determines effective collaborative learning, but teaching method and task. It is individual tuition for all pupils within class activities which requires that class size be cut down accordingly. A class size of twenty might well seem appropriate if: (a) it does not have several disruptive pupils in it, (b) it does not have more than one or two pupils with learning difficulties, and (c) every member of the class can read and write at the 7–8-year-old level. The reception-class teacher, for example, must provide a much greater degree of individual and small-group tuition than any other to help the pupils begin reading and writing. To do this really well, a class of 12–15 is more than enough, as phased versus cohort entry can show. In a study of five reception classes, it was found that as the class size increased the reading progress of boys decreased with each termly intake (Montgomery, 1977).

Classroom organisation and special needs

Classroom organisation as a subject has been much better researched in the special education needs area than in ordinary classrooms. In this respect, the text *Learning Together: Teaching Pupils with Special Needs in Ordinary Classrooms* (Hodgson *et al.*, 1984) is essential reading and provides an excellent summary of how the special needs of pupils with visual, hearing or physical impairment can be met in the ordinary classroom. This is done by describing the organisation of space, seating, resources, support teaching and task management in relation to each of these groups.

Children with learning difficulties, as has already been noted, have a higher proportion of associated difficulties and impairments from mild to severe than other groups of children. Clumsy children, those with mild visual anomalies or recently discovered hearing loss, are common in all classrooms and could benefit if their teachers used the checklists in Chapter 14 of *Learning Together* to make sure all conditions were as favourable to the pupil as possible.

BEHAVIOUR MANAGEMENT

General classroom management strategies have been evolved by generations of teachers over a hundred years of compulsory schooling, to keep the 'classroom crowd' in check when it did not necessarily wish to be where it was or to be doing what it was asked to do. These general strategies, once learned by each new teacher, provide the power and influence to maintain control of the class and to direct its behaviour to educational goals and purposes. Each new teacher is usually temporarily afforded this power by having the designated status 'teacher' but gradually loses this influence if his or her class control strategies are not appropriately used. Even the youngest pupils will put these powers to the test in a continuous struggle for dominance over someone whose job it is to direct their attention and behaviour to a specific task rather than to allow them to do entirely as they wish.

There seem to be two factors which need to be determined before any proposed intervention. First, it is important to decide whether an *individual programme* needs to be drawn up or if the *class management strategies* should be examined and revised. Second, consideration should be given as to whether a training or a retraining programme should be instituted. Behaviour management strategies for individual pupils derive much, according to Berger (1985), from social learning theory's principles (Bandura and Walters, 1963) of social reinforcement and modelling, and from the work of Skinner (1953) on operant-conditioning and behaviour-shaping procedures. Social reinforcement theory can be considered as an extrapolation of conditioning theory to the social arena for behaviour modification.

In Special Education many of the behaviour management techniques derive from industrial and clinical psychology and are referred to as Applied Behavioural Analysis. A wide range of materials and books are now available to help teachers in this area. These include Preventive Approaches to Disruption (PAD) for secondary schools (Chisholm *et al.*, 1986); Teacher Information Pack (TIPs) (Dawson, 1985); BATPACK (Wheldall and Merritt, 1984b); the Special Needs Action Programme (SNAP) of Coventry LEA (Ainscow and Tweddle, 1979; Ainscow and Muncey, 1984); Daily Teaching and Assessment for Primary Age Children (DATAPAC) (Ackerman *et al.*, 1983); and Observational Research and Classroom Evaluation (ORACLE) (Galton *et al.*, 1980a). Most of these packs are materials designed to bolster or be used as in-service training and updating programmes.

The decision to train or retrain rests upon whether the pupils know the rules of the 'classroom game' or not. Very young children coming to school for the first time often do not heed the teacher's general requests for quiet, or to 'come here and do this now'. Some may not know that swearing is not appreciated in schools or that there is anything unacceptable in the statements they have made. Older pupils, for a variety of reasons, may have wrested power from their teacher and the general classroom rules and mores may have completely broken down so that a class of adolescents behave as unconstrainedly as a class of egocentric nursery or reception-class children. The history of such a group is one of poor motivation and learning failure, particularly in secondary schools where a succession of teachers have been unable to cope with them or have just managed to cope by dominating and frightening them into a subdued but resentful state, using the drill sergeant's technique (Webb, 1962). Each new and unconstructive learning experience leads this group into lower self-esteem and more and more conflict with the established school order. This downward spiral is relieved only by voluntary withdrawal from the school in the case of truants or exclusions by the school governors on the recommendation of the head teacher.

If all the normal rules and routines have broken down and the setting is 'non-rule-governed', then the teacher has to learn to present the work in a *very* attractive fashion to gain the attention of the majority without waiting for all to join in. This means making it relevant and overtly useful, or explaining how it will be useful, in order to attract and maintain attention. This is *not* advice to be followed for a situation where classroom order has not broken down. 'Rule-governed' settings are, fortunately, the norm, and although pupils misbehave they respond by quietening *once the teacher uses the appropriate set of strategies.*

Classroom climate

Although some pupils were disruptive, Holt (1962) found that most of the rest spent their time in a fearful state. They were scared of physical punishment, verbal abuse, sarcasm, being shown up, and being generally demeaned. This is no environment in which learning is likely to be fostered. Withholding work or support, avoiding and evading are the only means such pupils have of exerting control over their own existence.

Setting an appropriate learning climate to help all the pupils is thus an important consideration. A simple first step is to draw a plan of the classroom and write out the first names of all the pupils so that they can be quickly learnt. Name learning is not only essential to classroom control but using them makes the pupils feel significant and known personally to the teacher. Pupils have expectations about the way they should be treated by teachers and a number of important studies have referred to this (Hammersley, 1976; Docking, 1980; Robinson, 1981). The general conclusions are that pupils expect teachers to be:

- *Firm* – and able to control the pupils and the class. The methods by which this is done, however, are not punitive or domineering.
- *Fair* – if reprimands or punishments are given then only the 'guilty' receive them. A whole class is not kept in because one child talks out of turn.
- *Consistent* – the teacher is well ordered and structured. Praise is given for worthwhile things and can be seen to be so.
- *Friendly* – the teacher is friendly, can 'take a joke' and laugh with pupils, but is not over-familiar.
- *Supportive* – the teacher helps pupils to achieve good results for their efforts and praises them for doing so. Most teachers are not supportive enough when carefully observed and not as supportive as they think they are.

and to:

- *Teach* – the teacher explains things well and gets work done. The pupils can feel they are making progress. Boredom is avoided.
- *Respect* – the teacher respects the pupils and allows them to retain a sense of dignity, receiving respect in return.

Teachers who can meet these pupil needs and expectations are the ones who have little trouble from potential disruptives.

These pupils' expectations are the attributes of those whom one could consider to be 'good teachers'. These teachers set the right classroom climate and they are fair and firm, they respect their pupils and take a kindly interest in them, as Wilson and Evans (1980) recommended. Such teachers provide good models for their pupils and have essential qualities for working with pupils with learning difficulties. Teachers good at dealing with disruptive pupils were found to be those good with all pupils. It is regrettable, however, that some teachers find it difficult to show compassion in their dealings with pupils and regard praising pupils for good work as 'going soft' or too 'feminine'. It is still unfortunately true in some classrooms and schools that 'teacher and pupil confront each other with attitudes from which the underlying hostility can never altogether be removed' (Waller, 1932, p. 196). Whilst education is conducted in this manner, and the drill sergeant (Webb, 1962) holds sway, the pupils with learning difficulties cannot be expected to prosper. But dominance, acrimony in relationships and hostility are not the necessary consequences of a process by which young persons must be inculcated into the values and purposes of their society. It is possible to achieve classroom control in other and more reasonable ways.

Classroom control

The 3 Ms strategy (management, monitoring and maintenance)

3 Ms represents a series of tactics which effective teachers use to gain and maintain pupils' attention whatever teaching method or style they subsequently use. It is a strategy which can be used with all age-groups of pupils from nursery to higher education.

(a) *Management phase* The teacher makes an *attention-gaining noise* such as 'Right', 'OK, class 3', 'Good morning, everybody', 'Uhumm!' or banging the door or desk. Some teachers just wait quietly until the noise ceases. Next the teacher gives a *short verbal instruction* such as 'Everybody, sit down', 'Get out your books', 'Listen carefully', 'Sit down and face this way now'. At this, most of the pupils will do as requested and fall silent but there are always a handful who do not. The effective teacher pauses, looks round, spots those who are not doing as requested and *quietly names* these pupils and individually instructs them to stop what they are doing and to listen. This is usually quite sufficient if a *check-back look* is given to bring the whole class to attention. The mistake that ineffective teachers make is to begin to shout 'Be quiet' and 'Sit down', as a general instruction to all the pupils. The raising of the teacher's voice and the general command to those who are already behaving as requested begins to engender hostility in them and seems to transmit information to the pupils that the teacher is not really in control and that he or she 'does not know the ropes'. There then can be a loss of confidence all round, with the teacher shouting more and more loudly and the pupils becoming more and more restive – a recipe for disruption.

The naming of individuals and the personal quiet instruction to them avoids creating resentment (O'Leary and O'Leary, 1973) in those who have done as they were told and emphasises the teacher's capacity to be firm and clear (Kounin, 1970). The naming also creates a *ripple effect* (Kounin, 1970; Scott MacDonald, 1971), for it silences others in the group around the one who is not attending. As soon as a lull in noise is produced and attention is directed towards the teacher, the *main theme* of the lesson should be introduced. A prompt start and a good pace at the start of the session will catch and retain the pupils' attention. Pupils with learning difficulties often have short attention spans and so long introductions and long monologues by the teacher will cause these pupils to 'switch off'. It is also essential that their written work is planned in short steps, allowing them to achieve each objective set before proceeding to the next.

(b) *Monitoring phase* Immediately the teacher *changes the activity* from the pupils listening or participating as a group in an introductory activity to moving back to their places or to getting out books, apparatus and so on, pandemonium can break out. Activity change of any kind is always an opportunity for tension release after a period of quiet and concentration, and pupils seldom fail to avail themselves of it, particularly where the methods of teaching are more formal and where there is less opportunity for independence and personal autonomy. In the move back to their places, for example, not all pupils will settle immediately and not all will want to. The teacher's usual response is to make a general request for quiet. If the pupils are well managed and know that the teacher will follow up this request, then the response is for the class to quieten. Kounin's firmness criterion (1970) is apparent. However, all pupils will at some time test this firmness and authority, and will do so particularly in the early stages of a relationship with a teacher. If the teacher fails to use the monitoring tactics, then the lesson will deteriorate into noise and disruption. Monitoring requires the teacher to follow up the general request for quiet with naming. The teacher should quickly cast an eye round the class, and on observing the focus of most noise quietly request that pupil by name to settle down, get out the book, stop talking, and so on. The whole class needs to be very quickly settled in this fashion before any individual is given specific help. Monitoring should only take about 5 to 30 seconds. It can be done in two different ways. First, by the teacher standing in one spot and using the control techniques from there. Second, if the room is large and with difficult acoustics such as in a science laboratory, or if it is an awkward shape as in some open-plan settings, then monitoring can be effected by the teacher quickly moving round to each group, settling them by naming and a few quickly delivered, short verbal instructions.

Once the round of monitoring has been completed, it can be reinforced by *non-verbal cueing*. Catching the eye of a pupil about to talk and frowning or giving 'stink look' can stop the unwanted behaviour and reinforce the notion that the teacher is all-seeing and all-knowing (Wragg and Kerry, 1979) and means what he or she has just said. Non-verbal cueing is a very restful way of achieving class control, and whole lessons can be conducted in this fashion once the teacher has mastered the techniques. Useful cueing behaviours are as shown in Table 4.1.

Table 4.1 *Cueing behaviours*

Visual cueing – eye contact	Auditory cueing	Proximity and contact cueing
simple looking	a light cough	calming hand on shoulder or top of head
raised eyebrow	snap fingers	remove object of distraction
frown	clap	walk towards
'stink look'	'ssh' noise	move towards and stand near
shake of head	quiet naming	sit next to
pointing with finger	tap on desk with pencil	gently turn and propel individual towards place
smile (wry, questioning, plain, etc.)	teacher waits silently	hold hand or arm and lead (younger pupils)
wink	tut-tut noise	put arm lightly round shoulder and guide (younger pupils)
nod	uh-uh (to encourage)	
head shake (tut-tut type)	aah! (to warn)	

Rushing quickly towards pupils, or standing facing them with severe or cross expression are aggressive acts and postures which can frighten many pupils and in others invoke corresponding aggression or, at least, hostility and resentment. Recently, Wheldall and Merritt (1986) report that teachers in their research programme who used physical contact found an improvement in their pupils' learning, but physical contact has to be used with caution and could become an embarrassment in secondary schools.

The monitoring phase in any lesson should be short but it can be repeated regularly throughout a lesson if the noise level *seems about to rise* when one or two pupils' voices rise above the general murmur, or if absolute quiet is needed when any pupil begins to talk. The final and most essential requisites in monitoring are for the teacher to:

- obey the *five-second rule*: having told a pupil to be quiet, the teacher checks back to that individual within five seconds to see that the request is being carried out;
- observe the *lowest likely level*: the teacher uses the quietest and lowest observable level of intervention to obtain the desired response. The noisier and more excitable the teacher the noisier and more disruptive the class will become.

(c) *Maintenance phase*   Once the pupils have been settled by the monitoring techniques to the task, it is then advisable for the teacher to move round the class to each individual to find out how the work is progressing. In the maintenance period all the requests and queries of individuals can also be dealt with. They should be deferred during the monitoring phase to this period. During a lesson or period of study, if each pupil can expect to receive some individual *constructive comment* (PCI – positive cognitive intervention) on his or her work, attention to task will be greatly enhanced (Montgomery 1988).

It is this individualised attention to the task which encourages interest and effort and helps to extend the concentration span. The time given to the individual's performance on-task can enable the teacher to keep track of each pupil's response and progress and can facilitate curriculum diagnosis and intervention. In using PCI, it is very important to find positive or good features of the work thus far and consider how to take this on to the next level. Where collaborative learning is in progress, PCI is still an essential feature but more time can be extended to the groups. Systematic PCI helps teachers to distribute their time evenly amongst the class so that no pupils are ignored, and enables small groups to be drawn together so that particular teaching points can be shared. Where teachers find that individual pupils need extensive help, then the task needs reconsidering or the pedagogy needs reviewing. The extensive help is usually required immediately the pupils with learning difficulties are asked to respond in writing or to read materials and then respond.

Other tactics used for gaining and maintaining attention

Observing Often observing and recording the frequency of mis-behaviours of an individual can cause the behaviour to disappear (Dawson, 1985). The teacher who at regular intervals stands back from the group work and just looks round to see what is going on (*monitoring*) may note a misbehaviour. If instead of naming she/he simply looks at the miscreant or appears to be looking this will cause attention to be directed to the work again.

Counselling Pupils who misbehave or spend time off-task need to be talked to about this. It is important to send the other pupils out of the room, sit beside the pupil and simply open the conversation by saying 'Now, what was all that about?' or 'I want to speak to you about your behaviour'. It is sometimes the case that the pupil does not know that his or her behaviour is causing concern or that, in any lesson, 80 per cent of the time is being wasted. A personal but kindly and interested talk to try to find what is the trouble can often ease the situation considerably. It is essential not to confront the pupil by standing opposite and bearing down. This is aggressive and will not lead to a constructive dialogue.

Counselling after a noisy outburst can be particularly helpful in regaining normal relationships. A confrontation may have arisen with a pupil who shouts or swears at the teacher in a way which cannot be ignored but which, if reacted to aggress-ively, could provoke further abuse and refusal to co-operate. A recommended set of tactics from work with teachers in the Learning Difficulties Research Project (Montgomery, 1983b) is:

- *Deflect* – the confrontation by saying simply 'I'll speak to you later', giving pause for both teacher and pupil to calm down and reflect on their next action.
- *Hold* – immediately settle all the pupils to the task in hand.
- *Systematic PCI* – work round the class giving help and sup-port. *Include* the disruptive pupil in this in a normal fashion – do not bear a grudge, separate the task from the 'scene'.

- *Counsel* – as soon as possible after this, talk quietly to the pupil on his or her own in the manner suggested. Do not leave any pupil waiting until the end of a whole session for some normal contact.

Video recording   If a video is available it is useful in a few cases to record an area of the classroom where a disruptive pupil is and then use segments of this to play back and discuss in a counselling session.

Threats   Threats are the least constructive of strategies for gaining class control, for pupils will always test out their validity by default or intent, and if they prove empty behaviour will deteriorate further. The general classroom rule is 'never make a threat which you cannot or do not intend to carry out'. Since threats are usually about punishment and the consequences of misbehaviour, they fall into the category of 'desist' behaviours which a number of researchers have found to be ineffective (Becker *et al.*, 1967; Kounin, 1970; Scott MacDonald, 1971; O'Leary and O'Leary, 1973).

Reprimands   These are also 'desist' behaviours and have complex consequences when used. Where a teacher feels they must be used, they should be kept very short and sharp, or short and very quiet, delivered to the individual concerned. Loud reprimands have been shown in certain circumstances to increase disruptive behaviours of other pupils, whereas soft ones decreased the frequency (O'Leary in O'Leary and O'Leary, 1973).

Managing individual problem behaviours in the classroom

Whilst little attention seems to have been directed in research to general classroom control procedures, there has been considerable attention given to the management of attention-seeking and disruptive behaviours of the individuals within it. Becker *et al.* (1967) demonstrated in their study that behaviour management procedures applied to target children also exerted a controlling effect on the rest of the class. Their study showed that increasing positive attention to the time the pupil was on-task, and ignoring where possible the time off-task, caused an improvement in behaviour and over a nine-week period a decrease of 50 per cent in disruption in the two target children in each class.

Scott MacDonald's *Battle in the Classroom* (1971) describes the 'power of the smiling teacher' and how teacher 'desist' statements actually created a worsening of pupils' behaviour and certainly no improvement. He showed that 'desists', at best, stopped unwanted behaviour temporarily but must be followed by some indication to the pupil of what is desirable behaviour. In some instances another child's behaviour (a model), which the teacher could praise, demonstrated the required response.

Scott MacDonald found that desist behaviour seemed to work entirely against the teacher's own interest. In half the instances when 'desist' was used the pupil's behaviour showed no change – the desist did not stop the unwanted behaviour. In most of the rest of the instances (34 per cent) it caused a deterioration in behaviour. Although teachers seemed to have little success with desist behaviour, the 17 per cent of cases where they were successful were with the stink look and the sharp gesture. He found that verbal criticism generated the most negative response, especially if lengthy, and also had a negative effect on the pupil's neighbours. Satire was one of the worst desist behaviours the teachers could use: only one or two teachers on rare occasions managed to use it in such a humorous way that they gained a positive attitude.

Scott MacDonald concluded that most often teachers seriously underestimated their influence and impact on their pupils. They often did not feel they had control when they clearly did. This made them nervous of experimenting with ideas and techniques. They observed the effect they had on the pupil they were talking to but did not notice the marked effect that this behaviour had on all the pupils nearby. Through his help they discovered the powerful, terribly simple, means of influencing pupil behaviour: the 'deliberate *smiling teacher*'. He then set out to help teachers apply systematic approval to their classrooms with considerable success.

Other researchers, such as Blackham and Silberman (1971), Poteet (1977), Berger (1983) and Wheldall and Merritt (1984a), have all adopted such techniques and recommend them to teachers for use with pupils with behavioural difficulties. Wheldall and Merritt (1984) present evidence for the success of their behaviourally based methods with sets of case studies illustrating their effectiveness. Typical of their approach and all others using behaviour modification is to establish baseline behaviours, for example time out of seat, and then show the pupils this record. The teacher then explains that she or he will continue to watch them and, if their 'out of seat' scores drop, they will earn a team point. The pupils are shown their progress charts and praised. As can be seen, extrinsic motivators are used.

Cognition is involved, but the system is behaviourally based. It is directed to changing the pupils' behaviours by overt attention to them. These methods have clearly worked in the variety of settings they describe to decrease unwanted behaviours. The researchers found that, in addition, although their teachers did praise children more for work than they disapproved of it, they did not praise good social behaviour but merely nagged when pupils exhibited inappropriate behaviour. They set out to change this aspect of teachers' behaviour, to encourage them to approve of socially acceptable behaviours and cease nagging unwanted ones. Where the BATPACK techniques differ from strategies developed at Kingston is mainly in emphasis. Their approach includes the use of tokens as motivators whereas the latter does not. Both use attention and praise as reinforcement and reward.

In some researches and programmes tangible rewards are given in the form of tokens to buy gifts (Becker *et al.*, 1967), time out of lessons or off-task playing sports (Wheldall and Merritt, 1984b). In the long run it can be argued that these are unconstructive in helping pupils in ordinary schools develop positive attitudes to school and school work. They may work in the short term but surely teach us that the task itself is wrong for not being seen as relevant and engaging by the pupil, who therefore has to be 'bribed' to stay with it rather than doing it for its own intrinsic interest.

Behaviour modification strategies

Behaviour modification strategies are mainly built upon Skinner's theory and research on operant conditioning (1971). In this he draws attention to the discriminant stimuli in the presence of which behaviour is emitted and subsequently reinforced. The rate of responding is increased in the presence of reinforcers which may be both negative and positive but which both maintain the response: 'Good things are positive reinforcers. The food that tastes good reinforces us when we taste it. Things that feel good reinforce us when we feel them. Things that look good reinforce us when we look at them' (Skinner, 1971). The removal of a negative or noxious reinforcer also increases the likelihood of a response occurring. Punishment is an attempt to present the aversive consequences in order to decrease the likelihood or frequency of a response, and according to Skinner is an unreliable mechanism. Its unreliability is probably a function of the complex nature of punishment.

Punishment in human concerns contains cognitive contents according to Hirst and Peters (1970) in which there are retributive and reformative dimensions. In other words, only if the pupil accepts that what was done was wrong is the punishment truly a punishment and accepted as such. Only if the pupil sees the error of his or her ways and does not do the misdeed again can the 'punishment' be seen as punishing. Moreover, what may be a mild punishment for one pupil may, to another, be more severe. Even a withdrawal of teacher approval or support may be seen by some children as punishing and this does indeed seem to be the way in which some very positive teachers operate. The mildest withdrawal of their approval for their pupils' efforts is sufficient to stop any misbehaviour and redirect them to time on-task.

Operant psychology looks at measurable behaviour and tries to identify the variables of which that behaviour is a function. In the process operant psychology rules out as explanations the hypothetical constructs located inside the pupil, such as cognitive structures and stages (Vargus, 1977). Progress is defined by observable behaviours such as 'Robert can recognise and read aloud the first ten words introduced in the reading scheme', 'Sarah has been on-task now for 45 seconds', and so on. As the consequences of punishment are so variable, most of the literature on behavioural change has concentrated upon the rôle of positive reinforcement and recording its observable manifestations.

As children spend more time on-task, so they may become more successful and perhaps begin to find schoolwork more rewarding. This is what Wheldall and Riding (1983) consider to be change in behaviour of a different order 'and is the ultimate aim of all good teaching' (p. 14). They refer to the three-term analysis of behaviour or the 'Behavioural teacher's ABC': *A* refers to the antecedent conditions, or what happens prior to the behaviour occurring; *B* refers to the behaviour, or what the pupil is actually doing; *C* refers to the consequences, or what happens to the pupil after the behaviour (consequences are the positive or negative reinforcers already mentioned).

Inhibition and positive reinforcement (IPR) and modelling and positive reinforcement (MPR)

In IPR the pupil learns to inhibit or suppress the unwanted behaviour so that it is unlikely to be triggered. It is *not* possible to unlearn or extinguish it. The teacher either ignores the unwanted behaviour or makes a cueing sign to stop it and immediately positively reinforces by attention or praise the desirable behaviour or its nearest equivalent. The pupil is not told or made aware of the ultimate purpose, the *pro-social goal*, towards which the teacher is shaping the behaviour.

This technique is often misunderstood and misused. The inexperienced teacher most often ignores the unwanted behaviour in the 'rule-governed' situation, such as murmuring during the teacher talk in class, rather than pausing and waiting for quiet, or does not immediately support some opposite and competing desirable behaviour when the pupils *are* working.

Teachers who have tried IPR often report that, for a time, the pupil's behaviour becomes worse before it gets better. Often the reason for this is that the positive reinforcement is not contingent on (following immediately as a consequence of) the desirable response. Teachers often argue that the child does nothing desirable to reinforce. In this instance, another child's behaviour can be reinforced (MPR – Blackham and Silberman, 1971), or any other response which is the closest approximation to the desirable response can be supported. If the teacher feels that the behaviour must be stopped, *non-verbal cueing* can often suffice as a warning to stop rather than giving verbal desists. Again, as soon as possible, it is essential to try to find and reinforce a desirable response.

There are problems with 'ignoring' in IPR in an ordinary classroom. If the technique is not accurately used, other children will begin to think that the misbehaving pupil is being allowed to 'get away with it' and they will begin to imitate him or her. This can lead to a rapid deterioration of the whole class's behaviour from which it is a long, hard climb back to order. The teacher who resorts to shouting to quell the class becomes progressively less effective and the work and behaviour deteriorates. These are the common sequences of events for inexperienced teachers whose classes gradually become beyond their control.

IPR is extremely effectively used by teachers during PE, games, drama and music lessons where behaviour can otherwise quickly deteriorate. For example, when the pupils are set to 'Move quickly and quietly, as though you were a very tiny person', the teacher should move through the group complimenting individuals on their performance, e.g. 'Very good, Emma', 'Very nice, Stephen', 'Good, Sarah', 'Well done, Jason', 'Good try, Ram'. All of this amounts to a *shaping procedure*, where small, silly behaviours can be ignored but approximations to desirable behaviours can be reinforced.

MPR can also be used to reinforce the desirable behaviours of a partner of misbehaving individuals, or to reinforce the nearest pupils to them. It too is a very powerful strategy.

Time-out from positive reinforcement (TO)

In time-out from positive reinforcement the pupil is placed in a situation in which reinforcement – for example, the attention of peers – is no longer available following unacceptable behaviour. Time-out may be extended to include sending to a separate space within the room, sending out of the room, or removing to a separate time-out room.

The use of time-out in ordinary classrooms is complicated by a number of factors such as:

- larger numbers of pupils and difficulty in finding time-out space;
- collusion between the pupil sent out and those left inside the classroom;
- regulations concerning sending of pupils unsupervised from classrooms;
- the manner in which time-out may be introduced – for example at a crisis point rather than as a pre-planned policy;
- the tendency of the pupil in time-out to clown or refuse to acquiesce and obey the procedural rules.

The time-out strategy therefore needs to be adapted to suit the needs and the particular constraints of ordinary classroom settings. Suggestions for these adaptations are set out below.

When a child becomes upset or angry and starts to shout, or becomes excitable, refusing to settle down, it can be useful to send her or him to sit on a time-out chair. It must not be treated as a punishment or as an old-fashioned dunce's stool – this would be cruel. Other pupils should be encouraged completely to ignore the pupil in time-out. The special chair can have beneficial side effects as a *neutral zone* for calming down and regaining composure. The time on the chair should be of a short duration, 10–30 seconds only, especially for younger children. At the end of the designated period, the child should be asked very quietly if he or she is ready to resume activities.

Some schools and psychiatric units for pupils with severe behaviour problems and autistic children have a time-out room to which the child is taken and left for a few minutes or longer. This room is bare, devoid of furniture and fittings, with a secure window. Once the routine is established it is often enough just to say 'Time-out' and the pupil marches off into the room. It is obviously most important that the teacher does not forget him or her.

Sending out of the ordinary classroom, however, is not

advised: it is often against school and LEA regulations and the pupil often runs home, wanders off, hides in the cloakrooms and vandalises, steals, or stands pulling faces through the window. If the pupil has an accident, the teacher is responsible. In the event of a pupil becoming highly disruptive or unmanageable, another pupil should be sent to fetch help. The teacher should not leave the classroom.

Cognitive intervention strategies

In many situations, behaviour management involves more than simply shaping a pupil's behaviour towards some pro-social goal of which he or she is unaware. Most often it is helpful for the pupil to *know* what the teacher considers desirable behaviour and to agree that it is desirable if it is to have any effect. When modification of behaviour only is practised, Wheldall and Merritt (1984b) have shown that the task or the work done does not improve. This is not surprising since the shaping is not directed to it but only to a symptom arising from it. If the pupil knows *how to* achieve a good result because of the teacher's comment on-task, both social behaviour and work output can be improved. This can happen with some of the following cognitive interventions.

Catch them being good (CBG)

This is a mixed strategy. Instead of waiting for pupils to start to misbehave and then trying to find a positive behaviour to reinforce, the teacher should move round the class, catching pupils on-task being good. This will extend the time on-task that they spend and will also give them some information on how they are progressing. 'Catch them being good' is one of those techniques which are used sometimes to *shape* pro-social behaviours and, at other times, to direct and inform on-task behaviours, giving some limited cognitive feedback.

CBG is an active, positive and supportive intervention like smiling. It has to be used unsparingly to social and task behaviours, but wisely. It has to be *genuine*, said in a way that is fitting. Gushing and saying 'good' to everything will be discounted by pupils and derided. Catching them being good takes practice, and it demands a genuine interest in pupils' learning, a real desire to help them and a pleasure taken in their small successes. It is here that the approach is sometimes called 'soft' or 'too feminine' and yet, in all company management training initiatives, 'stroking' and positive feedback are highly regarded training targets for the good manager (Handy, 1971; MacDonald, 1978).

Behaviour contract (BC)

The problem behaviour is discussed with the pupil and the teacher may say, for example, 'If you spent more time sitting at your desk, your work would improve. You are well able to do it. Remember the rule is – *sit at your desk*. If you do, I shall come and help you. Do you understand?' Pupil nods. When the pupil sits at the desk for any reason, the teacher immediately attends, smiles or praises, acknowledges the fact and helps with the work. This is a simple form of verbal contract.

In secondary schools, disruptive pupils are often put 'on report'. They agree to carry a card or paper which teachers must sign if no disruptive behaviour has occurred. The contract is discussed and 'good' behaviour defined. The daily and weekly results are examined with the pupil and often the parents. Exclusion may follow if the contract is broken. If the contract is kept well for several weeks it is discontinued. Keeping it gives a chance for teacher attitudes to the pupil to become more positive and supportive. In some instances, the contract is used as a weapon by teachers, a reminder of the sanctions which the school may have – to exclude the pupil, removal from friends, transfer to new school, parents' wrath. Where the parents are not supportive and the pupil is not missing work leading to an examination, and does not care in any case, the contract is seldom kept.

Behaviour contracting is often used by Social Services Departments who draw up a semi-legal document with parents whose adolescent son or daughter is out of control. The drawing up of the contract causes all participants to negotiate the issues and define their rôles and actions which can then be written into the contract and are held to be binding. The document is then signed by each participant. A behaviour contract is thus an outcome of a considerable amount of negotiation and frequently of counselling. This attention to a pupil's problem and the interest of a skilled teacher using counselling skills can be the therapy the pupil needs. The contract puts the two in contact at regular intervals and allows for some therapeutic release of tensions. If it is done well, as it often is, the teacher becomes a respected and significant adult to whom the pupil will refer when getting into difficulty. This formalised relationship may be just enough to set the pupil back on an even keel. Establishing the contract should, therefore, be carefully done, not in a perfunctory but in a probing and tension-releasing way.

Behaviour contract may be applied to any one of the behaviour modification strategies already outlined: in inhibition and positive reinforcement when the teacher discusses the behaviour to be inhibited and why; in time-out to explain the reason and what would be satisfactory behaviour; and in modelling and positive reinforcement to discuss the sorts of behaviour the teacher would like the miscreant to model and why.

Positive Cognitive Intervention (PCI)

PCI has already been outlined in Chapter 3. The essentials are that pupils should receive a comment indicating the good features of the progress already made, the next step which could be undertaken, how and why the work done was good, and how it could be improved or developed. The intervention should make a developmental teaching point and positively reinforce progress so far. The pupils should feel encouraged and know clearly in which direction to move or which goals to pursue. Where pupils have done no work thus far, or merely written a few words, it is up to the teacher's ingenuity to *find* something to support, for example good work in the previous session, good ideas put forward in the discussion, writing looking good and well formed, and so on. It is essential that every pupil should expect and receive some PCI during every lesson or session.

TASK MANAGEMENT

Good teaching: tasks and tactics

In order to reduce violence and disruption in schools, many strategies are being employed, including nurture groups, withdrawal and adjustment units, intermediate treatment centres, special counselling schemes, pastoral care systems, behaviour modification techniques, support teaching, and school-based social workers. Of increasing importance is the attention also being given to the curriculum task. Pupils themselves expect teachers to be good at teaching and expect to learn something from them (Robinson, 1981). Even so, a number of researchers in education would have us believe that good teaching cannot be defined and that there is no coherent theory of education. It is probably more accurate to say that good teaching is so complex that the descriptors and theories we currently use do it less than justice, and that, although good teaching can be recognised and agreed upon, it awaits a full analysis.

When Mongon (1985) suggests that in-service provision should allow teachers to share and contextualise their experiences, so that they develop a theoretical perspective which illuminates and enhances their own work, this sounds exactly right. But if this theory and practice endorses an expository method or a product-orientated pedagogy this can be disadvantaging for pupils with special needs. When some teachers, for example, are helped to make their implicit theories explicit, they are often found to be prescriptive, punitive, domineering and inflexible. Others reject the rigid and narrow perspectives of 'covering the syllabus' and of punishing 'deviance' and espouse a problem-solving philosophy, but nevertheless act quite differently when observed in the classroom and are unable to detect the mismatch between their 'theory' and their practice.

The tasks which we set all pupils need the most careful scrutiny for exactly what they will achieve for the pupils' own learning in terms of content, coherence, breadth, depth and relevance. In addition, the cognitive skills must also be taught which will enable these contents to be manipulated and used. In Chapters 2 and 3 these two particular task variables and their underlying rationale and relevance were explained at some length in an attempt to share the author's view of good teaching. Suffice here to reiterate (1) the emphasis upon process methods of teaching and learning to activate the cognitive skills and (2) the central objectives in teaching which were proposed to help teachers design and present tasks which enable the pupils to (a) think efficiently and (b) communicate those thoughts succinctly. Emotional tensions are released and needs met in the collaborative and supportive climate in which the work is undertaken.

The DES (1985) stated that the most important attributes of good teachers were that they are punctual, reliable and co-operative, command respect from their pupils and take an interest in what they say and do. Most of these so-called qualities need have little relationship or relevance to good teaching. They reflect an establishment's perspective on the well-groomed, well-ordered teacher. In retrospect, the best teacher I ever had was never quite punctual, was absent-minded, never marked our books but often read them and talked to us about them, was regarded by us as an indifferent teacher at the time, but gave us insights into arts, music, drama and literature which I have enjoyed and pursued ever since.

Good teachers may not always arrive on time but their pupils will begin to work without them or wait quietly until they arrive – they do not need to be policed. Constant unpunctuality, however, reflects a lack of respect for pupils and their needs and interests. Where DES fails, as Wolfendale (1987) points out, is that 'they list the ingredients of the meal but leave the making and the consumption to others'.

Pupils, too, have implicit theories about good teaching which for successful pupils often match those of their teachers. It is more often the difficult pupils who have a soundly-based understanding of what the attributes of a good teacher are and what constitutes a satisfying educational task, though even their accounts are not entirely to be relied upon. Grounded theory also needs to be empirically tested rather than accepted merely because a number of people agree.

Tactics

Wragg and his co-workers (1984, 1981), in observing several hundred lessons, defined a number of task-related practices which contributed to successful teaching. These were being well organised, having the appropriate resources ready, and making a prompt start. SED (1978) and HMI (1986) emphasise pace of lessons and timing of work, together with *matching* the task to the needs and abilities of the pupils. By 'matching' was meant the careful presentation of a task which is challenging to the individual learner but which is not too difficult to prevent him or her accomplishing it.

Tactical lesson planning

One of the effective ways of managing the classroom task which was tested in our research on appraisal has already been noted. This was to teach the teachers who were having difficulty managing their classes to develop a *tactical lesson plan*. This helped them avoid long informational sessions and long periods of monotonous work on one type of task so that the attention and motivation of the potentially disruptive pupils and those with learning difficulties was not lost.

Tactical planning thus involves activity change based upon the attention span of the class, for example from *listening* to *reading* to *writing* to *practical work* to *oral work* to *reading* to *practical work* continued to *writing*. For practical work in subjects such as social studies, English, French and history one could substitute group problem-solving, rôle play, drama, simulation exercises, mime and so on.

Group tactics

The practice of grouping was encouraged in the Plowden Report (1967) as a strategy for sharing out the teacher's limited time. By grouping children who were 'roughly at the same stage', i.e. ability grouping, the children would help each other along and all would benefit from the social and linguistic interaction. HMI have also frequently complained of late that there is too little group work going on in schools with a loss of all the benefits that should accrue (HMI, 1983, 1986; DES, 1985).

As Bennett (1986) has pointed out, there is little firm evidence to support these views. In fact there was more support for the view that, whilst most children sat in groups, they were most of the time engaged in individual work (Galton *et al.*, 1980b). Even when the pupils did interact, most of the interaction was not about the task. Bennett *et al.* (1984) and Bennett (1986) subjected task talk to a qualitative analysis, only to find that the talk was of a very low order: questions of how much, where, and how many, requiring one-word answers. They found that higher-ability groups tended to engage in more informational and extended talk than lower-ability groups. In these settings they found that teachers sat at their desks marking work with the pupil. This gave rise to queues and a lack of group teaching and of general supervision.

Group tactics of these kinds can be seen to be ineffective measures or vehicles for teaching. What is observed is akin to child-minding. If children are to learn, then the task needs to be designed so that they want to do it and by working together produce something better and more substantial than they do as individuals: synergy. Group tactics can then contribute to the whole rather than deflect the potential learning of individuals.

Task analysis

Some of the techniques of task analysis have already been referred to in Chapter 3. Close control of the task behaviours can help teachers manage pupils' behaviour, for on-task behaviours are most often incompatible with disruption and attention-seeking behaviour, and so assist classroom control.

SUMMARY AND CONCLUSIONS

Children who have learning difficulties often also manifest attention-seeking and disruptive behaviours in classrooms. These are often greater in scale than but not fundamentally different in quality from those of other pupils. Many of these problem behaviours are a direct result of the interaction between socio-emotional, interpersonal, cognitive and classroom factors.

Inconsistent socialisation strategies in the home can facilitate the display of difficult behaviours in a number of settings including the classroom. Lack of appropriate models and poor social integration and interpersonal skills can predispose children to be difficult to control, particularly in large groups. When such factors also interact with school and classroom failure, and attempts by teachers to confine and constrict pupils in negative and hostile ways, and to coerce them to engage in tasks which they find ego-threatening, tedious and irrelevant, then the scene is set for disruption. If the teachers' own social skills and classroom control strategies are poor, they seek to dominate, subdue and police their pupils. As these pupils grow older and enter fourth- and fifth-year secondary schooling, they become less likely to tolerate such controls, and hostilities and disaffection become entrenched. Such pupils become 'hard to reach' as well as hard to teach.

The more serious the behaviour problems, the lower the self-esteem of the pupils is found to be. A large proportion of pupils with behaviour problems and low esteem have, in addition, learning difficulties which may have precipitated the behaviour problems as a response to learning failure and frustration. If learning failure can be overcome and self-esteem for school work built, then pupils become less disruptive.

Pupils with behaviour problems, and with or without learning difficulties, profit from the same types of intervention. These interventions involve teachers taking a positive, supportive and constructive rôle in the management of the classroom, in the management of the pupils' behaviour and in the management of the task, so that all pupils can enjoy success. A number of ways in which these positive approaches to teaching and learning can be achieved have been discussed in the foregoing pages. The key constructs which teachers have found helpful to organise their teaching around, and in-service providers to develop programmes about, are: 'catch the pupils being good', 'positive cognitive intervention' and 'management, monitoring and maintenance'. When these were taught in appraisal sessions to teachers with disruptive classes, lessons were converted from failures to successes, and disruptive incidents waned and disappeared. Other researchers, such as Wilson and Evans (1980), confirm the effectiveness of firm but supportive control, kindness and warmth for the learner, and an interesting and enjoyable curriculum as the key factors in overcoming disturbed behaviour of children and adolescents in special units. These and similar strategies have been found to have a powerful effect in ordinary classrooms.

Access to the curriculum can be opened up on a very much broader scale for children with learning difficulties and behaviour problems if the teaching methods and strategies are changed to cater for them and the needs they share in common with many other children. Within this context, individualised tuition can prove even more effective, and here training in teaching to objectives and in precision teaching can act to strengthen and support the teacher's ordinary practice.

APPENDIX: RECORD SHEETS

Record Sheet A

A.   <u>RECORD SHEET 1</u>   TARGET PUPIL_____

DATE _____

Chronological Age _____

Position in Family _____

A. BASELINE RECORD (the level of a particular behaviour before it was changed)

TIME		DAY ONE	DAY TWO (multiple baseline)
a.m.			
	TOTALS		
p.m.			
	TOTALS		
BASELINE FREQUENCY AVERAGE PER DAY:			

1. DAYS ONE AND TWO – RECORD *FREQUENCY OF UNDESIRABLE BE-HAVIOUR.*
2. It may be possible before DAY TWO to develop a code to represent the different problem behaviours, e.g. H (hit) S (shout) W (wander).

Record Sheet B

| B. RECORD SHEET 1 | TARGET PUPIL_____ |
| | DATE _____ |

B. OBSERVATIONAL RECORD (copy extra sheets as necessary

TIME	OBSERVATIONAL RECORD	ACTIVITY/LESSON
(30 secs)		
(30 secs)		
(30 secs)		

Record Sheet C

C. RECORD SHEET 1	TARGET PUPIL_____	
	DATE _____	
HISTORICAL AND ANECDOTAL RECORD		
Note down from the other records the *main types of problem behaviour observed. Note down any additional observations.* Now identify the TARGET BEHAVIOUR which you wish to change ready to record in detail in Record D.		
	List of problems noted DAY ONE	List of problems noted DAY TWO
	Additional notes or activities	Additional notes or activities
IDENTIFY TARGET BEHAVIOUR		

Record Sheet D

D. RECORD SHEET 1	TARGET PUPIL_____
	DATE _____

TARGET BEHAVIOUR

When the target behaviour occurs write down an exact behavioural record of what you saw.

TIME	OBSERVATION	ACTIVITY/SETTING

Difficulties in learning and literacy skills

INTRODUCTION

Children with learning difficulties may or may not have difficulties with literacy skills and it is not uncommon to find some of them reading as soon as peers do. If this occurs, then their general learning difficulty tends not to be noticed until later, when their comprehension is found to be much poorer than their word recognition and they fail to understand instructions and the meaning of more complex prose. In secondary schools, if these pupils work hard and learn much of their test material by heart or are taught sufficiently well to achieve mastery learning (Carroll and Bloom, 1971), then they can also achieve success in public examinations. It is only when presented with new and complex material which requires advanced cognitive processing that these pupils can become vulnerable to failure, for their memory and practice routines are insufficient to cope. If they can be taught and given practice on higher-order reading and cognitive skills, then they can achieve good results. It is also possible to find students arriving at higher education who have never been obliged to exercise their full range of cognitive skills and whose learning strategies are weak. They, too, underfunction unless specific attempts are made to diagnose and help them. Students in FE may be found equally, if not more, vulnerable to these undiscovered learning difficulties.

It is more common, however, for teachers to regard learning difficulties as synonymous with reading difficulties (Croll and Moses, 1985; Clunies-Ross and Wimhurst, 1983). Pupils are often labelled 'remedial' and are withdrawn for special reading support or, particularly in secondary school, may be put into remedial groups or classes. These practices and definitions will need to be carefully considered if we are to meet these pupils' special educational needs.

Literacy difficulties and underfunctioning are to be found on a much broader scale than the onlooker might suppose. Thomas and Harri-Augstein (1972), for example, found that 50 per cent of students in university, polytechnic and college had difficulties in using higher-order reading strategies and could be considered inadequate readers. In-service training studies with teachers have shown that only some 5 per cent of them have well-developed study skills; the subjects included those who had taken first degrees at universities in subject areas as well as B.Ed. courses (Montgomery, 1983).

The Scottish Education Department survey (SED, 1978) found that some 50 per cent of pupils in their schools suffered from learning difficulties of some kind. Only 1½ per cent of this group had what were termed difficulties in acquiring basic skills which required specialist remedial help, the rest had more general difficulties in:

- understanding specialist terminology and concepts;
- using study skills or not being taught them;
- acquiring higher-order reading skills;
- seeing the relevance of school learning to daily life;
- pacing of lessons and of revision and reinforcement time;
- genuine pupil–teacher discussion to explore the learning problem;
- catching up with an accumulating work load when no help was given on how to catch up;
- presenting work with an image inappropriate to the age and stage of the pupils' development;
- too much broken attendance, and absences, too many different teachers in a week or a year in the same subject area.

To redress these problems and insufficiencies the survey recommended that attention should be directed to two major concerns – the curriculum and the pedagogy – if children with learning difficulties are to achieve more.

It is not uncommon to find that children with learning difficulties have the additional handicap of *specific learning difficulties* in reading, spelling and/or writing, so that without specific diagnosis and intervention they may never crack the code and have only a hotch-potch of reading knowledge; or they manage it so late in their school careers at junior or secondary stage that reading and spelling tuition is no longer available for 'learning to read' when pupils are expected to be 'reading to learn'. At this level remedial tuition may be made available, but children with learning difficulties need more than this form of help. Slow learners with specific learning difficulties tend to defy their classroom teachers' attempts to help them and by junior school stage their difficulties have compounded to such an extent that they cannot participate adequately in general classroom activities, for much of the work set by this time demands a considerable amount of independent reading and writing. These pupils have, until the recent moves towards integration, tended to find themselves referred for special schooling fairly quickly. Failure at an early stage in schooling may cause such depression and frustration that the pupil begins to become disruptive and so referral for special help or special schooling will be even more rapid. If the pupils' responses to failure are to withdraw and become quiet and subdued, then they remain unnoticed or unreferred for much longer. Girls tend to respond more often than boys in this way and demonstrate a slightly lower incidence of behaviour problems and a lower rate of referral. Regrettably, it is still true to say that many people, teachers included, mistakenly judge another's ability by the capacity to read and write.

THE DIFFERENT LEARNING NEEDS OF PARTICULAR GROUPS OF POOR READERS

On the whole, learning difficulties in the intellectual area also tend to permeate the areas of both reading and writing, so that pupils show a slower developmental profile than their age peers. They tend to be slower than peers to start to read and write and to make general progress with literacy skills. If progress is markedly slow in comparison with other children, unless the teacher is very careful and supportive the pupil can easily become disheartened and frustrated and lose motivation to try. If emphasis is placed upon reading in infant classes to the exclusion of valuing other skills and abilities, the scene is set for learning failure in 'cracking the code' of written symbols.

In addition to low intelligence there are a number of what Heaton and Winterson (1986) called extrinsic factors to the reading process which might cause delayed or slow progress. These are:

- interrupted or poor schooling
- socioeconomic disadvantage
- sensory and physical handicap
- neurological impairment
- emotional problems

The precise weighting which may be given to these factors in any individual's literacy development is as yet incalculable. The general result is that children in these sub-groups tend to be lumped together as a slow reader group. They may then be given the same form of reading support and the whole group may also be regarded as 'slow learners', when arguably this is not so and when there are often quite clear signs of higher ability.

Children who are slow readers because of their generally slow development and acquisition of concepts and skills would appear to need a *reading development programme*, one which reinforces the knowledge and skills which they have already acquired and which moves them steadily to the development of a wider range of skills and more advanced reading knowledge. It has already been suggested that this is best done through a cognitive process pedagogy which increases extended dialogue between pairs, encourages peer reading and provides motivation to communicate in writing. Composing and writing can be supported by the use of word processing facilities and overlays on the Concept Keyboard. This is a special computer keyboard which is used as an overlay; the overlays can be prepared by the teacher with pictures, words or phrases. When the 'concept' is touched it appears in writing or graphics on the screen, and thus sentences and stories can be written by touching appropriate parts of the keyboard. With appropriate printer facilities, these stories can be printed out. Concept Keyboard blanks are a flexible tool for teachers.

Teaching basic skills to slow learners thus becomes an across-the-curriculum approach to learning. This may be supported by task analysis strategies and direct instructional techniques (Carnine and Silbert, 1979) to overcome particular learning blocks where this seems appropriate. These techniques should not be allowed to dominate the curriculum, for implicit in them is the idea that the learner is the passive recipient and the teacher defines and sets all the learning goals. As can be seen, a curriculum weighted in this way is undesirable for children with learning difficulties (Wood and Shears, 1986) and does not help them in their need to establish autonomy (Green *et al.*, 1982).

Children who have had interrupted or poor schooling need a similar developmental programme to the above but skills and concepts about print together with learning-to-read strategies may need to be directly taught. Building in specific skills in this way can enable these pupils to make sudden and rapid progress as they incorporate this knowledge into their skills repertoire. In-class support teaching can be particularly helpful for these children. What they do not need is a withdrawal programme so that they miss more of the ordinary curriculum experiences.

Children who are socioeconomically disadvantaged may be

particularly deprived of experiences with print and with the more formal uses of language. In these circumstances an enriched range of experiences with print will be helpful, together with a curriculum which emphasises oralcy and offers a wide range of language experience activities. In this form of nurturing environment, steady and often rapid progress will be seen with many pupils revealing unsuspected talents and often creative and high potential. There are many new initiatives in the reading area which can be incorporated into the general curriculum of the school to help these pupils. Many of these, the Apprenticeship Approach to reading (Waterland, 1985), *Story Chest*, Parent Involvement Projects (Wolfendale, 1987), computer-assisted learning (Hope, 1986) and language experience methods, are already in use in infant schools. What is now needed is an opening up of junior, middle and secondary schools to these techniques. In this way it will become possible to cater for a much wider range of learning needs and development than currently seems possible. Junior school teachers need to be trained in teaching both the acquisition and development of reading. In most training courses only perfunctory attention is given to these areas and so it is not surprising that once a child begins to fall behind or fails to progress in reading this failure is most likely to be confirmed once the pupil has left the infant school. The 'remedial' tuition which many are then offered is given by untrained teachers (Croll and Moses, 1985) and proves insufficient to help them (Cowdery *et al.*, 1983; Gittelman and Gittelman, 1985). What needs to be questioned is whether 'remedial' provision is at all suitable to meet these particular pupils' needs. The assumptions behind the notion of remediation are that the pupil has fallen behind because of some intrinsic failure to acquire a particular range of skills and concepts, and that this can be 'cured' by applying a particular remedy. Once applied and given sufficient time to work the pupil will acquire the necessary skills to function at least at age level. This deficit model locates the problem as being within the child but as we have seen this is not always the case and even when it might be said to be so it can be argued that a more appropriate curriculum and pedagogy would have protected the child from failure (SED, 1978).

Poor literacy skills are not the necessary consequence of emotional problems (Rutter, 1975) but may develop because of the pupil's frequent absence from school or as a result of 'absence of mind' when teaching sessions are in progress. Characteristic of these pupils' 'reading profiles' are areas of conceptual and skills omission: skills learnt one day appearing to have been lost the next, only to return days later. It is very difficult for pupils to learn in a consistent way when their minds are upon their troubles. Their emotional needs must be satisfied if they are to progress. Apart from good teaching, these pupils need an emotionally satisfying curriculum and pedagogy and a positive and supportive school, ethos and learning climate. This can be provided by the language experience and negotiational problem-solving approaches already described and to be found detailed in Bowers and Wells (1985). These methods have been researched in a large variety of classrooms and found to be particularly helpful for pupils with emotional and behavioural problems. Their use and effectiveness with slow learners has already been recorded. A series of controlled studies are also in progress.

Most physical impairment does not affect the acquisition of literacy skills unless there is some specific neurological impairment as with motor skills in scanning and handwriting. Most often, technical aids can help to overcome or avoid these difficulties. The lowering of sensory input in vision can be overcome to varying degrees by the use of low-vision aids and classroom management strategies (Hodgson *et al.*, 1984, ch. 10), or if these fail then the pupil may learn Braille (or Moon in some circumstances).

The effect of perceptual impairment and visuomotor difficulties can prove to be more disadvantageous to the reader than lowered input. This form of impairment can affect the individual's ability to process the information obtained from the senses and is much more subtle in its effects. Nevertheless perceptual impairment is considered to contribute to only a small proportion of the difficulties observed (Vellutino, 1979; Yule, 1988).

The effects of lowered sensory input in the area of hearing can have much more profound and long-term effects. Most recently the condition known as 'glue ear' has been found to create many more problems for language, speech and reading than had hitherto been supposed (Wisbey, 1984, 1987). Reference should be made to Webster and McConnell (1987) to pursue the subject in more detail. The classroom teacher should be alert for cues to possible hearing impairment and should consult the special needs co-ordinator and also the peripatetic hearing impairment adviser or whoever is the key worker in this field. It may be helpful to know that under the provisions of the new Education Reform Act (July 1988) LEAs may now make provision for speech therapy. Whilst some previously did so, others left such provision up to the health authority even though it was contained in the statement of educational needs. Some possible cues to hearing impairment are when the pupil:

- looks intently at the speaker's face (young children may grasp another child's face and turn it so that the mouth can be seen);
- tilts own head or turns towards speaker;
- likes TV, tape recorder, etc. too loud;
- own voice may be loud or with a slightly strange and monotonous pitch;
- frequently asks 'Pardon?' or 'What?', misunderstands or needs instructions repeated;
- has difficulties with listening skills, sound discrimination and location;
- has difficulties with reading and spelling often characterised by sound substitutions, endings such as '-ed' omitted and indecision over high-frequency sounds in dictations, depending upon the type of hearing loss;
- tends to daydream or is easily distracted during listening activities, has short attention span in such tasks and a seemingly poor auditory memory;
- has language or speech problem, word-order errors, e.g. walk go me;
- often exhibits behaviour problems (one frustrated and un-diagnosed 4-year-old had a severe behaviour problem and was only referred for special help when he jumped off the top of the piano in the playgroup);
- has a history of hearing loss, ear infections or frequent colds;
- is 'catarrhal' or a mouth-breather.

CHILDREN WITH SPECIFIC LEARNING DIFFICULTIES

The Warnock Report (DES, 1978) gave official recognition to a group of children with a specific kind of learning difficulty. This difficulty is observable in their severe problems in acquiring reading and writing skills despite average, or even well above average, levels of intellectual ability. Nevertheless some LEAs do not distinguish this group in their diagnostic and referral procedures and group them with slow learners because they are slow to learn to read. Schools likewise often group children with general learning difficulties and those with specific learning difficulties together and offer them all so-called 'remedial' tuition or teach them in segregated groups for part of the school week.

Able children in these settings become frustrated by not having their potential recognised, being grouped with slow learners and receiving a watered-down or slow-moving curriculum. They can easily become depressed and unmotivated or may 'act out' their frustrations and become disruptive, with all the usual consequences including truancy and suspension.

The study of specific learning difficulties has had a long and complex history. Its roots may be found in neurological, clinical, experimental and psychological literature under the heading of 'developmental dyslexia'. 'Dyslexia' means that the individual has a difficulty with (*dys-*) words (*-lexis*), particularly in their written form. It is not a medical disorder or disease. The term 'developmental' indicates that the person has difficulty in learning to read, although most individuals with dyslexia do develop some reading skills. 'Acquired' dyslexia signifies that the individual was once able to read normally but has since lost that ability as a result of brain injury, insult or stroke.

Although it is usual in research literature to consider that 'dyslexia' refers to those cases where there is at least 2 years' decrement between reading and intellectual ability (Vellutino, 1979), or 2 years 4 months (Rutter and Yule, 1973), and that the pupil is of at least average ability, the same pattern of difficulties may be observed in some slow learners. In these circumstances the main difficulty is considered to be in the intellectual area, and so curriculum and pedagogy should be directed towards needs in this area. But additional and specialist help will be needed to develop the reading and writing skills within this developmental programme. These pupils can be considered to have two major types of learning difficulty and are therefore children with complex learning difficulties. They are the most likely referred to special school at the end of infant schooling as they fail to make progress and show negligible educational attainments.

Patterns of specific learning difficulties can be summarised as follows:

- reading *and* spelling difficulties (developmental dyslexia);
- spelling difficulties alone (developmental dysorthographia);
- handwriting difficulties (developmental dysgraphia).

Some pupils may have reading, spelling and handwriting difficulties. Firm evidence for a form of number difficulties (developmental dyscalculia), separate from the verbal processing difficulties found in the area of reading and spelling, is as yet not available.

Research over several decades has shown that remediation

techniques in the area are less effective than might be expected. For example, Chazan (1968) concluded that initial gains generated by participation in programmes of remedial reading were not sustained. This is not an uncommon finding where remediation is directed to only half the problem. It must be remembered that underlying any reading difficulty is an even more severe spelling problem. Remediation which deals only with phonics and not with linguistics can give initial gains which are not maintained as the needs change (Gittelman and Gittelman, 1985). Guthrie (1978) analysed the results from fifteen studies undertaken between 1969 and 1975 and found that in several studies a learning rate double that in normal readers was produced. Regrettably, in most studies carried out in this period the group of poor readers was not divided into those with and those without specific learning difficulties. In 1981, Tansley and Panckhurst were able to conclude that the definitive approach to poor reading had not turned up. This is still true, for poor readers have many different learning needs as already indicated. Pupils with specific learning difficulties are also a separate group with very specific learning needs, for whom some forms of remediation, for example the APSL (alphabetic–phonetic–syllable–linguistic) programme, are more effective than others.

Pupils with specific learning difficulties and at least average abilities can profit from a remedial tutorial programme (Gittelman and Gittelman, 1985; Cowdery et al., 1983; Hickey, 1977; Cotterell, 1974). This needs to be 'logical, structured and sequential' (BDA, 1981) and the tuition given *by a trained teacher*. When such specialist remedial tuition is given to no more than pairs of children at a time on two or three occasions per week, pupils can be brought back up to at least their age level (McMahon, 1982) within six months to two years (Schiffman and Clemmens, 1966). What remains to be seen is whether, now that we have been teaching these methods to primary teachers and students in initial training, class teachers can incorporate the teaching of the requisite concepts and skills into everyday classroom experiences. What they should not do is subject all pupils to the programme whether they need it or not.

According to Critchley and Critchley (1978) some 10 per cent of the school population are reading, writing and spelling less well than they should be and 'dyslexics' make up only a small proportion of these (this proportion is 4 per cent according to Rutter et al. (1970) in the Isle of Wight survey). The problem is defined as follows:

Developmental dyslexia is a learning disability which initially shows itself by difficulty in learning to read, and later by erratic spelling and by lack of facility in manipulating written as opposed to spoken words. The condition is cognitive in essence, and usually genetically determined. It is not due to intellectual inadequacy or to lack of socio-cultural opportunity, or to emotional factors, or to any known structural brain defect. It probably represents a specific maturational defect which tends to lessen as the child grows older, and is capable of considerable improvement, especially when appropriate remedial help is afforded at the earliest opportunity (Critchley and Critchley, 1978, p. 149).

The significance of this quotation is clear: reading difficulties are not the only problems these pupils have. There is now considerable evidence in the field to show that any pupil with severe reading problems will also have even severer spelling difficulties (Naidoo, 1972; Cotterell, 1974; Pollack, 1979; Frith, 1980; Miles, 1983b). In addition, the pupil may also have difficulties in handwriting co-ordination, orientation and so on. Thomson (1984) lists the problems which may be observed:

Specific Developmental Dyslexia should not be confused with learning disabilities resulting from dysfunction due to structural lesions of the brain. In MBD there is no family history of learning disability, neurological defects can be discovered on examination and there is usually a clear story of perinatal trauma, anoxia or ill health.
Evidence of impending dyslexia:–

1) Child lags behind peers in first steps in reading, e.g. gaining a basic sight vocabulary.
2) Gap widens and child becomes frustrated.
3) Child is late in learning the names or sounds of the letters of the alphabet.
4) Remains confused over the correct orientation of letters and numbers.
5) Often a delay in learning to 'join up' letters in script well into adulthood.
6) Confusion over the correct sequence of the alphabet, days of week and months of year, confusion over tables.
7) Difficulty in reading the time from a clock face.

The adolescent dyslexic

1) An unwilling reader, may even have an aversion to reading or a fear.
2) Prefers practical and outdoor activities to book work.
3) Slow reader.
4) Avoids writing.
5) Painfully slow at writing having to search even for words that s/he can spell.

6) Grammar, punctuation, literary style all imperfect.
7) Handwriting atrocious.
8) Verbally very good, logical, concise and impressive.
9) Slow copying or in dictation.
10) Polysyllabic words cause problems, chunks left out.

11) Mispronunciation – stress is put on wrong syllable *mis*cellanous instead of miscell*an*eous – of words expected to be in the pupil's vocabulary given socio-cultural condition.

12) Substitutes synonym for word to be read e.g. box for parcel, beer for ale.

Unfamiliar or longish words may be totally misread or not attempted.

Miles in his Bangor Dyslexia Test (1983a) confirms this constellation of potential difficulties and also includes digits forwards and backwards, b–d confusion, and reciting particularly the 6, 7 and 8 times tables as key areas of difficulty. Vellutino (1979, 1987) would interpret these difficulties as indicators of an underlying phonological processing difficulty rather than as significant in themselves. This is an important point in relation to remediation, for if memory for the sequences of letters in words, the days of the week, the digits in a series and the syllables in a word are considered the key assessment indicator the teacher might plan a remediation programme based upon teaching sequencing skills in each of these areas. This would be to little avail (Smith and Marx, 1972) when the underlying difficulty for the large majority of these pupils is in the verbal processing area (Vellutino, 1979, 1987; Snowling, 1985, 1987).

There is some considerable debate in the area of specific learning difficulties as to whether there is a separate pattern of problems constituting specific developmental dyscalculia (Kosc, 1974). So far, many of the number problems can be attributed to problems with verbal memory, reading difficulties, place order and spatial orientation problems associated with verbal processing difficulties. Difficulty in reciting tables is also attributable to verbal processing deficits (Wellings, 1980; Vellutino, 1979; Miles, 1983b; Hughes, 1986).

Modifications of the multisensory training for writing techniques and basic phonics of the APSL programmes have been developed by Bell (1984) for use with slower learners, and our teachers have found these helpful with groups of pupils and in support teaching.

METHODS OF INTERVENTION FOR CHILDREN WITH LEARNING DIFFICULTIES IN READING, SPELLING AND WRITING

There are a number of levels of intervention which Smith (1973) proposed in relation to the teaching of reading which can also be applied to spelling and writing. The first level is *developmental* intervention, in which the teacher helps a pupil to acquire new strategies, skills and information. The second level is denoted as *corrective* intervention, when a word has been misspelled and the teacher introduces a rule or strategy to correct the error. The third level, *remediation*, denotes a more systematic and structured programme of intervention to overcome a substantial reading, spelling and/or writing problem where the pupil has slipped well behind the level expected for his or her age and ability and is failing to develop new skills. It has already been suggested that the teacher should not wait until administrative borderlines are reached before intervening, but should make an analysis of daily errors and decide whether and where the pupil is failing to make progress and then apply the intervention appropriate to the pupil's needs. The essential feature of this style of intervention is the use of the curriculum task to diagnose the learning problems. This very simply means recording pupils' errors in the daily reading and writing tasks and then working out *with them* ways of overcoming the difficulties. The National Curriculum attainment targets and levels will facilitate this to some degree.

'Assessment through teaching' (Raybould, 1984; Pearson and Tweddle, 1984) and 'classroom-based assessment' (CBA) (Glaser, 1962; Vargus, 1977) are synonymous terms and represent formal behavioural approaches to teaching in the literature quoted. There are, in fact, two interpretations of the practice of CBA already described in Chapter 3. The type undertaken by the student teacher Elaine will be further developed here in relation to cognitive process methods of teaching reading, writing and spelling skills. The second method is that which has gained much prominence of late and is based upon behavioural principles. In this method, CBA is defined as 'the practice of obtaining direct and frequent measures of a student's performance on a series of sequentially arranged objectives derived from the curriculum used in the classroom' (Blankenship and Lilly, 1981).

Task analysis and direct instruction (DI) techniques give guidelines for helping prepare the curriculum, and precision teaching provides information which assists the placement of the pupil on the curriculum and gives feedback on the appropriateness or

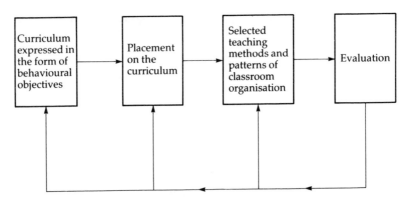

Figure 5.1 *CBA model (Glaser, 1962)*

otherwise of the teaching method (Solity and Bull, 1987). DISTAR (Direct Instructional System for Teaching and Remediation; published by Science Research Associates) has shown the capacity to improve the reading and spelling skills of pupils with general and specific learning difficulties in recent studies by Turner (1990). The precise nature of the criteria for framing objectives has already been indicated in Chapter 3. The instructional hierarchy established by Haring and Eaton (1978) is widely used. They have researched the hierarchy and found that different teaching methods are required for different stages in the model. The instructional hierarchy is as follows:

- *acquisition* – pupils are shown how to use a skill for the first time and learn to perform it accurately;
- *fluency* – pupils learn to perform the new skill with fluency as well as accuracy;
- *maintenance* – pupils are still able to perform the skill accurately and fluently even after a period of time when no teaching has taken place;
- *generalisation* – pupils are shown how to use the skill in different contexts;
- *adaptation* – pupils are set problems which require them to apply their newly acquired knowledge in novel ways.

As can be seen this model is mechanistic. It is a skills learning model in which the rôle of the learner is essentially passive, in the sense that he or she has little autonomy in the acquisition and development of the skill. The assumption made is that the teacher, or programme writer in the case of DI, knows all the sub-skills and their sequence in the hierarchy. Regrettably this is not the case, especially with respect to reading and spelling skills. For example, Carnine and Silbert (1979) suggest a set of phonics skills which should comprise a phonics curriculum as shown in Table 5.1.

Table 5.1 *A phonics curriculum and suggested placement probes (Solity and Bull, 1987, p. 72)*

Skill	Example	Placement probe
Letter sounds	a–z	Probe 1
VC	an, on	
CVC	sit, man, run	
CVCC	bend, sink	
CCVC	plod, grim	
CCVCC	stamp, blend	Probe 2
CCCVC	strum	
CCCVCC	string	
CVCe	pane, pole	
CCVCe	bride, grape	
ll	fall, call	
ck	pack, lick	
th	them, this	
er	fern, perm	
ing	sing, ring	Probe 3
sh	shop, wish	
wh	whip, when	
qu	quilt	
ol	bold, volt	
ar	farm, cart	
ea	beat, lead	

The arrangement of this hierarchy would not appear to be based upon any evidence from research, practical remediation, or logical structure in relation to English orthographic knowledge. For example, it is not wise to teach the letter sounds in alphabetical order and without their names in a *remedial* programme. Research and teaching experience to find out which knowledge is most successfully acquired prior to other knowledge in children with reading and spelling difficulties is in an advanced stage and APSL programmes and the work of Gillingham and Stillman (1956), Cox and Waites, (1972), Hickey (1977), and Cowdery *et al.* (1983, 1984) should be referred to. The order of teaching sounds organised into seven levels follows in Table 5.2 and is detailed in Cowdery (1987). Each level is associated with the teaching of linguistic rules and syllable structure of increasing complexity and is preceded by alphabet work taught in a multisensory fashion linking sound, name, symbol and grapheme. Table 5.1 leads one to suppose that the short closed syllable structure has many levels of complexity – for example CVCC, CCVC, CCVCC, CCCVC, CCCVCC – just by virtue of the number of consonants included, when in fact this is debatable. The principle of the short closed syllable is, however, the universal one to which blends and digraphs are assimilated in a slow progression across the programme according to the level of difficulty of their acquisition. The long vowel sounds are more difficult to acquire and are best taught in stages in levels 2, 3 and 7 (Table 5.2). The consonant digraphs (ch sh th th wh ph) are introduced together, not scattered throughout the programme as indicated by their placement in the probes suggested by Solity and Bull (1987). Spreading them in this way does not even meet the unifying criterion which DI seeks to find and teach to assist generalisation.

Table 5.2 *Structure and order in phonics versus psycholinguistic programmes*

Structure and order in phonics schemes	Structure and order in psycholinguistic schemes
	Level 1
1. Easy consonants: T N R M D S(sat) P B F	1. Sound–symbol correspondence: i t p n s using keyword system, make words and sentences for reading and spelling
2. Short vowels: A E I O U	
	2. Short vowels: only short vowels in closed syllables in early stages: a e i o u (y in middle and end of a word)
3. Consonant/vowel combinations: Use consonants and vowels learnt in 1 and 2 so that consonants in 1 precede vowels in 2, e.g. tap, nap, rat, man	3.i. Unequivocal consonants: With keywords and 1st and 2nd sounds: b c (k)(s) d f g (g)(j) h k l m n p r s t v x y z
4. Simple three-letter words: Using all vowels and consonants so far Ensure child knows alphabet names now as well as sounds Introduce new letters by name and sound	3.ii. Voiced and unvoiced consonants
	3.iii. Consonant blends: a) Initial l blends: bl cl fl gl sl spl Final n blends: -nt -nd -nk -ng
5. Less frequent consonants: V G(go) H W K J Q X Y Z. Second sounds of consonants C(cell) S(has) G(gem) should be introduced as they arise	•b) Initial r blends: br cr dr fr gr pr tr str spr scr shr thr Final m blends: mp c) Initial s blends: sc sl sm sn sp st squ sw sk Final s blends: -sp -st -sk
6. Consonant digraphs: CH TH *TH* SH WH PH	d) Initial w blends: tw dw Final others: -lt -lk -ft -ct
7. Silent 'E': here, ice, hope, use	4. Sound pictures: Words spelt exactly as they sound e.g. gŭn

8. Initial consonant blends
ST SP SC SK SL SW SM SN PR TR
GR BR CR DR FR PL CL BL FL GL

9. Final consonant blends: ND NT'
CT NG LD RT PT NK MP

10. Vowel digraphs:
AI AY EA EE OW OA UE ER UR
IR AR AR(vary) OR AV AW A(ball)
OR OW(cow) OO(room) OO(look)
OI OY EA(head)

11. Double consonants:
LL RR PP TT

12. Silent consonants:
C(black) K(knee) W(wrist) P(psalm)
H(ghost)

13. Treble blends:
spl, scr, str

5. Construction of English words:
Bases (run)
Roots (fer)
Prefix (re)
Suffix (ing)

6.i Types of syllable:
Closed and open syllables
Roots and bases
Affixing e.g. 1–1–1 rule

6.ii. Syllable division:
a) for reading – rabbit and robin words
b) for spelling change – add, double, drop, silent 'e'

7. Suffixes and their meanings

8. Prefixes and their meanings

9. Plurals
(rules to be introduced as required)

10. Simultaneous oral spelling for irregular words

11. Word families

Level 2 a–e, e–e, i–e, o–e, u–e
Levels 3 to 7
Including
• derivations and meaning
• Anglo-Saxon affixes
• less frequent letter combinations
  e.g. -igh
• accent and stress
[See also Appendix 2, page 242]

Thus, whilst task analysis and CBA can be of great assistance in teaching, a great deal of confusion and stress for the learner can be created if the analysis of the hierarchy of the sub-skills of the task is not based upon psycholinguistics and grounded research. Much remedial teaching therefore shows little result other than in a supportive atmosphere and a tutorial relationship. The pupil's attitude to learning improves, behavioural problems diminish, a few words and basic skills in reading are acquired, such as a knowledge and names of many of the letters of the alphabet, but the pupil makes little further progress in reading. He or she remains unable to use this knowledge in reading and writing and tends to sound every unknown word out, which leads to further failure and incomprehension.

Whilst CBA and its associated techniques have their uses, it is perhaps not wise to organise the whole of a pupil's curriculum and learning upon this basis, for it is much given over to rote training and practice routines. A cogent criticism of behaviourally based teaching methods and practices, especially in relation to children with severe learning difficulties, is offered by Wood and Shears (1986). The general thrust of their argument is that it does not teach for autonomy and self-motivation because it is authoritarian and directive. They also suggest that not much of that which is educationally worthwhile can be encapsulated into a skills based behavioural teaching programme.

PROMOTING LEARNING IN LITERACY SKILLS USING COGNITIVE PROCESS STRATEGIES

As has already been indicated, many children with learning difficulties in the reading area are simply slower to acquire and develop their reading skills. This is when reading teaching needs to be carefully structured and increased in quantity to help them progress. This does not mean that a task analysis approach is required but that a higher quality of what is ordinarily available might be appropriate. It is not always necessary to test formally the reading skills either. Few tests can provide teachers with more information than they already have at their disposal from daily classroom activities. Tests are sometimes helpful in the breadth of vocabulary they present for pupils to read and spell. No tests as yet, however, offer a coherent diagnostic analysis of error, although various 'miscues analyses' purport to do this (Spache, 1940; Neale, 1958; Goodman, 1969; Chambers, 1987).

Error collection can be a significant part of assessment of learning needs. The errors need to be studied and researched to find the most appropriate method to overcome them. In the following sections a range of cognitive process methods will be suggested which can assist the classroom teacher in helping children overcome difficulties, correct errors and build new skills.

Recent research (Read, 1971; Ferreiro, 1978, 1979, 1980; Ferreiro and Teberosky, 1982) has shown that young children's first literary impulse is to write rather than read and that they are absorbing a great deal of information about print which they are not demonstrating except through writing. It has been suggested, therefore, that children's *free writing* rather than copying and tracing should be encouraged and that developmental intervention strategies should be applied to reading and writing activities. Children who are late starting to read and write, and those who are progressing very slowly, can benefit from the new techniques for teaching being used in the early literary skills area. These developments concern an *emergent writing approach* to spelling, and a *cursive writing approach* to handwriting linked to spelling in a multisensory fashion. These two, spelling and writing, are taught separately as a cognitive skills development activity through spontaneous generation, whereas reading is taught as a pattern recognition skill (Montgomery, 1977) and as a psycholinguistic guessing game (Goodman, 1969) within an *apprenticeship approach* (Waterland, 1985).

The apprenticeship approach to reading

Those who promote an apprenticeship approach to reading hold the view that people learn things best by doing them. Most skills are in fact taught in this way. For example, we learn to drive by driving, to swim by swimming, to talk by talking and, *ergo*, to read by reading (Waterland, 1985). Waterland suggests that, instead of teaching the various sub-skills of reading, such as a sight vocabulary, sounds and blends, and expecting pupils to incorporate these into their reading of text, reading skills only become meaningful if they arise out of the experience of reading. The classroom should therefore be made more like a home, with books where there are no age-grade codes and where the children sit down and read any book they select with the teacher, a helper, a friend, and so on. In this type of setting story time takes place early in the day, using big books so that all the children can follow the text. These books and their small counterparts are left about to be picked up and read. Waterland finds that two five-minute sessions of shared reading are of more value to her beginning readers than one or two minutes every day. During all the reading sessions the psycholinguistic approach to teaching is adopted to teach word attack skills and meaning-accessing strategies. Sharing books, writing the children's own books, sharing reading, reading in pairs and involving parents and everybody around in the reading is part of the whole process. It is an absorbing and time-consuming process.

This method emphasises the rôle of meaning in learning and helps promote the development of comprehension strategies and the use of contextual cues.

Giving reading time so that children can learn

The time factor is a significant one in reading teaching and has received considerable attention in recent years. In the Effective Use of Reading project, Southgate-Booth *et al.* (1981) found that, though 7–9-year-olds might receive 3–4 minutes of individual reading time, the teacher was only able to spend an average of 30 seconds concentrating upon that individual read because her attention was continually required elsewhere. The teachers were working very hard but this higher teacher output was inversely related to pupil output. Similar results have been found in a more recent survey by Farquhar (1987) of top infant classrooms. To help overcome this and other problems, Southgate-Booth (1985, 1987) recommends group reading practice for 6–8 children with their teacher for ten minutes at a time each and every day, plus individual reading with classroom helpers trained to listen and parent involvement projects to support the general reading teaching programme.

Given the little time which these researchers have found to be available for children to learn to read it seems rather surprising that slower learners ever learn to read and write at all. It is no wonder that they have limited skills and abilities in these areas and become progressively more and more disadvantaged by their failures. It would seem that a first step in helping these children would be to ensure that they have sufficient time and support to practise and develop their skills in the best circumstances possible and using the most effective methods. Ensuring this quality of provision in the development of early reading skills can be more difficult than at first appears. Many teachers in junior, secondary and special school are not trained in reading development. They may have some knowledge of remediation, but remediation may not be appropriate.

Diagnosing and correcting reading difficulties

Clay's research in the early 1960s first shed light on the reading behaviour of pupils in their first year at school. In later research (1979) she found that the behaviour of high-progress readers involved anticipating or predicting what can occur in meaning and language structure, searching for cues, self-correcting and forming intuitive rules that took the reader beyond what she or he already knew. She found that the reading was organised at the phrase and sentence level and attention focused upon meaning, with the reader checking meaning cues with other cues related to syntax, concepts of print such as punctuation and direction, the visual impact of the print and sound to letter associations. Attention was directed to meaning and finding a fit within this integrated cue-searching behaviour, so that the reader was immediately aware when a mistake had been made and would search again for a better fit. This self-correction inevitably led to a greater independence in reading. The style was best encouraged by the psycholinguistic rather than the 'look and say' or 'phonics' methods of teaching. Clay found that the low-progress readers organised their reading at the letter and word level and used a narrower range of cues. They tended to rely on remembering words by sight and their attention to letters was usually restricted to the first letter. The resulting 'fractured utterances' caused the reader to lose track of what the message of the text was about. When a mistake was made, the reader was unaware of it and so self-correction did not occur. These differences between good and poor readers reflect not so much deficits in the poor readers as developmental differences in their progress. The poor readers were functioning more like beginning readers engaged in 'bottom up' processing, only progressing at a very slow rate and in some cases not making any progress at all.

Diagnostic inventories for early reading skills

Once the pupil begins to show an interest in books and stories there are some useful indicators to likely progress or difficulty.

Comprehension and whole-word knowledge

This is indicated when the pupil:

- is able to follow simple story lines;
- is able to predict what follows next in the story sequence;
- has the vocabulary knowledge and experience to follow the particular story in question;
- knows that words written in the book tell the story;
- can point to the words as they are said with good one-to-one correspondence;
- can predict from (a) pictorial, (b) semantic, (c) syntactic cues;
- recognises an occasional word in context;
- recognises one or two words out of context.

Pupils who fail to acquire knowledge of a few common words from their reading scheme or early reading books within the first month in school should be considered to be 'at risk' from learning difficulty in the area of reading. In a study of three years' entry to five reception classes, failure of this kind denoted those who were later to become low-progress readers (Montgomery, 1977).

Phonological knowledge

This is indicated when the pupil:

- can clap to the syllables in own and other children's names;
- has an appreciation of rhymes and enjoys and participates in them;
- enjoys and appreciates simple puns, and even tries to make them up;
- knows the names or sounds of about nine or ten letters of the alphabet by the end of the first half-term in school, even though these may not have been directly taught (children with learning difficulties who are just beginning to read should also be developing this knowledge);
- is able to segment the initial sound from words presented auditorially, e.g. cap – 'c' [k]
- is able to segment and reassemble the phonology, e.g. cap – 'c . . . ap, cap'.

Segmentation of the initial sound in this way is often inaccurately referred to in pre-reading tests as 'auditory discrimination'.

These two major categories, comprehension/whole-word and phonological knowledge, derive from the research and theory of Baron and Strawson (1976) who showed that there were two routes available which interact in the reader in the development of reading skills. In earlier decades, the teaching of reading tended to focus upon either a visual route in 'look and say' methods or the phonological route as in phonics programmes.

Miscues analysis

Through tape recordings from 1964 onwards the Goodmans began to analyse the mismatches between what the text presented and what the young reader read aloud. These mismatches they termed 'miscues', rather than errors, and used as a device to observe the strategies used by poor readers when processing text. This technique was first devised by Spache (1940) and incorporated by Neale (1958) into her Analysis of Reading test. This test is still widely used but needed the updating of the pictures and some of the vocabulary, such as the 'milkman's horse' which pupils now invariably read as the 'milkman's house', for obvious reasons, in its recent revision (1989).

The categories of miscue identified by Neale were: substitutions, omissions, additions, reversals, repetitions, mispronunciations. A more recent miscues analysis, detailed by Chambers (1987), records the types of miscue as both positive and negative and consisting of the categories: substitution, non-response, insertion, omission, pause, repetition, correction. Each response is coded and counted, and then analysed to determine the child's main reading problems. After one such analysis it was said that the child *'relies heavily on phonic clues'* and is *'unwilling to guess* even though many of her substitutions are nonsensical' (p. 89). In this particular analysis the girl made 33 positive and 22 negative substitutions, for example 'was' for 'were', 'Tuesday' for 'Thursday', 'scratched' for 'screeched', 'come' for 'came', 'when' for 'with', 'yane' for 'yawn', 'laughing' for 'laughed', 'he' for 'it', 'said' for 'sighed', and so on. It could equally be argued that because this girl has incomplete phonic knowledge she guesses well in context, using first sounds not digraphs or blends – for instance 't' led to the guess 'Tuesday' whereas knowledge of the 'th' digraph could have led her to 'Thursday'. In other words, she has incomplete phonic knowledge and no linguistic information or strategies, and resorts to using the visual strategy of guessing in context using the initial sound as a lead cue – a miscues misdiagnosis? It suggests that this is a pupil for whom the phonological route has only just been opened up and that sound segmentation and sound assembly skills need now to be developed.

In Neale's and also general miscues analyses it is the mispronunciation and substitution categories which prove to be most frequently recorded in assessments. These need to be analysed for phonological, linguistic and cognitive knowledge. Chambers (1987) goes on to explain that 'Though her repetitions and corrections show that she is struggling to process the print for meaning, basically she is attempting decoding accuracy at the expense of comprehension, and the meaning degenerates for her as the story progresses'. Chambers recommends on the basis of the miscues analysis that if the text is too difficult it should be replaced with another; if the child substitutes a special noun the original word should be given unless it is outside the child's experience, in which case the word or its equivalents should be discussed and accepted before the original is given; and finally teachers should help the child decode any word which is within his or her experience, drawing attention to its initial sound and to known syllables within the word. The author points out that,

NAME_____	CHRONOLOGICAL AGE _____
DATE_____	BOOK _____ PAGES _____
READING AGE _____	READING TEST(S) _____
SPELLING AGE _____	SPELLING TEST(S) _____

Categories	Examples
CONTEXT	Text too difficult – need to select another. Text stilted; child gives good prediction – text uses archaic form; text boring and mundane; unmotivating, uninteresting to this child; text stereotypic – sexist, racist, classist, etc.
WORD ATTACK SKILLS	No word attack skills observed; guesses from initial sound; tries sounds then names; tries blends; knows digraph; uses syllabification; uses analogy; self-corrects.
COMPREHENSION SKILLS	Can answer factual recall questions during or at end; answers inferential q.; answers abstract q.; can predict from picture, syntax, semantic content; grasps or loses sense as proceeds.
AUDIENCE EFFECTS	Engages in word-by-word reading, high-pitched monotone; observes full stops; observes commas; uses phrasing; observes speechmarks, questions etc; good use of expression, speed, voice.
BEHAVIOURAL SIGNS	Reading posture; reading distance of book – focal length; finger-pointing with the reading, swoops; finger or book mark below or above the words.
EMOTIONAL SIGNS	Tenseness and nervousness; fixed smile; jigging, especially when makes errors; regresses to finger-pointing; word-by-word reading and monotone; loses fluency; voice strained or shaky; hand and/or body shaking.
OTHER COMMENTS	Intervention selected (never pursue more than two related aspects at any one time).

Figure 5.2 *A hearing reading informal miscues inventory (Montgomery and Rawlings, 1986)*

as with any form of assessment, it is only possible to make informed guesses about the nature of the error the child has made. It is my view that if the teacher has a knowledge of the seven levels of orthographic information (Cowdery, 1987) she or he can make these guesses more informed and know which teaching input to organise next. Direct teaching of this information and skill, applied in a structured, sequential and developmental framework, can give pupils the necessary phonological, phonetic, syllabic and linguistic information to help improve their word attack skills. A somewhat more broadly-based miscues analysis, developed to help teachers in initial training become more adept at *hearing children* read, is outlined in the following section. This analysis can incorporate the full range of word attack skills outlined in the psycholinguistic programmes.

Examples of intervention strategies based upon the hearing reading inventory (HRI)

The categories in the HRI (see Figure 5.2) are, with their examples, mainly self-explanatory, except for some of the more technical aspects which are illustrated below. The HRI can be used with any book which the child elects to read or which the teacher selects. There are three main categories in which the interventions can take place: word attack skills, comprehension skills and audience effects. The other categories can be used for intervention or to monitor the effects of intervention in the other areas.

Example
TEXT: 'The train is going under the bridge.'
CHILD READS: 'The train is goin' under the [*pauses, looks at picture on left-hand page, fails to decipher it, reads*] tunnel [*begins to jig, is reading word-by-word in high-pitched monotone, fixed nervous smile showing both upper and lower teeth*]'.

During three pages of reading in this manner she makes no use of initial sounds to help guess words in context: her substitution of 'tunnel' for 'bridge' is but one example of this. Even when it is suggested to her that she tries the first sound she does not do so.

An illustration of a stage model for intervention during hearing reading is shown in Figure 5.3.

Proposed intervention   Present randomised letters of the alphabet to discover which sounds, if any, she does know and then persuade her to use this information in her next reading session. Concentrate very much on confidence-building and praising each small effort she makes. The finger-pointing is actually directing the word-by-word reading, and so after the word attack skills have been worked upon give her a book mark to place *above* the words and explain it is given because she is making such good progress. The book mark should be *above the words* so that the eyes can move on ahead and down to the next line to preserve and observe meaning. Once she is comfortable with the book mark and is using word attack skills as they are taught, the function of the fullstop for reading can be taught. This

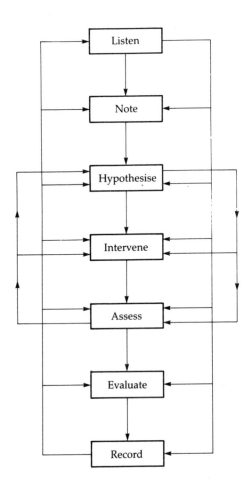

Figure 5.3 *Hearing reading stage model*

simply involves reminding her to *drop* her voice whenever she sees one and take a breath. It will be found that this simple device begins to ease the monotone and relax the voice and general tenseness. The pause also enables the eyes to move ahead and pick up more of the sense of the piece; this will assist both prediction and comprehension. To support each one of these strategies it will be found extremely helpful to teach the pupils how to record themselves reading and then replay the tape, reading along with themselves, first aloud then silently. This provides a most useful self-monitoring device after the reading session with the teacher. After this, several pupils can join together in a group reading session and in this way the twenty minutes per day reading teaching sessions can be built up.

Parent involvement projects in reading (PI)

Many schools are beginning to find enormous value in their parent involvement projects (Wolfendale, 1987). In these schemes, every day for five minutes or so the parent hears the child read or they engage in *paired reading* (Morgan and Lyon, 1979). The children, particularly those with learning difficulties and the unmotivated ones, are finding an interest in books and their reading is progressing by leaps and bounds. Paired reading is a system in which child and parent or teacher read along together, the child signals when s/he wishes the 'model' to stop and then continues until, when s/he falters, the 'model' joins in again, and so on. The system provides an instant reinforcement and correct model of fluent reading as a structure and context within which the pattern processing features analysers operate. Meaning is established through discussion of the book, through the pictures and in conversation following the reading. In a study undertaken by one of our teachers, it was found that paired reading with 6–7-year-olds was more effective in the early stages and with poorer readers, whilst psycholinguistic intervention was more effective in the later stages with able readers. In both methods, praise and encouragement was an essential ingredient.

In a study of 267 7–8-year-old children from a council estate in Dagenham, Essex, Hewison and Tizard (1980) found that reading achievement was strongly related to whether or not the mother regularly heard the child read. In a subsequent study, Tizard *et al.* (1982) found that pupils heard read at home showed more significant reading gains than those given extra tuition by teachers at school.

In a junior school project involving parents hearing reading, Sigston and Addington (1984) found that 31 out of 33 children showed significant reading gains and that their rate of reading progress had trebled, with most improvement found in those whose reading was the poorest. Our teachers, in their researches, have found similar differential results. Poorer readers make the most significant gains up to about the 8-year-old reading level and then progress levels out. There are always one or two pupils who make no progress. These few individuals are found to have specific learning difficulties and some of this group may have parents who are illiterate or semi-literate themselves and cannot hear them read or do not feel competent to do so. Such parents often fear to disclose their problem. Other parents are found who have no interest in the child and the project and refuse to hear reading. Some pupils in this group have extremely limited reading skills and a specific problem which, as yet, precludes them from making progress. It is this specific problem which will need to be diagnosed and overcome before normal reading development can ensue.

When the Belfield Reading Project test scores were re-examined (Hannon, 1987) it was found that the gains were not statistically significant. Hannon offers a series of hypotheses which might account for this. He suggested that there was less room for improvement than in the Haringey research (Tizard *et al.*, 1982), where only 2–3 per cent of teacher time in top infant classes was spent on reading. In Haringey there appeared to have been more ethnic minority parents and the supply of suitable reading books and improved school practice towards parents may have caused the greater improvement. The NFER Reading Test A, which was used in both studies, is a silent sentence reading, group administered test with multiple-choice answers. Hannon points out that a global score of 96 on such a test does not represent all the reading behaviours which might have improved. Attention was drawn to this problem in Chapter 1. Able and 'middle-class' children have less difficulty than disadvantaged groups and children with learning difficulties in completing such tests. Performance on such tests seems to be more than a simple product, reading. They tap other factors such as opportunities for learning and general cognitive strategies derived from initial teaching and/or ability, all of which contribute to reading ability. The pupils' reading of books may well have improved, but this may not have been picked up on the test. The research results in this area are much more complex than at first they seem. There is, however, one important and consistent finding from the studies: there are no negative effects of parent involvement. According to Tizard (1987) the best way forward is to train parents to support their children's reading and to research those features of PI schemes which make them effective.

Language experience approaches in the development of reading

The essence of the language experience approach is that it uses oral skills as a bridge between utterance and text (Olson, 1977).

First, the teacher establishes a partnership with the pupil and starts from the point the pupil has reached in literacy skills. Second, the pupil is helped to understand the necessary separation of the writing process into two parts requiring two rôles. These are the rôle of author and the rôle of secretary, both of which are essential to produce work of quality (Peters and Smith, 1982). The teacher works with the pupil and finds out the context of the subject and what it is the pupil wishes to say. The pupil then dictates the story to the teacher or on to a tape once the initial impetus for writing is established. The teacher writes or later types verbatim what the pupil says (here a classroom aide is useful) and then they read it aloud together. The first draft is studied and discussed and new sections written in until the author is satisfied with the product, when it is copied out, or retyped and displayed, or put into the 'story file' with suitable illustrations. Our teachers have often used this technique in a remedial withdrawal situation and have found that the pupils' interest and motivation to read and write have markedly increased. The stories then become reading material for the pupil. This is the approach which was being adopted in a modified form by Mary Yates, using pupils in pairs and the word processor.

When this approach was used in two long-term case studies with pupils with specific learning difficulties, it was found (Fisher, 1982) that there was little carry-over into spelling and that it was necessary to supplement the language experience method within a short space of time with alphabet work and psycholinguistic teaching from the APSL framework.

HELPING CHILDREN WITH SPELLING DIFFICULTIES

In a study of teaching spelling, Peters (1967) put forward the view that our teaching methods meant that spelling knowledge was largely 'caught' rather than taught during the process of reading. These teaching methods emphasised a visual approach and learning whole words by rote – a logographic method (Baron and Strawson, 1976), which did little to support spelling. Good readers and spellers derive essential spelling knowledge from their reading activities (Francis, 1982), whereas poor readers and spellers do not and seem unable to generate spellings for even the simplest of phonically regular words (red, bad, sip, etc.) which they have not previously learned by heart in copy writing. Teachers tended to correct misspellings for pupils, asking them to write them out several times in order to learn them. Recently this has been replaced by a more effective set of strategies in some classrooms, such as asking the pupil to guess at least the initial sound or to try the spelling out on a piece of paper which the teacher then corrects. Even so, many pupils do not learn to generalise this knowledge and fail to become adequate spellers.

Thus it was that Peters and Smith (1986) found that many pupils coming into comprehensive school were just as aware of their spelling as their reading difficulties. But whilst there had been consistent pressure upon them to read, the same pressure had never been placed upon their spelling. This had been to their disadvantage because, as Frith (1985) pointed out for pupils with specific learning difficulty, this delay was inextricably linked to their failure to progress from logographic to alphabetic stages. These pupils' difficulties according to Bradley and Bryant (1985) are more to do with delay in development of skills rather than deficit and so the pattern of difficulties is similar to that found in slower learners. Peters and Smith (1986) found that the secondary school pupils had been given six years of 'remedial' phonics, simple reading books and activity work books but that the teacher had always been on hand to give them their words and to correct their spelling mistakes. The result was that they had not learned to spell adequately and had developed a form of learned helplessness towards the problem. When these pupils' writing is examined, constant instructions to 'mind your spelling' and 'use a dictionary' may be seen to have been to no avail. Similar ineffective comments may be seen upon students' essays in higher education. It was to help these students that the cognitive strategies for spelling were first devised. Later they were tested out on pupils in schools.

A teacher working with pupils with spelling difficulties needs to understand that they are not lazy and do not deliberately make errors (Cotterell, 1974), and that they would use a dictionary if they knew the spelling was wrong (or knew in some cases how to use a dictionary in the first place). The first response of most teachers concerned with remediating spelling and reading problems is to put the pupil on a phonics programme. This is seldom found to prove effective when it is not linked to multisensory methods of teaching and to word building and word generation strategies. Even the use of the phonic knowledge in reading needs to be taught and these pupils encouraged to guess in context from initial sounds. What so often happens is that they then overgeneralise this strategy and try to sound out all new words, with disastrous and frustrating results for all concerned.

Often the needs of pupils with difficulties in the spelling area alone are not considered significant until they reach secondary school and by then they have much to unlearn as well as learn. Cognitive approaches to spelling try to address both these problems and are developed for use by subject and non-specialist teachers in an across-the-curriculum approach. They offer the opportunity for the development of a whole-school approach to spelling. As already noted, spelling difficulties may exist in the absence of reading difficulties whereas the reverse is rare. The 12 plus 1 cognitive strategies for correcting misspellings are outlined in a following section. For developmental interventions in spelling we need to examine work which has taken place in North and South America and which has been introduced into this country under the heading of 'emergent writing'. Good examples of this approach may be found in the 'Highscope' project in Bristol and in isolated schools in a number of LEAs. The emergent writing method emphasises the exploratory and problem-solving approach to beginning spelling. In the past teachers have pressed for accuracy and neatness and tended to dampen the enthusiasm of young spellers to try out their own spelling knowledge.

Emergent writing approaches

In helping the development of good spelling skills in young spellers, Cramer (1976) describes what he calls a creative writing route. He advocates that, as soon as children have assembled any notions of spelling or any skills at all, they should be encouraged to use them in writing. Others have argued (Chomsky, 1971; Clay, 1975; Read, 1986) that a child's first literate response is in fact to write, not read. This natural tendency, according to Cramer, should be encouraged. The teacher should not worry about misspellings but supply limited but helpful information, such as knowledge of sounds not yet learnt and rules if some problems persist – the rest will be learnt during reading. He found that, in this fashion, children themselves became critical of their own performance and could see their often rapid improvement. Parents would need to have this strategy carefully explained as they are more intolerant of spelling errors than teachers, strangely seeming to expect young children's spellings to be near perfect. Cramer emphasises the need to take a positive approach to misspellings and illustrates it in the following manner by analysing the spellings in a poem written by David, aged 7, without assistance:

My Ded cate
Ones I hade a cate
He was white and yellow
One night my father
Came fame my grandfathers house
Wenn father come home fame
my grandfathers house he said
Ruste is ded.

David made six separate misspellings and gave eighteen correct spellings, which gives him a spelling error ratio of 0.33 (actual divided by total). Cramer argued that David's superior spelling skills are demonstrated in his correct spellings of father, grandfathers, white, night, house, said and yellow, and analyses his misspellings as common but near miss good equivalents. The misspelling, he says, will gradually disappear with further writing practice as he becomes more familiar with orthographic conventions through reading. Cramer counts 'ded' for 'dead' as a good generalisation from basic knowledge since /e/ as in 'bed' is the most common way of spelling that particular sound. 'Hade' for 'had' is counted as an overgeneralisation of the final 'e' rule, of which he has good knowledge for he spells 'home', 'come' and 'white' correctly. 'Wenn' for 'when' is a good phonetic equivalent when one takes into consideration that the use of double 'n' is common particularly in the middle of words (tunnel, funnel). His 'Ruste' for 'Rusty' indicates that he needs to learn that the /i/ sound at the end of *English* words is always represented by 'y'. 'Fame' for 'from' shows lack of knowledge and sensitivity to the two-letter blend /fr/ but he correctly uses /f/ and /m/ for the first and last sounds. The vowel in 'from' is a 'shwa' /ə/ or 'uh' sound which can be represented by several graphemes depending upon its morphemic context. He adds an 'e' possibly because he is aware that there are four letter places in the word – this place knowledge is not an uncommon finding in memory span research (Baddeley, 1978) – and adds silent 'e' as that is a common ending.

If one were to suggest teaching strategies to help speed up David's spelling development, he might be taught the 'wh' words as a group – e.g. where? who? what? why? when? (later, whither? whether? and whence?) – and their formal pronunciation with aspiration, which, for fun, he could listen for in different speakers' accents. Later, not at the same time, he could be taught the closed syllable structure with short vowel sound which does not require the addition of 'e' (had, bed, pig, lot, but) and, when this was absorbed, the use of final 'e' to denote the long vowel sound in the closed syllable, e.g. fade, cede, ride, mode, rude. The sound and use of 'y' in the final position in English words would be taught and pointed out in practice games. The difficult and irregular word 'once' would be best taught by a writing route as a whole motor unit so that it becomes automatic. This could be undertaken whilst using a simple 'look–cover–write–check strategy' (Figure 5.4).

The research by Ferreiro (1978) in Buenos Aires, in which she interviewed 68 4–5-year-olds in nursery schools and 6-year-olds who had just entered school, none of whom knew how to read, is a fascinating study of their views about writing. From these views, she found that their responses fell into categories in a developmental sequence. She showed that, by the time children entered school, they had quite a well-developed idea of what writing was. She gave them written sentences and asked them about their ideas of correspondence between written segments, in capitals and cursive, and those which were spoken, e.g. *elosocomemiel* (thebeareatshoney) and *papa patea la pelota* (papa kicks the ball). She found that initially the children thought that only nouns were written, not verbs. Articles were extra noises attached to the nouns. For these children, written text only represented the people and objects in the utterance. This rather resembles an infant learning the names of people and objects when beginning to speak. Ferreiro also found that the child

Figure 5.4 *Look–cover–write–check strategy linked to cursive writing*

located the whole utterance in one key word or phrase of the text, e.g. Papa kicks the ball in 'papa patea', the rest of the sentence was used to generate other contextually relevant sentences such as 'I kicked the ball' etc. At first the children found it impossible to segment the utterance in any way which corresponded exactly to the text but when asked to point to the position of a word in a sentence, it was possible for a 6-year-old to say the sentence to herself and, as she did so, follow the words in the text and come up with the correct position.

Ferreiro (1980) monitored for two years the development of 33 6-year-olds from both non-literate and highly literate families. When she asked these children whether various letters and number strings could be read, their judgements were that you needed at least three signs and a variety of them. This is presumably the beginning of an awareness of the basic syllable structure which so often has to be taught in remedial programmes (Cowdery *et al.*, 1984). At first, she found a child's writing can mean whatever he or she wishes. Later, all the messages written are accomplished with the letters the child knows at the time, for the discovery is made that letters can be combined and recombined to produce varied messages. This discovery, according to Ferreiro, is made even before it is learnt that letters correspond to sounds. What the child appears to search for is some governing principle segmenting individual words. The first notion to develop is that each letter corresponds to one sound; as the ideas of syllable develop it is represented by three letters rather than two for reasons 'given' that most words cannot be made with two letters, the minimum requirement is three – a quantitative notion of importance to the young child. Another criterion used by the 'middle-class' children but not the others was that of truth: only truthful utterances could be written down.

From all of this, Ferreiro concluded that children construct a series of hypotheses about writing before they realise it is based upon an alphabetic system with correspondence between sounds and spellings; in this sense, each one is 'reinventing' the writing system in coming to understand it. This is very much a Piagetian notion. She suggests that the function of pre-school and primary education was not to introduce children to written language but *to help them refine their own conception of it*. This is very much the approach which Cramer (1976) has adopted, and which has been suggested by Goodman (1969) and Smith (1973) in viewing reading as a psycholinguistic guessing game. Now we see the development of this same approach with writing and that, if anything, it precedes learning to read by several years. It has been found that 3-year-olds could distinguish pictures from writing although they could not distinguish one type of writing from another. Some 4-year-olds could distinguish writing from scribbles and by 5 they could all recognise writing well, although none of them could read. The developmental sequence was first that writing is not pictorial, then it is linear, then horizontal and finally it consists of Roman characters (presumably this was a contextual factor).

Once children are in school and have grasped the alphabetic principle, Read (1971, 1975, 1986) shows how they use this knowledge to generate new spellings for words which they do not yet know how to spell. He calls this 'children's creative spelling' (1986). His creative spellers spontaneously used the same spelling for different sounds; they did not expect the sound–symbol relationship to be consistent and regular as it more often is in Dutch, Spanish and Turkish. They would write 'sed' for 'said' (phonetic transcription), 'ckup' for 'cup' (a standard spelling in the wrong position), and 'rodot' for 'robot', and were not surprised to see visual reversals. According to Read, these creative spellings look bizarre to adults but are based upon reasonable principles that spelling represents sounds, and that similar sounds may have similar spellings. He argues that children who make these kinds of error are actually on the right track, for different sounds *are* spelled alike in standard spelling but because of historical and morphological reasons, not phonetic ones. A teacher should realise that such a child is perceiving words correctly and spelling them reasonably.

Teachers adopting these strategies will find that their pupils' spelling *and* reading skills develop rapidly and that they begin to have difficulty coping with all the writing that their pupils suddenly begin to generate spontaneously and enthusiastically. It will also be found important to share these new techniques with parents and other colleagues in the school to avoid some of the initial misunderstandings which may occur. Teachers who may feel the approach is worthwhile will also need to be supported and encouraged, for such a radical change in teaching technique can induce considerable anxiety. Again we see that what is considered to be good practice, and what good spellers tend to do, can prove to be practice which is particularly suitable for helping children with learning difficulties to achieve autonomy in learning and to learn new skills with the aid of developmental inputs from the teacher. This system of teaching and developing spelling could equally be regarded as an apprenticeship approach.

Both of the children whose copy writing is shown in Figure

Figure 5.5 *Examples of children's copy writing: (a) Harry, aged 4½ years; (b) James, aged 7 years*

5.5 are beginners in writing and not able to read independently. Both show a form of 'picture manuscript'. They copy the shapes of the letters slavishly without insight into their structure and function in the word. They draw them as picture symbols as best they can, starting where they may. No doubt they will, through reading and hand co-ordination practice, eventually build up a repertoire of words which they can recognise and commonly write.

Chomsky (1975) found that nursery, kindergarten and first-grade children, when encouraged to write using invented spelling, could (providing they knew the letter names) teach themselves that:

- letters have some relation to sounds;
- one-to-one correspondence does not exist in English;
- a system exists and rules do operate;
- this process can generate products beyond the remembered;
- there are more abstract regularities (orthographic rules).

'This hypothesis construction was an active process taking the child far beyond the rules that can be offered him/her by the best patterned, programmed or linguistic approaches. The more the child is prepared to do for her/himself the better off she or he is' (Chomsky, 1979). Although teachers might worry about them learning incorrect spellings, it has been shown that children who begin with invented spelling shift easily to more conventional spelling (Chomsky, 1979; Ehri, 1980; Henderson and Chard, 1980; Read, 1986). These creative spellers can be regarded as potentially good spellers and are those who progress easily into early spelling development and to full orthography. The researchers have shown that poor spellers are those who fail to abstract the alphabetic principle from the words they read and who fail to establish sound-to-symbol correspondence in the early stages of reading and spelling. Frith (1980), Snowling (1985) and Bradley and Bryant (1985) suggest that this is because of a phonological encoding problem which later delays the acquisition of orthographic knowledge.

Leah (Figure 5.6) has some letter features knowledge, particularly of capitals, but as yet most of them are reversed. She has not yet organised all her letters into word-like clusters and syllables, but she appears to be on the verge of discovery. She has some word spacings with vowel insertions. Lower-case 'e' appears several times and, like 'l', could be made into a special learning feature as both appear in her name. Teaching a cursive

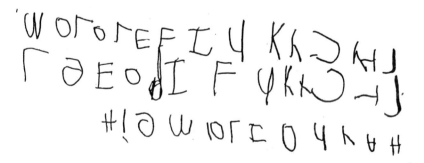

Figure 5.6 *Emergent writing from Leah, aged 5 years*

form of writing from the outset would reinforce the left to right progression through the word and stop the reversals (Morse, 1984). This pupil's teacher has been using the more traditional copy writing thus far. Leah would appear to be making good progress in her unaided development of spelling skills. This will speed up as she is encouraged to become an emergent writer.

The piece of writing, by Yacob from the same class (Figure 5.7), shows a more advanced state of spelling knowledge and is typical of what pupils can achieve at this age. This pupil is likely to develop good literacy skills.

For the first time Marcus has been asked to generate some spontaneous writing as a 'creative speller' or 'emergent writer'. His writing (Figure 5.8) shows some incorrect formation of letters even for a print script and tendencies to reversal which could be overcome by introducing cursive writing and by teaching some whole words as writing units, for example starting with 'me', 'in', 'to' and 'you'. He has just begun to break the phonetic code and his alphabetic and sound knowledge needs to be checked so that sounds he does not know can be gradually introduced as required in spelling. The notion of beats or syllables in words could be introduced with the information that each must have its own vowel sound. Distinctions between consonants which have an identifiable contact pattern in the mouth, as opposed to vowel sounds which do not, need to be

'I went to bed.'

Figure 5.7 *Yacob's writing*

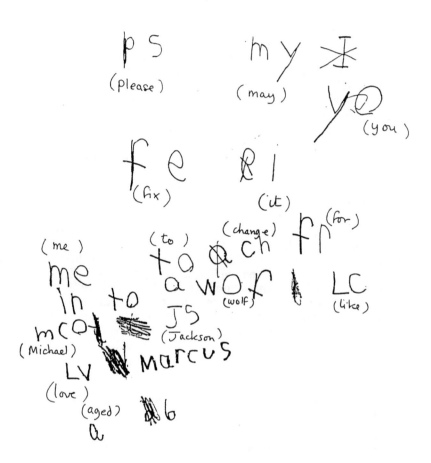

'Dear Jim,
Please may you fix it for me to change into a
wolf like Michael Jackson.
Love Marcus
aged 6'

Figure 5.8 *Emergent writing from Marcus, aged 6 years*

taught so that the pupil can differentiate between them. His spelling of 'please' (ps) and 'wolf' should be complimented and the two blends 'pl-' and '-lf' could be taught. If these interventions are carefully planned and slowly phased in, this new knowledge should begin to appear in his writing. If this does not happen either the knowledge has been introduced too precipitately or a much more systematic approach is required to overcome the learning block or delay. Again an APSL programme which is multisensory in its early stages would be recommended. It will also be found helpful to Marcus to give him some lines to write upon in order to guide the position and placing of words upon the page (Burnhill *et al.*, 1975).

Figure 5.9 shows samples of emergent writing produced by two pupils, James and Caroline, with specific learning difficulties. Their writing indicates how little they have learned from the copy writing system and remedial phonics. They will need the support of a multisensory APSL programme before they can begin to make any progress.

Caroline has some whole-word knowledge – my, is, Caroline, I, and, mum, dad (inverted ds). She also has some initial consonant and vowel knowledge, but often expresses this with capital letters – 'Nsole' (name), 'asol' (am), 'isn' (years), 'asli', (old). She also has some notion of syllable structure – 'noli', 'bon', 'noi', 'nos', 'non', 'noo', 'myoli', etc. The 'oli' and 'NO', 'NOLI' combinations from her name are scattered throughout her writing; they signify her knowledge and express her confusion, showing the degree to which the visual strategy alone has failed her.

Using cognitive strategies for correcting and developing spelling

The research began with the development of a series of cognitive strategies for the correction of students' misspellings, by evolving with them the ways in which they tried to spell difficult or new words. In this process their *meta-cognitive events* were discussed and made explicit. When 480 students in teacher training and 200 teachers on in-service courses were asked how they helped pupils or corrected their own misspellings, the few 'taught the rules' (and some were complex and incomprehensible to other teachers in the group), while the rest asked the children to write them out correctly and the special needs teachers, mainly primary teachers, asked the children to use the look–cover–write–check strategy.

When their metacognitive events were discussed in relation

(a) Wn n mmm m m Y

JAMes

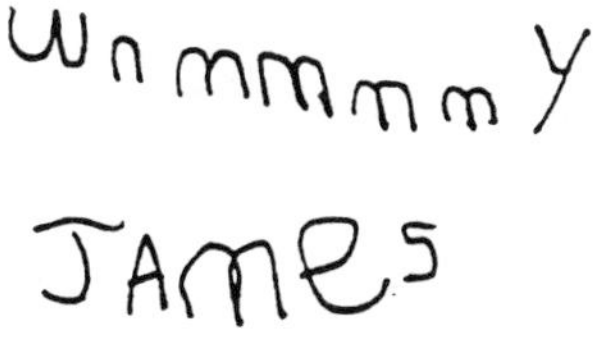

(b)

MY   NSOLE   IS CavoLiNe aND I asoL 7
SN ASLi. I NoLi   3 .aND 3 oNoʹʒL .
NoLi boN. NoLi Noi NoSCG NoSo .
Nos NoLi NoLb ʟOLYE NoN Noo
MY MuM (aND PoP oLNS
It   Muas ʃ a ND MY LNoGT .
Pua BoLiNo aNḆ MyoLi aNoLi IVoNoe .
GEoL . iNoL aNMe NyL RoAE 4 LNeP Me .
Pua IS   21 BYoLYo is 2l NoLi iS 22 .
MY. NoLi Brcᴳ aNP � ᴍⁿrꭒeiⁱₛ Men
Mᴟl.

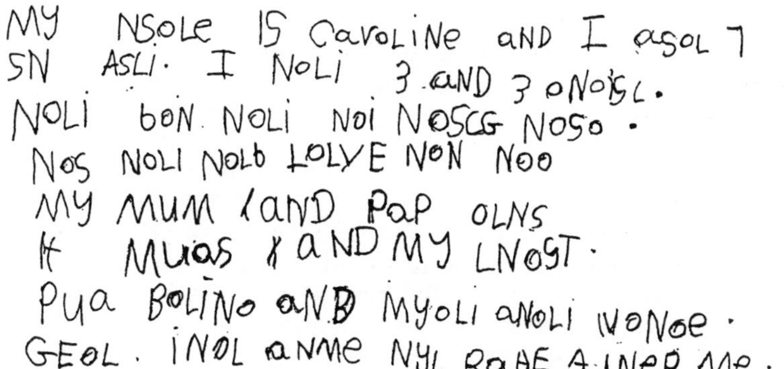

'My name is Caroline and I am 7 years old. I have 3 brothers and 3
sisters. Some of them live at home and some of them do not. My mum
and dad live at home and so do my goldfish.
Paul Breda and Mark still live at home. They are a lot older than me.
Paul is 21. Breda is 21. Mark is 22.
My other brothers and sisters are a lot older than me.'

Figure 5.9 *Emergent writing of pupils with specific learning difficulties: (a) James, aged
7 years (the only two words he knew); (b) Caroline, aged 7½ years*

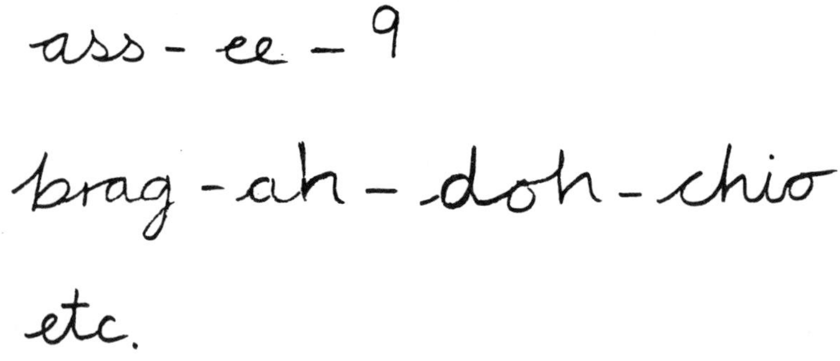

ass - ee - 9

brag - ah - doh - chio

etc.

Figure 5.10

to a special misspelling test it was found that each teacher used a range of strategies, of none of which they were necessarily aware. They were asked, 'Consider how you try to spell . . . ', and words such as those in Figure 5.10 were written on the screen.

This process of making explicit the metacognitive events would be what Thomas and Harri-Augstein (1984) would explain as helping each one to hold a 'learning conversation'. The largest number of student errors were found to arise from their incomplete knowledge of affixing the base words or stems (*philol.* 'the base of a word to which inflectional suffixes are added' – *Chambers Dictionary*, 1945). In these instances, there are a number of remedial strategies which can be directed to correcting the problem. To correct bases, direct attention to the root from which the word is derived, associate it with other words from the same root, explore its particular meaning and so on. To correct affixes, that is, prefixes and suffixes, of which there are a limited number to learn with each student deficient in a different group, each student is taught self-help to examine affix structures and meanings and to master learning the family groups. When short vowel and long vowel syllable structures are understood, then the 'add, double, drop and change' rules for suffixing can be applied. Where there are articulation errors, these can be pointed out and clear enunciation practised for difficult spellings. Sometimes 'over-articulation' is appropriate to cue the memory for spelling, e.g. in 'parli-*a*-ment', 'gover*n*ment'. Some errors still give rise to several different possible interpretations but these are relatively few in number. This form of remedial intervention at student level is still being evaluated but results thus far seem promising. Only a handful of cases each year are thrown up but the investment of tutorial time is small (one hour followed by a few minutes per week for about four weeks) and the students quickly become independent of the support and continue on their own.

So far, out of fifteen cases studied in detail two have been resolved as a handwriting co-ordination problem and specific remedial strategies have been planned and implemented with some resolution of the problem. Six cases have been spelling problems with which there was an associated original reading difficulty and slow reading problems left at student level. The rest were cases in which there was no known, or at least remembered, previous reading problem.

Since any misspelling is usually confined to a specific and predictable location in a word – for example at the schwa point or the syllable/prefix boundary – a *critical features* identification strategy was used to draw attention to it (Gibson and Levin, 1975; Farnham-Diggory, 1978). This simply meant a ring was drawn round the error letter or the omission area, e.g.:

accom◯odation,   practi⬭e

All attention was then directed to correcting this error item rather than attending to any part of the word already known. First, students were taught how to remediate any two of their misspellings at any one sitting, no more. On each occasion, several remedial strategies were shown them and they were sent off to remediate two more of their errors using similar strategies and to report back in three days to explain how the strategy worked and orally to spell the words correctly.

Although during this process the students found they might still misspell the word in essay writing, whenever they came to it they had warning bells or signs that this was one of their 'specials'. They would misspell it and then correct it, using their special strategy. As they used the word more often, they could begin to correct it before writing it down, for they were cued to attend carefully and avoid the old error. Eventually, they found that words frequently used were spelled easily and correctly without pause as the old motor programme was substituted by the 'higher profile' new one. In some cases, practice in writing the word in full cursive was a means of overriding old writing habits.

Simultaneous oral spelling (see Table 5.3) is used in preference to the look–cover–write–check strategy, for Bradley (1981) found that it was the more effective. Copywriting and tracing were also found to be ineffective methods for teaching spelling. Our studies show that combining SOS with cursive writing of the word so that it is completed as one motor unit is the most effective of all.

Table 5.3   *The 12 plus 1 cognitive strategies for spelling*

(1) Articulation	Make sure the misspelled word is correctly and clearly articulated for spelling, e.g. chim(l)ey should be corrected to chimney and skel(ing)ton to skeleton. These are common errors of speech.
(2) Over-articulation	Remind the student of difficult parts of a word, e.g. parli(a)ment and gover(n)ment.
(3) Cue articulation	Say the word incorrectly to remind the student of the area of difficulty and to cue the correct spelling, e.g. necessary spoken as neckessary to remind one that the 'c' comes before the 'ss', or Wednesday for We'n'sday.
(4) Syllabification	It is easier to spell a word broken down into short syllables than to spell it as a whole. Syllabifying helps avoid contractions, e.g. misdeanour – mis/de/mean/our; criticed – crit/i/cise/d. Contractions of polysyllabic words are typical of the student misspeller. They must learn to spell a difficult polysyllabic word syllable by syllable.
(5) Phonics	This is assigning a grapheme, a written unit, to a phoneme, a sound unit. For most words in English there is not direct sound-to-symbol correspondence, it only occurs in regular words in its simplest form, e.g. bed, bred, bled, pin, tram, plan. After this, orthographic rules have to be applied. However, the application of these simple one-to-one correspondences denotes progress in spelling and can act as the framework for developing correct spelling. It provides a comprehensible skeleton and can be read correctly, e.g. marstr (master); mstry (mystery); nite time (night time). This last misspelling is more advanced than basic phonics, incorporating orthographic knowledge beyond phoneme–grapheme correspondence. This is knowledge of the long vowel sound in a syllable denoted by the silent 'e'.

(6) Funnies

It is sometimes not possible to apply any of the foregoing, but something funny or rude can aid the memory, e.g. one subject used 'knickers' to remind her, another 'cess pit' which is also an analogy strategy to spell *necessary* correctly.

(7) Meaning

Words such as *separate* are commonly incorrectly spelled as sep(e)rate. You may know you spell it wrongly but cannot remember which is the correct version. 'Parting' or 'paring' can be used as meaning cues to correct spelling. The word's origin from *parare* can be a second clue.

(8) Origin

The word's roots in another language often provide the framework for correct recall, e.g. sen(c)ation was misspelled as well as 'sen(c)e'. The origin is *sens* in both French (feeling) and Latin and helped to put the word right. For the word *opportunity*, commonly misspelt opp(u)rtunity, the origin is *port* or harbour, an effective or timely opening. This revelation clears up the misspelling.

(9) Rule

e.g. 'i before e except after c': receive, perceive; and 'when two vowels go walking the first one does the talking': breath, breathe, main, steal. There are always a few exceptions to the general rules, or another less common rule applies.

(10) Family

This is often helpful in recalling silent letters and correct representations of the schwa (ə) or 'uh' sound in some words, e.g. for Canada, Canadian; telephone, telepathic, telescope, television (the *meaning/origin* clues can also be used for *tele*); bomb, bombardment, bombardier.

(11) Analogy

This is comparison with similar words or parts of words. Students should learn to say, e.g., 'it is like' braggart with two gs in *braggadocio*, or it is like a maze with only one z in *hazard*.

(12) Orthographic or psycholinguistic structure

This is affixing and syllable structure rules, e.g. effects of short and long vowel sounds in closed syllables:
short – bid (CVC)
long – bide (CVCe)
when affixing short vowel closed syllables – double and add suffix, e.g. bid/ding
when affixing long vowel closed syllables – drop 'e' and add suffix, e.g. bid/ing
when stress occurs in the second syllable – doubling occurs, e.g. reference, referral.

Table 5.3 *continued*

(13) Simultaneous oral spelling (SOS)	This system, devised by Stillman (1932), is the plus 1 to be used when all else fails: 1. Identify area of difficulty. 2. Write correctly from dictionary once, lower case. 3. *Name* letters as you do so. 4. Fold paper to cover word. 5. Spell word aloud (naming) as you write it. Repeat 3, 4, 5 until word is spelled correctly three times in a row. Check each time with original.

The 12 plus 1 strategies for remediating misspellings were also tested by Parrant (1986) with a group of 11-year-olds in an ordinary middle school. In the class group of 21 pupils, eight were identified as having specific special needs in relation to reading and spelling problems. A parallel class of 23 pupils was used as a control group. For six weeks during normal curriculum activities the teacher offered cognitive strategies to the experimental group pupils instead of the usual practice of using look–cover–write–check (Peters, 1970) or repeat copying of words misspelled. The control group did not receive the cognitive strategies, only look–cover–write–check. The pupils were given a dictation pre and post training and the total number of errors for both groups fell: the experimental group's errors fell from 273 to 162 on the post test. This difference was significant at $p < 0.01$ level for the experimental group and not significant for the controls. The control group's errors on the post test showed a highly variable pattern of improvements and deteriorations. The experimental group's error scores all diminished markedly, except for one subject who made one error on each and one who made no errors on the pre test and one on the post test. A change in attitude was reported by the experimental group pupils from a learned helplessness or neutrality to positive interest and self-esteem through finding a way to improve their own spelling. The special needs group's spellings also improved but less significantly ($p < 0.05$). They were observed to be making steady but slower progress. This is an important finding, for such children by this time are usually failing to make any progress at all. Similar findings were reported by Vincent (1983) with top infants and by a range of our teachers in detailed case studies, especially where the strategies were carefully adapted to suit the age and ability of the pupils. It was also found that many classroom dictionaries contained insufficient information for spelling purposes.

HELPING CHILDREN WITH HANDWRITING DIFFICULTIES

It is not an exaggeration to say that thousands of children in our schools from 4 years old to 19 are daily being handicapped by their poverty in handwriting skills. They bring this handicap with them into further and higher education and yet so much of the anguish and stress caused by these problems can be created by the teaching method and the handwriting curriculum, or sometimes the lack of any teaching at all. Teachers are extremely insistent that pupils should write with a neatness and clarity of hand, and this pressure for neatness grows as the pupil leaves the reception class and is expected to have learned the basics of a 'good' hand. Scattered throughout particular pupils' writing books can be found admonishments such as: 'You must try to be neater', 'Rewrite this untidy work!', 'Careless work!', 'Untidy, see me!'. It does not seem to have occurred to any of these teachers that the pupil cannot help it and would write neatly and tidily if it was at all possible. Untidy work is usually considered a product of laziness and carelessness (Cotterell, 1974), which is most often very far from the truth. These pupils may be observed tense and hunched over their papers, pen held in a vice-like grip to try to gain control of it, white knuckles, strain and tension evident in every movement (Alston, 1983; Sassoon, 1983). After ten minutes of such intense effort they become exhausted and the writing increases in size and wobbles and swoops across the page. Content and spelling are sacrificed to the huge effort expended on the motor act. At the end of it all if the comment is 'Careless work' it is not surprising that pupils with such problems become disheartened and unwilling to make an effort for such an unhelpful return (Myklebust, 1965).

It has been found that remedial handwriting programmes which teach a cursive script can prove very effective in helping these pupils overcome their co-ordination problems (Gillingham *et al.*, 1940; Gillingham and Stillman, 1956; Wedell, 1973; Hickey, 1977; Cowdery *et al.*, 1983, 1984). There are however a number of problems in changing to cursive. Some pupils on a cursive programme are not able to use the cursive hand in ordinary classroom work: it is often forbidden or the pupil thinks it is and so dares not practise it. Pupils often feel safer with print and copying and even think that cursive looks untidy.

Recent research by Laszlo (1987) has shown that one in ten pupils in ordinary schools suffers from co-ordination problems with no neurological impairment to be found. Eighty per cent of the cases were boys. The remedial treatment which was found

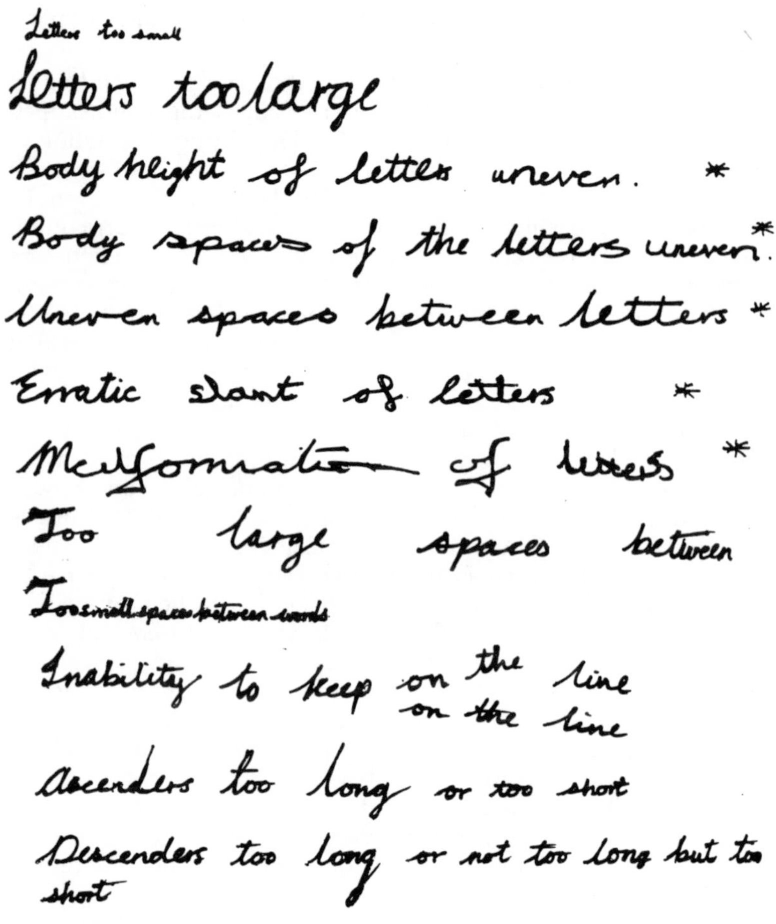

Letters too small

Letters too large

Body height of letters uneven.   *

Body spaces of the letters uneven. *

Uneven spaces between letters *

Erratic slant of letters   *

Malformation of letters *

Too   large   spaces   between

Too small spaces between words

Inability to keep on the line
on the line

Ascenders too long or too short

Descenders too long or not too long but too short

Figure 5.11 *A checklist for identifying handwriting difficulties*

to be most successful in these cases was to select one skill which the child had not successfully mastered and to teach it over a period of weeks or even months. During this period, as the one skill is acquired and its perceptuo-motor organisation is achieved, it suddenly seems possible for other such skills to be developed. A case example given was of a boy, trained on a specific ball skill, who after several months showed a marked improvement in handwriting.

In most APSL programmes (Gillingham and Stillman, 1956; Hickey, 1977; Cowdery *et al.*, 1983) it is the handwriting skill itself which is singled out for systematic training. Wedell (1973) recommends that training in cursive is especially used for pupils with handwriting difficulties. When these pupils lift the pen from the page in print script they have difficulty in relocating it and forming the next letter. It is particularly helpful for them to learn words or syllables in words as whole writing units, so that they do not have to keep lifting pen from paper.

Figure 5.12 shows the work of Mark, a 9-year-old who has a handwriting problem. At first glance a teacher might be more concerned about the spelling but will not have seen the effort which has gone into producing this. The work was written with a line guide. The problems are illustrated in such diagnostic features as:

- variations in pressure seen in thickness of stroke and faint and dark areas of writing;
- capitals and lower-case letters in inappropriate places (use of capital 'B' for 'b' indicates reversal problems with 'b' and 'd' in spelling);
- wavy/shaky strokes on some letters;
- certain letters poorly formed: e.g. 's' often too large, almost capital; 'w' tending to be too large or too open; 'k' appearing almost as capital; letters open which should not be;
- variation in slope of letters;
- variation in size of body of letters;
- variation in length of ascenders and descenders;
- variation in body space taken up by each letter;
- overall size of body of letter too large;
- uneven space between letters and words;
- writing swerving in towards the mid line from margins;
- 'rivers': large spaces run down from the top of the writing through the rest of the page.

Mark was given tuition in cursive (Morse, 1984) over several weeks and very pleasing results were quickly obtained which his class teacher was able to encourage in classwork. Transfer to open-ended writing from the set-piece exercises is more gradual. The results shown here are after two weeks' tuition, for a few minutes per day within the ordinary class lesson time.

Cursive provides a fluent, through-the-whole-word movement which prevents excessive pressure and eventually allows a good speed to be built up. The fluency and speed enables the brain to concentrate more fully upon meaning and spelling.

In order to train the hand to make a fluid movement, it is helpful to practise tracing the letter in the air, to write it on the

(a)

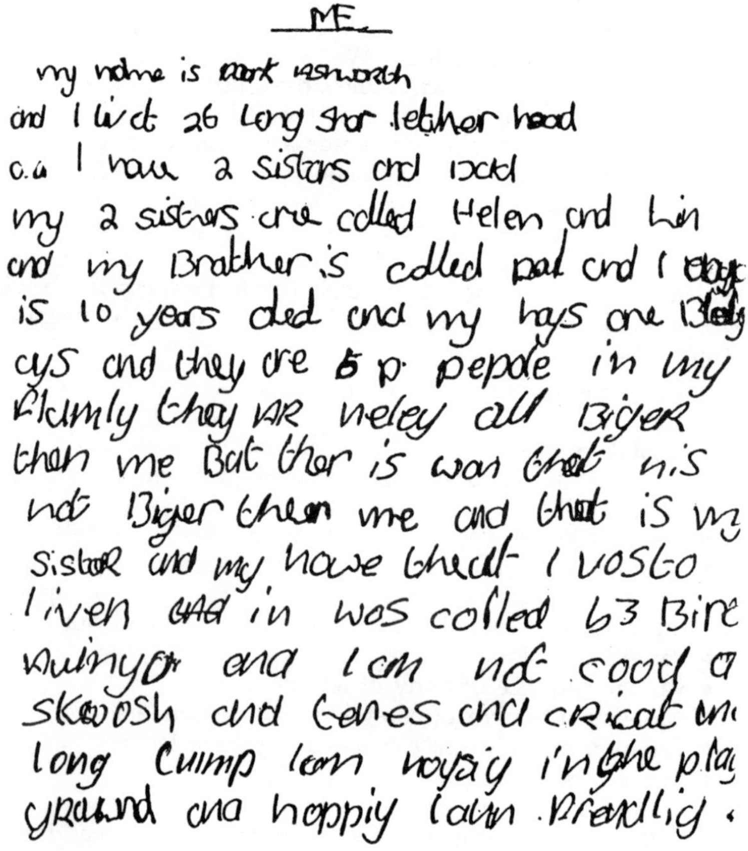
ME

my name is mark ashworth
and I livct 26 Long Stor lethor head
o.a I have 2 sistars and 1dad
my 2 sisters are called Helen and Lin
and my Brather is called pal and I age
is 10 years old and my hays are Black
cys and they are 5 p pepole in my
flamly thay AR neley all Biger
then me But ther is wan that his
not Biger then me and that is my
sistaR and my have thedt I vosto
liven and in wos colled 63 Bire
nuinyor and I cam not good a
skwosh and Genes and cRicat and
long cump lam noyaiy in the play
grawnd and hoppiy lam Draklig.

Figure 5.12 *Work of Mark ('Me') (a) before, (b) during programme. (Teacher's writing in brackets)*

children's backs for them to identify, and to encourage practice using finger paints, drawing in sand and crayons and paints.

Figure 5.13, based on Morse (1984), illustrates how to proceed with the business of teaching the letter. Sometimes it is necessary for the pupil to produce a whole book devoted to one letter before it is of a reasonable size and shape. It is only found necessary to proceed in this laborious fashion with the first few letters; after this the pupil seems to gain mastery of the motor skill as Laszlo (1987) pointed out, and this transfers to the learning of other letters and syllable combinations.

(b)

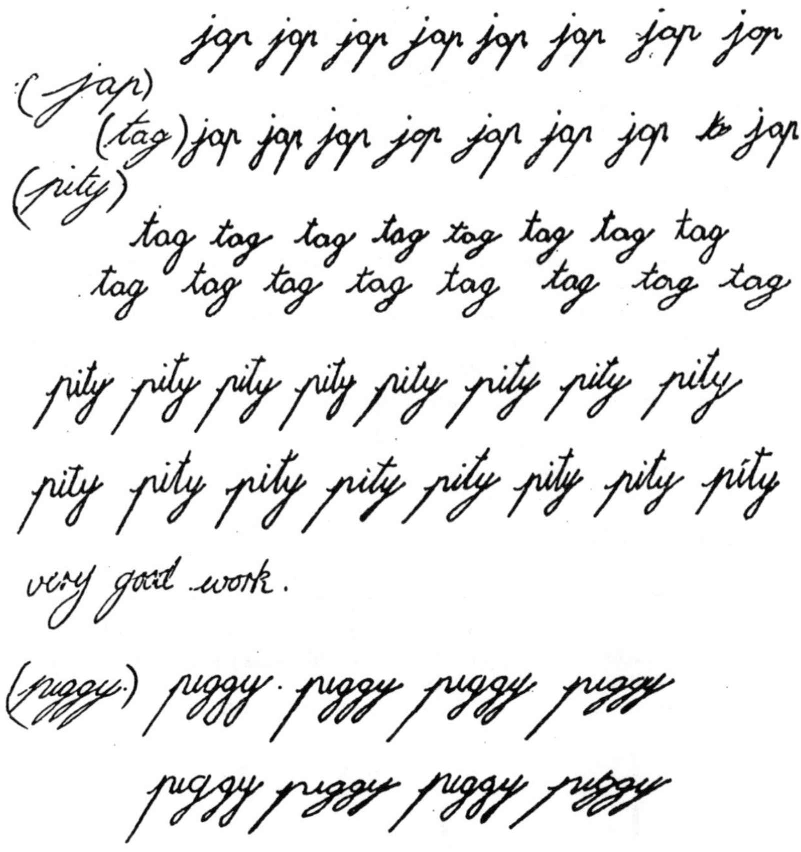

(jar)

jar jar jar jar jar jar jar jar

(tag) jar jar jar jar jar jar jar to jar

(pity)

tag tag tag tag tag tag tag tag
tag tag tag tag tag tag tag tag

pity pity pity pity pity pity pity pity

pity pity pity pity pity pity pity pity

very good work.

(puggy.) puggy. puggy puggy puggy

puggy puggy puggy puggy

Motor impairment and handwriting

There are some children who have suffered mild to severe physical impairment which can affect their fine motor skills in handwriting (Gubbay, 1975). In such cases it can be of more educational value to provide the pupil with a word processor from the age of 5 in the reception class rather than insist that handwriting is practised. Handwriting can always be taught later at the age of 7 or 8, when and if the pupil is developmentally ready.

Quite the reverse has unfortunately happened to Stephen.

Every letter has an *approach stroke* and a *carry-on stroke*. This means that the pupil can join his/her letters as soon s/he has learned two or three.

It also gives the directional flow from left to right and same starting point for every letter and word. When writing on lined paper s/he should be asked to place his/her pencil or pen on the line to start, every time, with an approach stroke. (This is invaluable for the pupil whose writing floats off all over the page. The use of this 'anchoring point' helps to overcome this problem very quickly.)

Using this procedure the letter shapes will be introduced in the order given.

Example: Teaching the letter

1. Teacher *writes the shape* fairly large (about 15 cm) on the blackboard saying (ĭ) as s/he makes the shape.

2. Pupil stands *square to the board,* places different coloured chalk on the beginning of the approach stroke and goes over ι in chalk, saying (ĭ) as s/he does so. (Some children may need to repeat step two several times.)

3. Pupil moves along to the right and copies another ι on the blackboard.*

4. Pupil cleans board *from left to right* and writes ι on his/her own.*

5. Pupil moves to right again, places chalk on board (or cleans board again), *closes his/her eyes* and writes ι .*

* Child says (ĭ) each time.

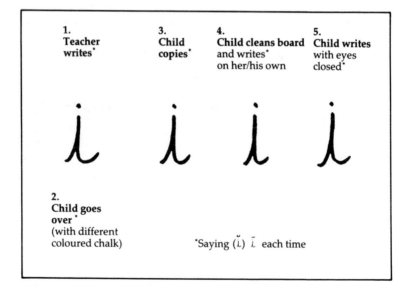

1. Teacher writes*	3. Child copies*	4. Child cleans board and writes* on her/his own	5. Child writes with eyes closed*

2. Child goes over* (with different coloured chalk)

*Saying (ĭ) ī each time

Figure 5.13 *An example of how to introduce the first letter of the Teaching Reading Through Spelling (TRTS) programme (Cowdery* et al., *1984)*

Stephen has a moderate physical impairment following birth difficulties which affects his gross and fine motor co-ordination skills. He gained a place in an ordinary school after his parents had exerted considerable pressure, but no additional resources were made available by the LEA to assist the school to help him. He spends many hours a day trying with extreme difficulty to write his work neatly and legibly for his teacher to read (Figure 5.14), but it takes a huge amount of effort and more than three times as long as other pupils. Now at the age of 7 he is becoming very frustrated at his lack of writing fluency and speed and is beginning to lose heart. His ideas flow much too fast for him to be able to capture them on the page. His parents are now on the horns of a dilemma. In order to obtain additional resources for Stephen, such as the word processor he should have had since the age of 5, he will need to be 'statemented'. The LEA considers he has made good progress comparable with his peers and that invoking the statementing procedure is unnecessary. The parents see the effort which he has to apply and know that the quality of what he could produce is much better than is written in his books. They feel his real potential is not being recognised because his impairment means that lower standards are expected of him. They are also concerned that once a 'statement' is made for Stephen he will be put on a direct route for entry to the local school for physically impaired children. Whilst this debate continues Stephen's educational progress and his literary skills are being held back: he is being disadvantaged by being where he belongs, in a mainstream setting, but without necessary technical support. In the special school the word processor would be readily available but his career aspirations would become narrowed by the limited curriculum available in a small school and by the stigma which regrettably can attach to 'special' schooling. Stephen's case shows the dangers which can arise from examining only the final product which a pupil produces rather than looking at both the process and the product.

James, at 7, also has handwriting difficulties, caused by a mild co-ordination problem typical of the 'clumsy child' described by Gubbay (1975). His mother reported:

> He always manages to spread food over himself at mealtimes. When he was younger he kept falling off his bicycle but just persisted and finally learnt not to. Even when he went to school he still had problems in dressing, his clothes were always in turmoil with shoes on the wrong feet.

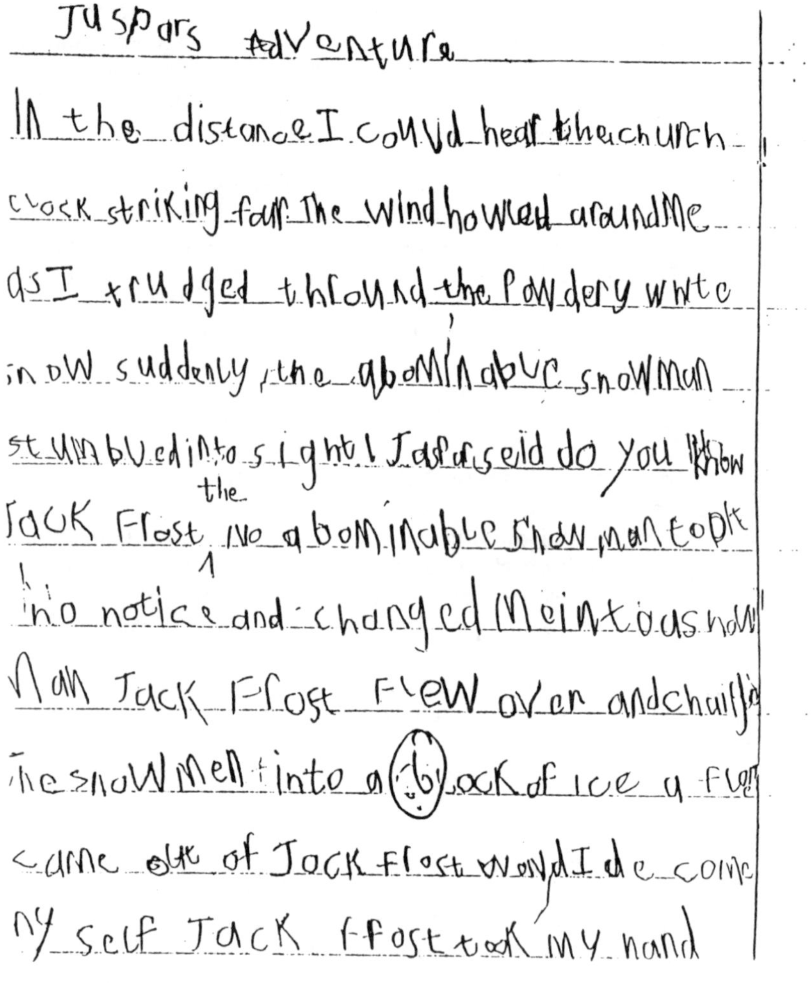

Juspars Adventure

In the distance I could hear the church clock striking far. The wind howled around me as I trudged through the powdery white snow suddenly, the abominable snowman stumbled into sight. I ask said do you know the Jack Frost no abominable snow man took no notice and changed me into a snow man Jack Frost flew over and chilled the snow men into a block of ice a fire came out of Jack Frost would I de come my self Jack Frost took my hand

Figure 5.14 *An example of Stephen's handwriting*

James was not markedly late in walking and talking. At 7 he is keen on sports but cannot read or write. There is no tradition of reading books in his family. The extract of his copy writing of one of our standard exercises – 'Baa Baa Black Sheep' – is shown in Figure 5.15. This is the one nursery rhyme which most young children seem to know by heart and can attempt to write from memory at 6, 7 or even earlier in some cases. Any similar simple nursery tale from the pupil's cultural back-

...and Left ...into. the (Night sky'.
through the woods, I
safely on the ground

how many times have I told
not to do your 'b' like 'this.

m m m.
Otherwise a good story Stephen

ground will suffice. James cannot even begin to write the rhyme from memory, but agrees to copy it line under line because he says he becomes muddled when all the writing is together. He was observed as he copied and it could be seen that he was *drawing* the letters rather than writing them. The drawing is indicated by the arrows showing the point where the letter was begun, large tails on the 'a's in 'Baa Baa' where he noticed a slight curve on the down stroke, the 'H n' in 'three' where the

Table 5.4   *A screening questionnaire to identify clumsiness (Gubbay, 1975)*

1. Is the formation and neatness of this child's handwriting much below average?

2. Is the child's sporting ability and body agility much below average?

3. Is the child unduly clumsy?

4. Does the child fidget excessively in class?

5. Is the child's conduct much below average?

6. Is the child unpopular with schoolmates?

7. Is the child's overall academic performance much below average for his/her age?

Screening examination questionnaire
1. Whistle through parted lips (pass or fail).

2. Make five successive skips (without skipping rope) (pass or fail after three attempts, with two demonstrations by examiner if necessary).

3. Throw a tennis ball up, clap hands up to four times, then catch ball with two hands or dominant hand (no. of claps – fails if only claps twice or less).

4. Roll tennis ball with dominant foot in spiral fashion around six matchboxes at 30 cm intervals (18 seconds allowed).

5. Tie single shoelace with double bow (15 seconds allowed).

6. Thread 10 beads (in 38 seconds) (beads 3 cm diameter, bore of 0.8 cm, string stiffened end).

7. Pierce 20 holes in graph paper (in 24 seconds) (use hat pin, two rows in 0.1 in x 0.1 in squares).

8. Posting box: fit six different plastic shapes into appropriate slots (seconds) (fails if takes longer than 18 seconds)

The clumsy children were selected on the following basis:

8-year-olds	6 or more failures
9-year-olds	5 or more failures
10-year-olds	4 or more failures
11-year-olds	3 or more failures
12-year-olds	2 or more failures

model shows 'th' joined. Note the more fluent writing of 'one' where he becomes interested in the technicalities of joining: he succeeds in relation to 'o' and 'n' but needs to have learnt a flowing 'n' before he could attach the 'e'. Because he finished the 'o' in the correct place he was able to carry straight over to the 'n'.

At the 5-year-old level pupils with difficulties in co-ordination in fine motor movements are not difficult to detect. Compared

Baa baa black
Baa baa black

Sheep have you
sheep have you

any wool, Yes
any wool, Yes

sir, yes sir three
sir' yes sir three

bags full, one
bags full, one

for the master
for the master

Figure 5.15 *James's copy writing/drawing*

with peers their drawings are unformed scribbles, performed shakily or fiercely until holes are poked through the paper. They show difficulty in making the smooth to and fro movements required for colouring, spill the colours over the edges and boundaries, may have an immature pencil or paintbrush grasp, and expend a great deal of effort in producing an indecipherable mess. These children often also show a range of signs of immaturity in the development of fine motor skills such as difficulties in drawing, colouring, using scissors, tying shoelaces, doing up buttons and zips, and so on. Young children with fine motor co-ordination problems will be seen to have great difficulty in drawing controlled, regular patterns such as those presented in early screening tests.

When these same 5-year-olds are asked to do the Draw a Person test (Harris and Goodenough, 1963), the figures drawn are minimalistic and poorly formed for the age-group. This can lead teachers to conclude wrongly that the pupil is intellectually less able than he or she actually is, and can lead to lower expectation and then lower achievement. As an assessment tool this test needs to be used with caution and the results with reservation because of the inherent problems with reliability and validity.

There are some pupils who have more severe difficulties in handwriting which makes their writing intensely spidery and difficult to read. This, according to Myklebust (1965), derives from cerebellar ataxia and may be seen in a few pupils in various degrees. An example is given in Figure 5.16.

Guidelines for helping with handwriting

Although some teachers will be concerned that to introduce the cursive form to 5-year-olds will confuse them, Jarman (1979) thinks that this is not the case, and the history of handwriting teaching in this country, of copperplate and then 'civil service' cursive, would support him. In North America and Europe teaching cursive from the outset is common practice. Once the ability to write a few letters of a reasonable size has been established, lined paper can be introduced to help structure and support the writing act. The use of lines does not hamper the child's creative flow as some teachers suggest: they help the child locate the place to begin the letters and help to produce a much neater and more well-ordered piece of writing (Burnhill et al., 1975).

In addition to the rigid ideas which have grown up around print versus cursive, and lined versus plain paper, irrational

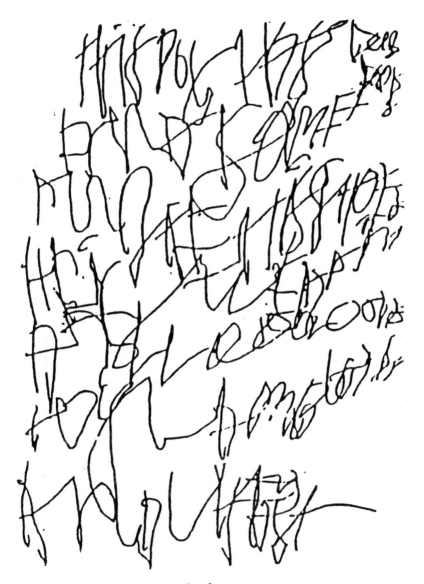

This boy has dolls and some books.
He has shoes. He is wearing a
warm coat and has a toy lamp shade.

Figure 5.16 *An example of cerebellar ataxia and writing (Myklebust, 1965)*

ideas also appear to have grown up around styles of writing, loops and slopes. If calligraphy is required for display then strict adherence to style can improve the look of the work. Most often, however, the pupil writes to communicate ideas and to record them as rapidly as possible during thinking or listening – here speed and legibility are paramount. Therefore excessive use of loops may confuse the writing and too great a slope either way will give rise to cramped and illegible writing because of the shortening of the connectors. Different letter shapes or forms are to be encouraged to maintain writing speed, thus two different 's' forms in the word 'sister'

Sister

are not an error or a failure to obey rules but are necessary to the writer for speed and fluency. Similarly, it is perfectly correct to use different 'd's within a word:

decided

For reasons not always possible to determine some teachers become unnecessarily upset by these legitimate and necessary differences.

In order to help pupils overcome their untidy writing, encouraging joining can greatly assist those with minor problems, together with asking the pupils to concentrate upon two main rules:

- body sizes of all the letters should be the same;
- slopes of heads and tails should all flow the same way.

Schools often introduce italic to tidy up pupils' writing but, although fluent and able writers will soon learn this and enjoy using it, it presents even more severe problems for those with learning difficulties because of the stroke differences of thick down strokes and thin connectors. There is also a lack of fluidity in connections, for joining is more often achieved by precise placing of each letter. Pupils with difficulties often finish up splaying their nibs, digging holes in the paper and making blots. To insist that italic is used as a handwriting style is most unwise, although it can be taught and used for *calligraphic* purposes.

The physical position of the writing act needs to be carefully established, with desk top at least 30 cm from the eyes to bring the book within the average focal distance. Pupils need to be noted who lie on their desks and squint sideways at their books with one eye – they could be compensating for a lack of fixed referent eye (Fowler, 1982). This can be checked using the Dunlop test (1974, 1975).

The paper for right handers should be angled towards the left-hand side and held still by the writer with the left hand. A reverse and even greater slope should be allowed on the paper for left handers. The bigger slope is so that they can pull the pen across the page without blotting or covering the results. For this reason some left handers will be found who write vertically down a page placed horizontally. It is not necessary or even helpful to persuade them to change this. What should *not* happen is that the page of any pupil should be placed straight in front of them or corrected to be straight – this defies the natural organisation of the motor movement of the hand from one side of the paper to the other as it pivots from the elbow. If pupils are asked to try this the correct slope of the paper for them can be discovered. Left-handed pupils should sit on the left-hand side of mixed pairs and right handers on the right side. This prevents the pivoting writing arms of each partner from hitting. So few courses of teacher training seem to include these simple but important points in their classroom management courses, or teach about handwriting with any degree of insight into children's problems, that students are obliged to learn what to teach from those already in the field. As has already been indicated, this fund of teaching wisdom can be in direct opposition to children's needs.

Guidelines for teaching handwriting to help overcome learning difficulties

- Teach the basic letter shapes as a single fluid motor movement *not* in copy writing or in tracing.
- Teach the letters singly but encourage joining to make two- and three-letter words and syllables, and blends.
- Teach the letters in use order with their sounds and names, not in alphabetical order.
- Use lined paper.
- Start each letter on the line.
- Teach joining as soon as two letters are learnt.
- Teach base word and affixes as one writing unit wherever possible.

As we have seen, this set of guidelines contradicts practically everything which is undertaken in the name of handwriting in reception classes.

HELPING CHILDREN WITH NUMBER DIFFICULTIES

Curriculum modification for children with learning difficulties is seen in its most prevalent form as an objectives-based approach. It was advocated for this purpose by Ainscow and Tweddle (1979). Definitive programmes of objectives are not offered, however, it is left to the teacher to specify these. Womack (1984) challenges the view that there is a general model for generating steps in a mathematical hierarchy and suggests that the teacher is better employed observing the child's mathematical behaviour. An analysis of how the child works and the errors made in that working will suggest the learning needs the child may have and the teaching objectives the teacher should establish. This can be regarded as a miscues approach to mathematics.

Miscues analysis in mathematics

Early examples of this approach may be found in the work of Davidson and Marolda (1975), Gibbons (1983) and Hughes (1986). Recently the work of Miles (1983b) has shown the errors of pupils with specific learning difficulties where problems are seen particularly in reciting the 7 and 9 times tables. The pupil may recite for example:

> A correct 7 times table up to –
> four sevens are twenty eight
> five sevens are thirty two
> six sevens are thirty eight,
> thirty nine. What am I up to?
> Was it six sevens?
> Seven sevens are forty two – that's wrong.
> Forty two yes, I think it is . . . forty nine,
> fifty six, sixty three, etc. (Miles, 1983b, p. 124).

Miles also analyses their errors in addition and subtraction, pointing out the many idiosyncratic features. Vellutino (1979 and 1987) ascribes the dyslexic's difficulties to a verbal processing deficit. The research of Wells (1981) and Tizard and Hughes (1984) suggests that the way language is used in the home may be significant in the development of mathematics, and so exploring the way pupils have learned to solve problems outside school could prove helpful to our understanding of their problems. The relationship between language, reading and mathematics has been extensively explored by Shuard *et al.* (1980), to which reference should be made.

A miscues analysis of Gemma's approach to solving an addition problem is very revealing. In this instance just looking at the result can indicate her problem. Most often the teacher will need to ask the pupil to explain the working out aloud so that notes can be made:

$$
\begin{array}{c}
27 \\
\underline{41} \\
68
\end{array}
\qquad
\begin{array}{c}
29 \\
\underline{54} \\
713
\end{array}
$$

Here the carrying strategy is incorrect and it is very likely that the concept of place value is not understood. This can then be explored with the child and strategies devised to help her to understand the sum. As Walkerdine (1982) has pointed out, the errors that children make are not random or irrational. They very often have their own form of logic limited by their ability to remember the steps in their quite often lengthy verbal process.

Cognitive process approaches to mathematics

The Cockcroft Committee (DES, 1982) underlined the need for a more problem-solving orientation in mathematics, directed to real-life issues, if the teaching of the subject was to be improved, not a 'back to basics' approach. Regrettably, drill and skill, or back to basics, is a common approach in the teaching of children with learning difficulties (Daniels, 1988).

The DES Lower Attainment in Mathematics Project at West Sussex Institute of Higher Education (Ahmed, 1984) was established to try to overcome the difficulties of a wider group of pupils than those with learning difficulties, but their findings have done much to promote good practice for all pupils. Lower attainers include both pupils with learning difficulties and thereby low attainment and their more able peers with equally low attainments. The specific aims of the project are to:

1. encourage teachers to change their attitudes about ways in which low attainers learn mathematics;
2. help teachers to interpret the Cockcroft Committee's 'Foundation List' (paragraph 458) in the spirit of paragraph 455 to 457 and 460 to 466. That is, suggest activities which should involve low attaining pupils in a wider range of mathematics than the usual restrictive diet of 'basics';

3.   provide teachers with ideas and strategies which should enable pupils to change their perceptions of mathematics, encourage them not to view the subject just as a body of knowledge which has to be 'passed on' fact by fact;

4.   suggest ways in which teachers can continually gain insight into pupils' mathematics without having to rely on formal tests;

5.   suggest ways in which pupils can arrive at conventional methods and terminology through their participation in problem solving activities and investigatory mathematics;

6.   suggest ways of working which should enable pupils to see links between mathematics and other subject areas;

7.   suggest ways of working which should help teachers to develop pupils' confidence and independence in handling mathematics;

8.   suggest approaches which should help teachers cope with different rates of learning amongst low attainers (Ahmed, 1984).

Not only is miscues analysis encouraged but also real problems are presented for resolution. Such approaches involve setting a problem such as 'Which soap powder would be the best buy?' and presenting the pupils with a range of brand boxes for them to resolve the problem. The resolution involves project pairs or teams working together to decide what the issues are and how they might test and solve them. This is very much in the style of the cognitive process model already outlined, with its emphasis on co-operative and negotiational learning. As can be seen, the project relies upon some of the basic skills having been learnt at some time, but similar problem-resolving approaches can be designed for learning basic skills and concepts.

Chris Robson, one of our project teachers, found that her group of 10-year-old slow learners could not grasp the concept of a standard unit of weight until she set up a rôle play for them. She introduced 'Weight Street' to them. Weight Street had three sweet shops and no standard weights. Each pupil was given 4p and invited to go into each shop and buy some real sweets. Shop A used 4 marbles as weights, shop B used 4 wooden blocks and shop C used 4 plastic cubes. The pupils soon realised that they were all choosing to buy their sweets at the same shop, and they were able to discuss the concept of standard weight, fairness and so on with vigour. This was a lesson they did not forget, even though shop play might be thought suitable only for 5- and 6-year-olds.

Learning styles and learning difficulties

Since the research by Witkin (1959) into field dependence/independence and his subjects' habitual ways of making judgements about the perceptual field, there has been an increasing interest in style. Particularly relevant here are styles of learning and cognitive style. Cognitive processes refer to the manner and the strategies which people use to solve problems or learn new material. Style refers to the habitual ways in which they do this, preferring one set of strategies to another. Bruner *et al.* (1963) refer to variants of focusers and scanners, detailing the way in which subjects select and reject concept attributes to solve particular problems involved in concept attainment. There is, however, insufficient evidence to show a strong connection between their laboratory modelling and problem-solving in real life. Guilford (1960) in his model of intellect put forward the notion of convergent and divergent thinking styles, which provided a useful critical framework for looking at intelligence test items and more general approaches to problem solution. De Bono's lateral thinking strategies are another example of this type of approach.

It is perhaps in the area of mathematics that it has proved easiest to pursue the notion of learning style based upon such models. According to Davidson and Marolda (1975) there are two distinct learning styles in mathematics: the 'recipe' approach, in which the person follows a step-by-step sequence of operations moving towards a solution, and the 'estimator' style (Table 5.5). Estimators are impatient with step-by-step procedures and are likely to make mistakes when using them. They prefer to be more adventurous. When confronted with a set of instructions for putting together a model, they prefer to ignore them and risk-take, trying to put the model together on the basis of hypothesising and testing as they go along. If they fail they then revert to reading the instructions. The recipe followers proceed in an orderly manner, reading the instructions, laying out the pieces in the recommended manner, and so on. If they do not find instructions or obtain clear guidelines from the teacher in lessons they become upset, even disturbed, and find it difficult to learn. The lack of clear instructions seems to make them feel insecure, and unless they already have a routine of their own which they can follow they become upset and unable to make progress. They may even follow a routine which they know is incorrect in desperation.

It can be noticed that anxious people tend to want to follow routines and perhaps the tendency for many children with learn-

Table 5.5   *Davidson and Marolda's concepts of mathematical style (1975)*

Recipe style	Estimator style
(1) Prefer a step-by-step approach moving forward to a solution.	Impatient with step-by-step procedures, likely to make mistakes doing them.
(2) Seldom estimate.	Good at estimating.
(3) Tend to remember parts rather than wholes.	Superior at recognising large-scale patterns, picturing geometric situations and visualising in 3 dimensions.
(4) Better at counting forwards than backwards.	Good at counting backwards.
(5) Better at understanding addition and multiplication.	Understand subtraction and division.
(6) Have a need for talking themselves through procedures.	
(7) Once the recipe is mastered are often very precise in carrying it out and obtain correct answer, but may remain totally unaware of the logic that gives meaning to what they are doing.	Have a better general understanding of what is involved in a particular mathematics problem, but often get the wrong answer because of their impatience and imprecision.

ing difficulties to want recipes or to use trial-and-error methods is an indicator of their anxiety and proneness to failure. It is little wonder in the end that they lapse into a state of learned helplessness, pleased only if they are allowed to copy work neatly into their books – unless of course they also have the misfortune to have a handwriting difficulty.

Loviglio (1981) linked the work of Davidson and Marolda (1975) to hemispheral style. The left hemisphere style is to process information in a sequential, linear and analytic fashion, and so plays a primary rôle in language, reading, writing and computation (Gazzaniga 1967). The right hemisphere tends to specialise in a non-verbal, simultaneous and holistic processing approach to learning.

Having identified the two basic styles of mathematics learning, Davidson and Marolda (1975) have developed a series of teaching techniques that allow the same material to be taught in at least two different ways. They use alternate strategies that allow the child to arrive at the solution by the most comfortable route.

For example: To add 8 + 6
A child with learning style 1:
Pretend to take the 8 in one hand and tap child's head as if

to store the 8. The child then counts on 6 more to get 14: 9–10–11–12–13–14.

A child who prefers learning style 2:

Since these pupils usually know doubles, they may be taught –

add 6 + 6 for a total of 12

since 8 is 2 more than 6

2 is added on to 12 to make 14.

Once a teacher begins to sense the way a child thinks and works, s/he should use that knowledge to begin presenting mathematics in a compatible form. Davidson believes that teachers need opportunities to broaden their own appreciation of the richness of mathematics. Too much emphasis is placed on computation at the expense of other aspects, so that spatial and geometric topics may not be taught because there is no time. 'If children had some time to work in the area of mathematics they can enjoy and shine in, they would have a better chance of developing mathematical competence and confidence!' She argues that if teachers took a less strictly computational approach in instruction in the early years, especially with girls, aversion to mathematics might be ameliorated.

Davidson suggests that teachers tend to prefer the orderly and neat, and that this is easier to obtain from girls and tends to be strongly reinforced. It is this she believes that sets the stage for girls' later downfall, for girls come to prefer the recipe rather than the estimator approach. They need to build spatial and manipulative experiences into the curriculum for girls, not let them avoid it and leave the boys to Lego building. Only by positive steps to balance the curriculum in this way does she think that mathematical thinking can be well developed and each style of learning used as appropriate to the problem. She points out with regret that the current climate of schools (in the USA) militates against equal opportunities, for the activities which stimulate such developments do not lend themselves to behavioural objectives and the goals of accountability.

Bias against girls and ethnic minority groups in Britain in relation to GCSE in mathematics, science and modern languages was also noted by Gipps *et al.* (1987). Teachers in these areas have to select pupils for different courses and different papers for different abilities. She writes that:

> some pupils will know before they enter the exam that they cannot get higher than a grade D for example. This I suspect will do much to counter the notion of positive assessment. Also I wonder how confident we can be that girls and ethnic minority students

will be entered at the level for which they are truly capable (Gipps
et al., 1987, p. 78).

SUMMARY

In this chapter the assessment and remediation of learning and
specific learning difficulties in reading, writing and number have
been discussed. In each case a developmental analysis of errors
has been outlined. The error categories themselves have suggested the focus for the teacher's intervention. The interventions
are recommended to take place as an integrated provision by
the class teacher within the ordinary classroom and as part of
the daily curriculum, except where the pupil has severe specific
learning difficulties and needs short-term specialist help
urgently.

In relation to reading it was suggested that developmental
assessment should be undertaken as the pupil reads his or her
ordinary reading book. Teaching intervention should be corrective and developmental, in the context of an apprenticeship
approach in which reading is a psycholinguistic guessing game.
Spelling development should be encouraged through an emergent writing approach across the curriculum, supported by the
structured teaching of spelling skills in context. These teaching
inputs should have regard to the hierarchical nature of spelling
development and include cognitive strategies to overcome
learned helplessness.

Where pupils have fallen many years behind peers in reading
and spelling skills, only average ability and able pupils should
be withdrawn for remedial tutorials. Children with learning difficulties who are slower to grasp concepts and principles out of
context should be taught their reading and spelling skills and
strategies within the ordinary classroom in an integrated provision. These skills and strategies should be incorporated into
across-the-curriculum activities, not taught within a narrow basic
skills provision. In order to undertake this developmental work,
class sizes will need to be reduced accordingly.

The teaching of handwriting should be coupled with the
teaching of spelling in a multisensory method. A cursive style
is particularly recommended both for remediation of handwriting
difficulties and for beginning writers.

A similar miscues and developmental analysis of error was
suggested in relation to mathematical difficulties. To overcome
low attainments in this subject, pupils need to learn to develop

strategies for solving problems geared to real situations in mathematically relevant contexts.

Epilogue

Children with learning difficulties will be able to prosper in ordinary schools when teachers are helped to develop a more learner-relevant curriculum and pedagogy. When teachers can successfully meet the needs of slow learners in their classrooms they will begin to appreciate what good teaching really involves and all pupils will benefit.

This book has attempted to bring together examples of successful practice and bind them into a coherent framework from which teachers can learn and be enabled to develop their own techniques. The framework suggested is a cognitive process methodology which can stimulate learning and help pupils overcome their learned helplessness, achieving personal autonomy and self-advocacy. The examples given are from lessons with pupils with mild to moderate learning difficulties and show how they can be taught in mixed-ability settings to the advantage of all. Similar techniques are beginning to be developed in the teaching of children with severe learning difficulties, particularly by the self-advocacy movement, although it has not been possible to include them here. These methods, assisted by behavioural objectives approaches, will bring nearer the possibility of integrating all children into mainstream education.

I have tried to show how a classroom teacher in primary or secondary school can help pupils with learning difficulties even though he or she has no classroom aides, no support teacher and no special resources. There are texts in this series, for example Wolfendale (1987), Webster and McConnell (1987) and Hegarty (1987), which develop these themes or deal with specific needs or curriculum areas. The main theme of this book has been that it is the teacher who is the most important classroom resource and that the teacher's attitude and style of teaching can promote or deny pupils' learning opportunities. Examples have been given to show how a positive and supportive learning climate coupled with a language experience and problem-resolving approach can help children with learning difficulties achieve far more than they or their teachers ever thought possible. It embodies a set of principles and practices which are emotionally sustaining, cognitively challenging and motivating for both teachers and learners.

At the outset it was intended that the needs of children with severe learning difficulties should be included in this book, but in the writing it has proved impossible to do this and keep within a reasonable length. These pupils' needs and their integration into ordinary schools will therefore be addressed in a separate book. A summary table of their position on the intellectual and attainment continuum may be found in Appendix 1.

POSTSCRIPT: SUMMARIES OF HMI SURVEY OF SECONDARY SCHOOLS, 1988 (*Times Educational Supplement*, 5 August 1988, p. 9)

Curriculum and pedagogy

As in 1979, there were clear indications of the constraints that preparation for external exams could have.

These included the 'slavish adherence to a narrow interpretation of examination syllabuses', the over-preparation of pupils by excessive note-taking and use of poor worksheets and too much teaching of exam techniques.

The classroom atmosphere in most lessons in more than four-fifths of schools was 'generally conducive to learning' and disorder was rare.

But the emphasis was usually on 'benevolent control, with challenge and excitement a lower priority. Instruction by the teacher was more common than active involvement in learning by the pupil. Good order was often the result of a passive and uncritical conformity rather than of an intrinsic interest in what was offered.'

Teaching and learning for most pupils seemed to have changed little since 1979 either in pace, content or approach, HMI found. Youngsters continued to spend a large part of their time in the classroom listening or writing. Lessons often contained little to help them apply what they had learned more widely.

Only a quarter of schools were setting expectations that were appropriate for all pupils. Low expectations were more common than unreasonably high ones. Schools catered less well for those of just below average ability.

Special educational needs

Nearly all special needs provision was for pupils with learning difficulties, the inspectors found.

The most common practice, seen in 45 per cent of schools, was to withdraw pupils in years one to three, usually from English and maths lessons, but, often from subjects such as modern languages and humanities, in order to concentrate on basic language and numeracy.

But in a growing number of schools, special needs teachers worked alongside subject teachers in the normal classroom setting.

Separate grouping in remedial classes frequently meant specialist teaching, good accommodation and well-chosen resources, the inspectors say. But more often 'such advantages were outweighed by a variety of problems: isolation from peers provided a sense of security for some pupils, but at the same time it could lock them into a cycle of low achievement, poor motivation, and even disruptive behaviour'.

HMI conclude that the variety of special needs provision means there is still confusion about the best way forward. There were signs of more appropriate provision but in general, 'too little attention is given to the diagnosis of need before attempting to meet it'.

Appendix 1 *Mental Impairment Continuum*

17th–20th centuries	World Health Organisation	Pre-Warnock	Warnock (1978)		Clarke and Clarke (1978)
Idiots	Profound IQ 0–20	ESN(S)	Slow L.(sev.)	0–5 yrs	Gross retardation needing nursing care.
				6–21 yrs	Obvious delays in all areas, few learn to walk or have simple speech.
				Adult	Incapable of self-maintenance.
	Severe IQ 20–30	ESN(S)	Slow L.(sev.)	0–5 yrs	Marked delay in all development.
				6–21 yrs	Some understanding of speech.
				Adult	Can perform simple daily tasks but needs constant supervision.
Imbeciles	Moderate IQ 30–50	ESN(S)	Slow L.(sev.) 0–55	0–5 yrs	Noticeable delay in motor and language development.
				6–21 yrs	Can learn simple communication skills and safety habits. May read but with little understanding. Likely to remain very childish in behaviour and interests.
				Adult	Needs supervision to carry out simple tasks. Can travel alone in familiar areas. Usually capable of self-maintenance.
	Mild	ESN(M) IQ 50–75	Slow L.(mod.) 55–70	0–5 yrs	Often not noticed as retarded until goes to school. But probably slow to walk and more probably slow to talk.
				6–21 yrs	Can acquire practical skills and may become literate.
				Adult	Can usually maintain self, although guidance and support may be needed especially over financial matters.

2/3: cause unknown

23 children in every 1,000 are mentally handicapped on basis of IQ figures.
Prevalence: 1 in every 100 children are profound to borderline.

Level 1   i t p n -nt s sn sp ă st l ll pl sl d spl f -ff -lt -ss -nd h fl -ft g gl -ng ŏ m -mp sm r dr fr y gr pr ě tr y/i spr str u/i ŭ k -nk c(k) -lk c(s) sk sc -ck cl -ct cr scr b bl br j -ed w dw qu wa qua sw v tw z squ x

Level 2   a–e e–e i–e o–e u–e ye -ke

Level 3   er ur ir or wor ar war g(j) ge dge sh shr ch ch(k) ch(sh) tch th thr wh ph -es

Level 4   ā ē ī ō ū -ce -se -ze

Level 5   ee ea (ē) ea (ě) ea (ā) ear (ěr) ōō˘ ǒo ai ain ay oa oe ou (ou) ou (ōō ǒo) ou (ŭ) ow (ou) ow (ō) au aw oi oy ue ie (ē) ie (ī) ei (ē) ei (ā) ey eu ew ui ey (ā) ous (ūs) us (ŭs)

Level 6   o (ŭ) al eigh igh ind old ble ckle stle el et v/v -tion -sion -ssion -cian sion ant (etc.) ary (etc.) silent letters ist est ine -tune tu i (y) final (sh) (ū) (à)

Level 7   Silent e, one-one-one rule, two-one-one rule, y, plural y, plural f, plural o, irregular plurals, plural letters, possessives, prefixes, -ble and -ity, -cular and -gular

Negotiated agreement (using Snowballing)

This activity can begin with a brainstorm. From all the ideas obtained, each person lists what s/he believes to be the five most important qualities, in order of priority. If time allows, each person then teams up with another person and they agree a list of five, these two then team up with another two and so on. Each group member should be in broad agreement with the group list. Groups can combine again and endeavour to agree a list acceptable to all its members.

What are our rights?

Additional material if there is time.

Triangle of rights

List under three headings:

(1) your rights which you think are abused by others;
(2) other people's rights that you abuse;
(3) other people's rights that you see abused by other people.

Review and discussion:
How widely did your personal list differ from your final group list?
    If it was very different, were you happy with the group list?
    To what extent did members of the group really listen to each other in the discussion and decision-making?
    To what extent did everyone participate?
    Was the decision-making shared or did one or more people dominate?
    To what extent were any conflicts resolved, or were they 'swept under the carpet?'
    What process did you use to come to a decision (voting, consensus, authority or dominant member)?
    What sort of authority (superior knowledge or louder voice)?
    What are the advantages and disadvantages of:
    voting
    consensus

authoritarian dominance?
Which of these methods is used in:
your family
college
clubs you belong to
politics
internationally?

Source: Bowers and Rawlings, 1988

Broken squares

Five individuals have an envelope containing pieces of five small
broken squares. Their job is each to make up *one* of these small
squares. Each person may only give pieces, not take them from
anyone else. The whole task must be done in silence.

Observers record what the group did for presentation to the
whole class. Few groups perform well or as a team; they misbehave, flout the rules, demonstrate greed and selfishness. Each
aspect is discussed at the end of the task to help promote group
collaboration. The task is an enjoyable one.

Source: Bowers and Rawlings, 1988

In 1989 the National Curriculum Council published documents and Statutory Orders covering English, mathematics, science and technology. History and geography should follow shortly, delayed by difficulties in coming to agreement within the Working Parties. At this point we might well ask, where are the arts in education? Why are they not considered to be equally important?

A National Curriculum is now specified for the first time in Britain. This in itself is no bad thing, for as has been suggested, there was always an implicit common curriculum which pupils have had access to on the basis of teacher and school decisions. What is likely to prove problematic is the enforcement of such a curriculum through policing by local education authority advisers turned inspectors.

The disadvantages of the system are that some teachers, lacking in pedagogical and curriculum expertise, will, as in the worst excesses of former secondary education, press to *cover the syllabus*, leaving concerns for the learning of individuals behind. Where this occurs, children with learning difficulties, who make up 20–50 per cent of the population in ordinary schools, will be put under pressure 'to catch up' or be 'statemented out' of the curriculum. Teachers who teach to the middle ability, making up two-thirds of the classroom group, will create more learning difficulties and a lowering of self-esteem in an even larger group than before. Even teaching to the assumed three levels of attainment within the class group can seriously underestimate what individuals of all ability levels may achieve when well taught by defining their place on the curriculum and teaching to that. This could mean a progressive lowering of attainments across the nation. We shall all know the same and can set our sights lower by comparison. Perhaps the most serious disadvantage for both teachers and learners are the thousands of assessment statements which have to be recorded on pupils, so that teaching and talking time will be at a premium. Until this administrator's concept of what makes good education is modified over the next ten years, children with learning difficulties could be just as vulnerable as they have been in the past, although for different reasons. In Eastern European countries, the results have been to consign such individuals to 'defectology clinics' and in Japan to fee-paying crammer night-school classes from the early years.

Formerly the general aspects of provision for these children might be characterised as 'Type one' teaching errors, that is, much of what should have been put in was left out: i.e. 'child-minding'. Now we can have visions of a widespread 'Type two' teaching error, in which much of what should have been left out is put in: i.e. content ramming.

Other groups with special learning needs could also be seriously disadvantaged by the present arrangements. Able learners who need to work through early stages of subjects very quickly or not at all will, in many classrooms, be made to mark time whilst they wait for others to reach their level of attainment under a particular curriculum target. This typifies curricula specified by contents rather than levels of intellectual operation upon contents (Bloom *et al.*, 1956). It demonstrates that those educators with relevant experience had no place in this scheme of things.

Children with specific learning difficulties will become particularly vulnerable to failure in a curriculum which requires a preponderance of written and read material in lessons and assessments. They will fail to thrive in a school curriculum which does not value achievements in the arts, in communication and social skills, and in practical intelligence and ability. In addition, the compulsion at secondary stage to learn a second or foreign language will prove a serious handicap when they lack the necessary phonological abilities to become literate in their own language. If second language teaching is confined to oral communication in real contexts, then some of the hardships will be removed. It is recommended that these pupils should be statemented out of traditional foreign language teaching and be provided with specialist remedial tutorial support on a multisensory psycholinguistic reading, spelling and handwriting programme. This tuition should be given in groups of no more than two pupils to one trained specialist tutor, for in-class support at this late stage is a less effective and, in the long run, less economical system, as now shown by research.

In the next decade, the progress and learning needs of slower learners and lower attainers will need to be monitored very carefully if their career aspirations are not to be jeopardised by such a hastily constructed basket of provisions.

References

ACE (Advisory Council for Education) (1980) *Survey of Disruptive Units*. London: ACE.

Ackerman, I., Gunelt, D., Kenwood, P., Leadbetter, P., Mason, L., Matthews, C. and Winteringham, D. (1983) *DATAPAC: An Interim Report*. Birmingham, UK: Department of Psychology, Birmingham University.

Ahmed, A. (1984) *West Sussex Institute of Higher Education: Lower Attainment in Mathematics Project*. Bognor Regis: WSIHE.

Ainley, J. and Clarke, R. (1980) *Early Language Programme*. London: Globe Education.

Ainscow, M. and Muncey, J. (1981) *Special Needs Action Programme (SNAP)*. Coventry: Coventry LEA.

Ainscow, M. and Muncey, J. (1983) Learning difficulties in the primary school, an inservice training initiative. *Remedial Education* **18**(3), 116–124.

Ainscow, M. and Muncey, J. (1984) *SNAP*. Cardiff; Drake Educational Associates.

Ainscow, M. and Tweddle, D. A. (1979) *Preventing Classroom Failure: An Objectives Approach*. Chichester: Wiley.

Alston, J. (1983) A legibility index: can handwriting be measured? *Educational Review* **35**(3), 234–242.

AMMA (Assistant Masters and Mistresses Association) (1986) *The Reception Class Today. AMMA Report of 1984 Survey*. London: AMMA.

Anderson, J. R. (1980) *Cognitive Psychology and its Implications*. San Francisco: Freeman.

Arter, J. A. and Jenkins, J. R. (1979) Differential diagnosis – prescriptive teaching: a critical appraisal. *Review of Educational Research* **49**(4), 517–555.

AWMC (Association for Workers with Maladjusted Children) (1984) *Report on Maladjustment*. London: AWMC.

Baddeley, A. D. (1978) In Foss, B. (ed.) *New Horizons in Psychology*, vol. 2. Harmondsworth, Middx: Penguin.

Bakker, D. J. (1972) *Temporal Order and Disturbed Reading*. Rotterdam: Rotterdam University Press.

Bandura, A. and Walters, R. H. (1963) *Social Learning and Personality Development*. London: Holt, Rinehart & Winston.

Barker-Lunn, J. C. (1986) Report of NFER survey on teaching basic skills in primary schools. *Times Educational Supplement*.

Baron, J. and Strawson, C. (1976) Use of orthographic and word specific knowledge in reading words aloud. *Journal of Experimental Psychology: Human Perception and Performance* **2**, 386–393.

Barton, L. and Tomlinson, S. (eds) (1984) *Special Education and Social Interests*. London: Croom Helm.

Baumgart, R. (1986) In Broadfoot, op. cit.

BDA (British Dyslexia Association) (1981) *British Dyslexia Association Guidelines for Teaching Dyslexic Children*. Oxford: BDA.

Becker, H. S. (1963) *Outsiders: Studies in the Sociology of Deviance*. New York: Free Press.

Becker, H. S., Madsen, C. H. *et al.* (1967) The contingent use of teacher reinforcement and praise in reducing classroom behaviour problems. *Journal of Special Education* 1, 287–307.

Bell, D. (1984) *Multisensory Teaching for Reading and Writing*. Ewell: Surrey Learning Resources Centre.

Bennett, N. (1976) *Teaching Styles and Pupil Progress*. London: Open Books.

Bennett, N. (1986) 'Co-operative learning: children do it in groups – or do they?' Paper presented at the Conference for Development, Education and Child Psychology. Published in *Journal of Educational Child Psychology* (1987).

Bennett, S. N., Desforges, C. W., Cockburn, A. and Wilkinson, B. (1984) *The Quality of Pupil Learning Experiences*. London: Lawrence Erlbaum.

Berger, M. (1983) *Bulletin of the Association for Child Psychology and Psychiatry* **5**.

Berger, M. (1985) Applied behaviour analysis in education. *Bulletin of the Association for Child Psychology and Psychiatry* **7**.

Bernstein, B. (1960) Language and social class. *British Journal of Sociology* **11**.

Bernstein, B. (1970) 'Education cannot compensate for society'. In Cashdan, A. and Grugeon, E. (eds) *Language in Education*. London: Routledge & Kegan Paul.

Bindra, D. and Stewart, J. (1966) *Attitudes*. Harmondsworth, Middx: Penguin.

Blackham, C. J. and Silberman, H. (1971) *Modification of Child Behaviour*. Belmont, California: Wadsworth.

Blagg, N. (1987a) Instrumental enrichment: a report of work in three comprehensive schools in Somerset. *Times Educational Supplement*.

Blagg, N. (1987b) Unwillingly to school. *Times Educational Supplement* (24 July).

Blank, M. and Solomon, F. (1969) How shall the disadvantaged child be taught? *Child Development* **40**, 47–61.

Blankenship, C. and Lilley, M. S. (1981) *Mainstreaming Students with Learning and Behaviour Problems*. New York: Holt, Rinehart & Winston.

Bloom, B. S. *et al.* (1956) *Taxonomy of Educational Objectives*, vol. 1. London: Longman.

Bogen, J. (1969) The other side of the brain I II III. *Bulletin of the Los Angeles Neurological Society* **34**(3).

Booth, A. (1982) *Special Biographies*. OU Course E241. Milton Keynes: Open University Press.

Booth, A. and Potts, P. (1983) *Creating Integration Policy*. Oxford: Blackwell.

Booth, A., Potts, P. and Swann, W. (eds) (1987) *Preventing Learning Difficulties*. Oxford: Blackwell.

Bowers, S. and Rawlings, A. (1988) *Research Workshop Materials*. Kingston, Surrey: Kingston Polytechnic Learning Difficulties Research Project.

Bowers, S. and Wells, L. (1985) *Ways and Means*. Kingston, Surrey: Kingston Polytechnic Learning Difficulties Research Project.

Bradley, L. (1981) The organisation of motor patterns for spelling: an effective remedial strategy for backward readers. *Developmental Medicine and Child Neurology* **23**, 83–91.

Bradley, L. and Bryant, P. (1985) *Children's Reading Problems*. Oxford: Blackwell.

Brennan, W. K. (1974) *Shaping the Education of Slow Learners*. London: Routledge & Kegan Paul.

Brennan, W. K. (1979) *Curricular Needs of Slow Learners*. Working Paper no. 63. London: Evans/Methuen Educational.

Brennan, W. K. (1985) *The Curriculum in Special Education*. Milton Keynes: Open University.

Brennan, W. K. and Tomlinson, S. L. (1982) *Changing Special Education Now: Children with Special Needs*. Milton Keynes: Open University.

Broadfoot, P. (1986) *Profiles and Records of Achievement*. London: Cassell.

Bruner, J. S. (1966) *Toward a Theory of Instruction*. New York: Norton.

Bruner, J. S. (1972) *The Relevance of Education*. New York: Norton.

Bruner, J. S., Goodnow, J. and Austin, G. (1963) *A Study of Thinking*, 2nd edn. New York: Wiley.

Burgess, T. and Adams, E. (1985) *Records of Achievement at 16*. Windsor: NFER-Nelson.

Burnhill, P., Hartley, J., Fraser, L. and Young, D. (1975) Writing lines: an exploratory study. *Programmed Learning and Educational Technology* **12**(2) (March).

Carnine, D. W. and Silbert, J. (1979) *Direct Instruction Reading*. Westerville, Ohio: Merrill.

Carroll, J. B. and Bloom, B. J. (1971) In Block, J. H. (ed.) *Mastery Learning*. New York: Holt, Rinehart & Winston.

CERD (Council for Educational Research and Development) (1980) *Study Skills*. Lancaster: CERD.

Chambers, P. (ed.) (1987) *Reading*. Leamington Spa: Scholastic Publications.

Chazan, M. (1964) The incidence and nature of maladjustment amongst children in schools for the educationally sub-normal. *Journal of Educational Psychology* **34**(3).

Chazan, M. (1968) *Compensatory Education*. Bulletin no. 1. London: Schools Council.

Chazan, M. (1974) 'The treatment of maladjusted pupils: research and experiment 1960–69'. In Pringle, M. L. K. and Varma, V. P. (eds) *Advances in Educational Psychology*, vol. 2. London: University of London Press.

Chazan, M. and Jackson, S. (1971) Behaviour problems in the infant school. *Journal of Child Psychology and Psychiatry* **12**, 191–221.

Chazan, M., Laing, A. F., Shackleton-Bailey, M. and Jones, G. (1980) *Some of Our Children*. London: Open Books.

Child, D. (1977) *Psychology and the Teacher*. London: Holt Education.

Chisholm, B., Kearney, D., Knight, G., Little, H., Morris, S. and Tweddle, D. (1986) *Preventive Approaches to Disruption*. London: Macmillan Education.

Chomsky, C. (1971) 'Write first read later'. *Childhood Education* **47**(6), 296–299.

Chomsky, C. (1979) 'Approaching reading through invented spelling'. In Weaver, P. and Resnick, L. B. (eds) *The Theory and Practice of Early Reading*, vol. 2. Hillsdale, New Jersey: Lawrence Erlbaum Associates.

Clarke, A. M. and Clarke, A. D. B. (eds) (1978) *Mental Deficiency: The Changing Outlook*, revised edn. London: Methuen.

Clarke, T. (1984) 'Mathematical difficulties'. Kingston Polytechnic Learning Difficulties Conference.

Clay, M. M. (1975) *What Did I Write?* London: Heinemann Educational.

Clay, M. M. (1979a) *The Early Detection of Reading Difficulties*. London: Heinemann.

Clay, M. M. (1979b) *Reading: The Patterning of Complex Behaviour*. London: Heinemann.

Clunies-Ross, L. and Wimhurst, S. (1983) *The Right Balance: Provision for Slow Learners in Secondary Schools*. Windsor: NFER-Nelson.

Cotterell, G. (1973) *Diagnosis in the Classroom*. Reading, UK: Reading University School of Education.

Cotterell, G. (1974) In Wade and Wedell, op. cit.

Cowdery, L. L. (1977) Unpublished thesis, Kingston Polytechnic.

Cowdery, L. L. (1987) *Teaching Reading Through Spelling (TRTS): The Spelling Notebook*. Kingston, Surrey: Kingston Learning Difficulties Research Project.

Cowdery, L. L., McMahon, J., Montgomery, D., Morse, P. and Prince, M. (1983) *Teaching Reading Through Spelling (TRTS): Diagnosis*. Kingston, Surrey: Kingston Polytechnic Learning Difficulties Research Project.

Cowdery, L. L., Montgomery, D., Morse, P. and Prince, M. (1984) *Teaching Reading Through Spelling (TRTS): Foundations of the Programme*. Kingston, Surrey: Kingston Polytechnic Learning Difficulties Research Project.

Cox, A. and Waites, L. (1972) *Language Training Programme*. Scottish Rite Hospital, USA.

Cox, A. R. (1975) *Structures and Techniques of Remedial Language Training: Multisensory Teaching for Alphabetic Phonics*, revised edn. Cambridge, Massachusetts: Educators Publishing Service Inc.

Cox, B. (1985) *The Law of Special Educational Needs*. London: Croom Helm.

Cox, T. (1978) *Stress*. London: Macmillan.

Cramer, R. L. (1976) Diagnosing skills by analysing children's writing. *Reading Teacher* **30**(3), 276–279.

Critchley, M. and Critchley, E. A. (1978) *Dyslexia Defined*. London: Heinemann.

Croll, P. and Moses, D. (1985) *One in Five*. London: Routledge & Kegan Paul.

Daniels, H. (1988) Misunderstandings, miscues and maths. *British Journal of Special Education* 15(1) (March), 11–13.

Daniels, J. C. and Diack, H. (1958) *The Standard Reading Tests*. London: Chatto and Windus.

Davidson, P. and Marolda, M. (1975) *The Mathematics Diagnostic/Prescriptive Inventory (MDPI)*. Boston, Massachusetts: Children's Hospital Medical Center.

Davie, R. (1988) Summary of NCB Report. *Times Educational Supplement*.

Davie, R., Butler, N. and Goldstein, H. (1972) *From Birth to Seven*. London: Longman.

Dawson, R. (ed.) (1985) *T.I.P.s (The Macmillan Teacher Information Pack)*. Basingstoke: Macmillan.

de Bono, E. (1976) *CoRT Thinking Action Programme*. Blandford Forum: CoRT.

de Bono, E. (1983) *CoRT Thinking Programme*. Oxford: Pergamon.

Delecco, J. R. and Crawford, W. R. (1974) *The Psychology of Learning and Instruction*, 2nd edn. Englewood Cliffs, New Jersey: Prentice-Hall.

DES (Department of Education and Science) (1946) Pamphlet No. 5: *Special Educational Treatment*. London: HMSO.

DES (1971) *Education Act (Handicapped Children)*. London: HMSO.

DES (1975) *A Language for Life* (The Bullock Report). London: HMSO.

DES (1978) *Special Educational Needs* (The Warnock Report). London: HMSO.

DES (1981) *Education Act*. London: HMSO.

DES (1982) *Mathematics Counts* (The Cockcroft Report). London: HMSO.

DES (1983) *Assessment and Statements of Special Educational Needs*, Circular 1/83. London: HMSO.

DES (1984) *CATE Criteria*. London: HMSO.

DES (1985) *Better Schools*. London: HMSO.

DES (1987a) *The National Curriculum 5–16*. London: HMSO.

DES (1987b) *Primary Schools: Some Aspects of Good Practice*. London: HMSO.

DES (1989) *Discipline in Schools* (The Elton Report). London: HMSO.

Dobinson, E. (1987) Unpublished thesis, North East London Polytechnic.

Docking, J. W. (1980) *Control and Discipline in Schools: Perspectives and Approaches*. London: Harper & Row.

Donaldson, M. (1978) *Children's Minds*. London: Fontana.

Douglas, J. W. B. (1964) *The Home and the School*. London: MacGibbon & Kee.

Dreeben, R. (1968) *On What is Learned in School*. New York: Addison Wesley.

Dreeben, R. (1970) *The School as a Workplace*. Glenview, Illinois: Scott Foresman.

Driver, R. (1988) Interim report on learning and teaching targets in science. *Education* (February).

Dunlop, D. B. (1974) Orthoptic assessment of children with learning difficulties. *Australian Journal of Ophthalmology* 2.

Dunlop, D. B. and Dunlop, P. (1975) A new orthoptic technique in learning disability due to visual dyslexia. *Australian Psychology and Education for Learning Disabilities.*

Dyke, M. (1986) *Collaborative Learning and Language: Report.* Manchester: Manchester Special Education Resource Centre.

Ehri, Y. (1980) In Frith (1980) op. cit.

Evans, M. (1981) *Disruptive Pupils.* London: Longman/Schools Council.

Eysenck, H. J. (1966) *Handbook of Abnormal Psychology.* New York: Basic Books.

Farnham-Diggory, S. (1978) *Learning Disabilities.* London: Fontana/Open Books.

Farquhar, C. (1987) Little read books. *Times Educational Supplement* (8 May).

Farrell, P. (ed.) (1985) *EDY: Its Impact on Staff Training in Mental Handicap.* Manchester: Manchester University Press.

Ferreiro, E. (1978) What is written in a written sentence? A developmental answer. *Journal of Education* 160(4), 25–39.

Ferreiro, E. (1979) 'Towards a theory of spelling development'. In Read (1986) op. cit., ch. 5.

Ferreiro, E. (1980) 'The relationship between oral and written language, the children's viewpoints'. In Read (1986) op. cit.

Ferreiro, E. and Teberosky, A. (1982) *Literacy before Schooling.* Exeter, New Hampshire: Heinemann Educational.

Feuerstein, R. (1980) *Instrumental Enrichment: An Intervention Programme for Cognitive Modifiability.* Baltimore: University Park Press.

Fisher, J. (1982) Unpublished thesis, Kingston Polytechnic.

Fontana, D. (ed.) (1984) *Behaviourism and Learning Theory in Education.* British Journal of Educational Psychology Monograph Series no. 1. Edinburgh: Scottish Academic Press.

Formentin, T. and Csapo, M. (1980) *Precision Teaching.* Vancouver: Centre for Human Development and Research.

Forsyth, C. (1987) Unpublished thesis, Kingston Polytechnic.

Foster, J. (1971) *Recording Individual Progress.* London: Macmillan.

Fowler, S. (1982) 'Orthoptics and fixed referent eye'. Paper presented to School of Nursing, Berkshire Hospital, UK.

Francis, H. (1982) *Learning to Read: Literate Behaviour and Orthographic Knowledge.* London: Allen & Unwin.

Freeman, J. (ed.) (1985) *Psychology of Gifted Children.* Chichester: Wiley.

Freud, A. (1958) *Adolescence: Psychoanalytic Study of the Child*, vol. 13, pp 255–270. London: Hogarth Press.

Frith, U. (1980) *Cognitive Processes in Spelling.* London: Academic Press.

Frith, U. (1985) 'Beneath the surface of developmental dyslexia'. In Patterson, K. E., Marshall, J. C. and Coltheart, M. (eds) *Surface Dyslexia: Neuropsychological and Cognitive Studies of Phonological Reading*, ch. 13. London: Erlbaum Associates.

Frostig, M. and Horn, D. (1964) *The Frostig Programme for the Development of Visual Perception.* Chicago: Follett.

Gagné, R. (1969) In Gagné (1973) op. cit.

Gagné, R. (1973) *The Essentials of Learning.* London: Holt, Rinehart & Winston.

Gagné, R. (1977) *Conditions of Learning and Theory of Instruction,* 2nd edn. London: Holt, Rinehart & Winston.

Gains, C. W. and McNicholas, J. A. (eds) (1979) *Remedial Education: Guidelines for the Future.* Papers from National Association for Remedial Education (NARE) Conferences August 1975 and January 1977. London: Longman for NARE.

Galloway, D., Ball, T., Blomfield, D. and Seyd, R. (1982) *Schools and Disruptive Pupils.* London: Longman.

Galloway, D. and Goodwin, C. (1987) *The Education of Disturbing Children.* London: Longman.

Galton, M., Simon, B. and Croll, P. (1980a) 'Observational Research and Classroom Evaluation Project (ORACLE)'. In Galton *et al.* (1980b) op. cit.

Galton, M., Simon, B. and Croll, P. (1980b) *Inside the Primary Classroom.* London: Routledge & Kegan Paul.

Gazzaniga, M. S. (1967) Split brain in man. *Scientific American* (217), 24–29.

GCSE (General Certificate of Secondary Education) (1988) GCSE Guidelines. Southern Examinations Board.

Gentry, R. J. and Richardson, E. H. (1978) Three steps to teaching beginning readers to spell. *The Reading Teacher* **31**(6), 632–637.

Gibbons, R. (1983) Evolving appropriate methods of assessment. *Struggle* **10**, 1–4.

Gibson, E. J. and Levin, H. (1975) *The Psychology of Reading.* Cambridge, Massachusetts: MIT Press.

Gillingham, A. and Stillman, B. (1956) *Remedial Training for Children with Specific Disability in Reading, Spelling and Penmanship.*, 5th edn. New York: Sackett and Williams/Better Books.

Gillingham, A., Stillman, E. and Orton, S. T. (1940) *Remedial Training for Children with Specific Disability in Reading, Spelling and Penmanship.* New York: Sackett and Williams.

Gipps, C., Gross, H. and Goldstein, H. (1987) *Warnock's Eighteen Per Cent.* London: Falmer Press.

Gittelman, R. and Gittelman, S. (1985) Controlled trials of remedial approaches to reading disability. *Journal of Child Psychology and Psychiatry* **26**(6), 843–846.

Glaser, R. (1962) *Training Research and Education.* Pittsburgh: University of Pittsburgh Press.

Golinkoff, R. M. (1978) 'Phonemic awareness skills and reading achievements'. In Murray, F. B. and Pikulski, J. J. (eds) *The Acquisition of Reading.* Baltimore: University Park Press.

Good, T. L. and Brophy, J. E. (1972) In Good, T. L. and Brophy, J. E: *Educational Psychology: A Realistic Approach* (1977). London: Holt, Rinehart & Winston.

Goodman, K. S. (1969) Analysis of oral reading miscues: applied psycholinguistics. *Reading Research Quarterly* **5**, 9–30.

Graham, D. (chair) (1985) *Those Having Torches: The Suffolk Report.* Ipswich: Suffolk Education Authority.

Gray, K. (1970) Thinking abilities as objectives in curriculum development. *Educational Review* **24**(3), 237–249.

Green, F., Hart, R. and Staples, I. (1982) *Microcomputers in Special Education.* York: Longman Resources Unit.

Grönlund, N. E. (1970) *Stating Behavioural Objectives for Classroom Instruction.* New York: Macmillan.

Groves, P., Griffin, J. and Grimshaw, N. (1983) *Steps: Basic English Course,* Step 2. Harlow: Longman.

Gubbay, S. S. (1975) *The Clumsy Child.* London: W. B. Saunders.

Guilford, J. P. (1960) In Wiseman, S. *Intelligence and Ability.* Harmondsworth, Middx: Penguin.

Gulliford, R. (1969) *Backwardness and Educational Failure.* London: Routledge & Kegan Paul.

Gulliford, R. (1985) *Teaching Children with Learning Difficulties.* Windsor: NFER-Nelson.

Guthrie, I. D. (1978) 'The sociology of pastoral care in an urban school'. Unpublished MA thesis, Kings College, University of London.

Hammersley, M. (1976) 'The mobilisation of pupil attention'. In Hammersley, M. and Woods, P. (eds) *The Process of Schooling.* London: Routledge & Kegan Paul.

Handy, C. (1971) *Psychology of Organisations.* Harmondsworth, Middx: Penguin.

Hanko, G. (1985) *Special Needs in Ordinary Classrooms.* Oxford: Blackwell.

Hannon, P. (1987) Parent involvement. *Times Educational Supplement* (3 April).

Hannon, P. and Jackson, A. (1987) *The Belfield Reading Project Final Report.* London: National Children's Bureau.

Hargreaves, D. (1976) *Deviance in Classrooms.* London: Routledge & Kegan Paul.

Hargreaves, D. (1978) What teaching does to teachers. *New Society* **43**(9) (March), 540–542.

Hargreaves, D. (1982) *The Challenge for the Comprehensive School.* London: Routledge & Kegan Paul.

Hargreaves, D. (1984) *Improving Secondary Schools.* London: ILEA.

Haring, N. G. and Eaton, M. D. (1978) 'Systematic instructional procedures'. In Harling, N. G. *et al.* (eds) *The Fourth R – Research in the Classroom.* pp. 23–40. Westerville, Ohio: Charles Merrill.

Harris, D. and Goodenough, F. (1963) *The Goodenough–Harris Draw-A-Person Test Manual.* New York.

Hart, S. (1986) In-class support teaching: tackling Fish. *British Journal of Special Education* **13**(2) (June).

Heaton, P. and Winterson, P. (1986) *Dealing with Dyslexia.* Bath: Better Books.

Hegarty, S. (1987) *Meeting Special Needs in Ordinary Schools: An Overview.* London: Cassell.

Hegarty, S., Pocklington, K. and Lucas, D. (1981) *Educating Pupils with Special Needs in Ordinary Schools*. Windsor: NFER-Nelson.

Hemming, J. (1987) 'The capability of the young child'. World Education Fellowship (Great Britain section) Conference, Kingston Polytechnic.

Hemming, J. (1988) 'Quality or control in education?' World Education Fellowship (Great Britain section) Conference, Kingston Polytechnic.

Henderson, L. and Chard, M. J. (1980) 'The reader's implicit knowledge of orthographic structure'. In Frith (1980) op. cit.

Herbert, M. (1975) *Problems of Childhood*. London: Pan.

Hewison, J. and Tizard, B. (1980) Parental involvement and reading attainment. *British Journal of Educational Psychology* 50, 209–215.

Hewitt, L. E. and Jenkins, R. L. (1946) *Fundamental Patterns of Maladjustment: The Dynamics of their Origin*. Springfield, Illinois: Springfield.

Hickey, K. (1977) *Dyslexia: A Language Training Course for Teachers and Learners*. Wimbledon: K. Hickey.

Hinshelwood, J. (1917) *Congenital Word Blindness*. London: H. K. Lewis.

Hirst, P. (1966) Language as thought. *Proceedings of the Philosophy and Education Society of Great Britain*, 63–75.

Hirst, P. (1968) 'The contribution of philosophy to the study of the curriculum'. In Kerr, J. F. (ed.) *Changing the Curriculum*. London: University of London Press.

Hirst, P. and Peters, R. S. (1970) *The Logic of Education*. London: Routledge & Kegan Paul.

HMI (Her Majesty's Inspectorate) (1964) *Slow Learners at School*, pamphlet no. 46. London: HMSO.

HMI (1979) *Aspects of Secondary Education*. London: HMSO.

HMI (1981) *The School Curriculum*. London: Welsh Office/HMSO.

HMI (1983) *Science in Primary Schools*. London: HMSO.

HMI (1984) *Slow Learning and Less Successful Pupils in Secondary Schools*. London: HMSO.

HMI (1986) *Lower Attaining Pupils Project*. London: HMSO.

HMI (1988a) *Better Mathematics: Low Attainers in Mathematics Project (LAMP)*. London: HMSO.

HMI (1988b) *Secondary School Survey*. London: HMSO.

Hodgson, A., Clunies-Ross, L. and Hegarty, S. (1984) *Learning Together: Teaching Pupils with Special Needs in Ordinary Classroom*. Windsor: NFER-Nelson.

Holt, J. (1962; frequently reprinted) *How Children Fail*. London: Pitman.

Holt, J. (1967) *How Children Learn*. Harmondsworth, Middx: Pelican.

Hope, M. (ed.) (1986) *The Magic of the Micro: A Resource for Children with Learning Difficulties. Readers 7*. London: Microelectronics Education Project/Council for Educational Technology.

Hughes, M. (1986) *Children and Number: Difficulties in Learning Mathematics*. Oxford: Blackwell.

ILEA (Inner London Education Authority) (1984) *Improving Secondary Education*. London: ILEA.

ILEA (1985) *Educational Opportunities for All?* (The Fish Report). London: ILEA.

Jarman, C. (1979) *The Development of Handwriting Skill*. Oxford: Blackwell.

Jenkins, R. L. (1966) Psychiatric syndromes in children and their relation to family background. *American Journal of Orthopsychiatry* **36**, 450–457.

Jenkins, R. L. (1968) The varieties of children's behavioural problems and family dynamics. *American Journal of Psychiatry* **125**, 1440–1445.

Johnson, R. (1964) Another study method. *Journal of Developmental Reading* **7**, 269–282.

Johnson, R. (1979) 'Helping people succeed'. Paper given at British Association for Commercial and Industrial Education Conference.

Johnson, R. (1981) Manpower policies: helping people to succeed. *BACIE Journal* (October).

Judd, R. (1982) Unpublished thesis, Kingston Polytechnic.

Kelly, G. A. (1955) *The Psychology of Personal Constructs* (2 vols). New York: Norton.

Kempe, R. S. and Kempe, C. H. (1978) *Child Abuse*. Cambridge, Massachusetts: Harvard University Press.

Kerry, T. L. (1979) In Wragg and Kerry, op. cit.

Kingman, Sir J. (chair) (1988) *Report of the Committee of Enquiry into the Teaching of English* (The Kingman Report). London: HMSO.

Kingslake, B. (1983) The prediction accuracy of school screening procedures. *Special Education: Forward Trends* **10**(4), Research Supplement, 23–26.

Kingston Friends Workshop (1985) *Ways and Means*. Kingston, Surrey; Kingston Learning Difficulties Research Project.

Kinsbourne, M. and Warrington, E. K. (1963) Developmental factors in reading and writing backwardness. *British Journal of Psychology* **54**, 145–156.

Kirklees LEA (1986) *Parental Involvement in Reading Videotape*. Kirklees LEA.

Kolvin, I. *et al.*, (1981) *Help Starts Here: the Maladjusted Child in the Ordinary School*. London: Tavistock.

Kosc, L. (1974) Development dyscalculia. *Journal of Learning Disabilities* **7**, 46–59.

Kounin, J. S. (1970) *Discipline and Group Management in Classrooms*. New York: Holt, Rinehart & Winston.

Krech, D., Crutchfield, R. S. and Ballachey, E. L. (1962) *Individual in Society*. Tokyo: McGraw-Hill.

Laslett, R. (1977) Disruptive and violent pupils: the facts and fallacies. *Educational Review* **29**(3), 152–162.

Laslett, R. (1977b) *Educating Maladjusted Children*. London: Crosby Lockwood Staples.

Laslett, R. (1982) *Maladjusted Children in Ordinary School*, Stratford upon Avon: NCSE.

Laszlo, M. (1987) Children with perceptuo-motor difficulties in schools. *Times Educational Supplement* (3 September).

Lawrence, J., Steed, D. M. and Young, P. (1977) *Disruptive Behaviour in a Secondary School*, Goldsmiths' Monographs No. 1. London: Goldsmiths' College, University of London.

Lawrence, J., Steed, D. and Young, P. (1984) *Disruptive Children – Disruptive Schools*. London: Croom Helm.

Leach, D. (1980) In Leach (1983) op. cit.

Leach, D. (1983) Early screening techniques. *School Psychology International* **4**, 47–56.

Leach, D. and Raybould, E. (1977) *Learning and Behaviour Difficulties in School*. London: Open Books.

Leavitt, H. J. (1951) Some effects of certain communicative patterns on group performance. *Journal of Abnormal Psychology*.

Lerner, J. W. (1971) *Children with Learning Disabilities*. Boston: Hougton Mifflin.

Levy, S. and Trevarthen, C. (1972) In Springer and Deutsch, op. cit.

Liberman, I. Y. (1973) Segmentation of the spoken word and reading acquisition. *Bulletin of the Orton Society* **23**, 365–377.

Liberman, I. Y., Shankwerter, D., Liberman, A. M., Fowler, C. and Fischer, F. W. (1977) 'Phonemic segmentation and recording in the beginning reader'. In Reber, A. S. and Scarborough, D. (eds) *Towards a Psychology of Reading*. Hillsdale, New Jersey: Erlbaum.

Lindsay, G. (1984) *Screening for Children with Special Needs*. London: Croom Helm.

Lindsay, G. and Pearson, L. (1986) *Special Needs in Primary Schools: Identification and Assessment*. Windsor: NFER-Nelson.

Loviglio, L. (1981) Mathematics and the two sides of the brain. *Massachusetts Teacher*.

Lowenstein, L. F. (1976) *Report on Vandalism and Violence in Schools*. London: NUT.

Luria, A. R. (1973) *The Working Brain*. Harmondsworth, Middx: Penguin.

McBrien, J. and Weightman, J. (1980) The effect of room management procedures on the engagement of profoundly retarded children. *British Journal of Mental Subnormality* **26**(1), 38–46.

MacDonald, E. (1978) *Women in Management*. London: E. MacDonald.

McGrew, W. C. (1972) *An Ethological Study of Children's Behaviour*. Cambridge, UK: Cambridge University Press.

McMahon, J. (1982) 'An analysis of the spelling patterns and remedial interventions with a group of dyslexic children'. Unpublished thesis, Kingston Polytechnic.

McMahon, J. (1983) In Cowdery *et al.* (1983) op. cit.

McNicholas, J. (1981) *Early Screening Inventory*. London: Macmillan.

Maidenhead Group of Teachers (1985) *The Motorway Project*. Wisbech: LDA.

Marland, M. (1986) Appraisal and evaluation: chimera, fantasy or practicality? *Education Management and Administration* **14**, 169–189.

Marshall, C. and Wolfendale, S. (1977) 'Screening and early identification of children with problems'. In Gilliland, J. (ed.) *Reading: Research and Classroom Practice*. London: Ward Lock Educational.

Masheder, M. (1986) *Let's Co-operate*. London: M. Masheder.

Meek, M. and Thomson, B. (1987) *Study Skills in a Secondary School*.

Miles, T. R. (1981) In Pavlidis, G. T. and Miles, T. R. (eds) *Dyslexia Research and its Applications to Education*. Chichester: Wiley.

Miles, T. R. (1983a) *The Bangor Dyslexia Test*. Wisbech: LDA.

Miles, T. R. (1983b) *Dyslexia. The Pattern of Difficulties*. London: Granada.

Ministry of Education (1913) *Mental Deficiency Act*. London: HM Government.

Mitchell, S. and Rosa, P. (1981) Boyhood behaviour problems as precursors of criminality: a 15 year follow-up study. *Journal of Child Psychology and Psychiatry* **22**(1), 19–33.

Mittler, P. and Mittler, H. (1982) *Partnerships with Parents*. Stratford upon Avon: NCSE.

Mongon, D. (1985) 'Patterns of delivery and its implications for training'. In Sayer and Jones, op. cit.

Mongon, D. and Hart, S. with Ace, C. and Rawlings, A. (1989) *Improving Classroom Behaviour: New Directions for Teachers and Pupils*. London: Cassell.

Montgomery, D. (1977) Teaching pre-reading skills through pattern recognition training. *Reading Teacher* **30**(6), 216–225.

Montgomery, D. (1979) *Visual Pattern Recognition Test and Training Materials*. Windsor: NFER.

Montgomery, D. (1981a) The nature of modern teaching. *School Psychology International* **1**.

Montgomery, D. (1981b) Do dyslexics have difficulty in accessing their articulations? *Psychological Research* **43**.

Montgomery, D. (1982) Teaching thinking skills in the school curriculum. *School Psychology International* **2**.

Montgomery, D. (1983a) *Study Skills: Teaching and Learning Strategies*. Kingston, Surrey: Kingston Polytechnic Learning Difficulties Research Project.

Montgomery, D. (1983b) *Managing Classroom Behaviour Problems*. Kingston, Surrey: Kingston Polytechnic Learning Difficulties Research Project.

Montgomery, D. (1984a) *Evaluation and Enhancement of Teaching Performance*. Kingston, Surrey: Kingston Polytechnic Learning Difficulties Research Project.

Montgomery, D. (1984b) In Cowdery (1987) op. cit., ch. 6.

Montgomery, D. (1985) *Helping Able Learners in Ordinary Classrooms*. Kingston, Surrey: Kingston Polytechnic Learning Difficulties Research Project.

Montgomery, D. (1988) Teacher appraisal. *New Era in Education* **68**(3).

Montgomery, D. and Hadfield, N. (1989) *Practical Appraisal in Secondary Schools*. London: Kogan Page.

Montgomery, D. and Rawlings, A. (1986) *Classroom Management*. Leamington Spa: Scholastic.

Mordecai, S. and Lloyd, C. (1988) *National Association of Curriculum Enrichment and Extension Newsletter* **12** (Summer), 16–24.

Morgan, . and Lyon, . (1979) In Wolfendale and Topping, op. cit.

Morse, P. (1984) In Cowdery *et al.* (1984) op. cit.

Mortimore, P., Sammons, P., Stoll, L. *et al.* (1988) *School Matters.* London: ILEA.

Myklebust, H. R. (1965) *Development and Disorders of Written Language,* vol. 1. London: Grune & Stratton.

Myklebust, H. R. (1973) *Development and Disorders of Written Language,* vol. 2. London: Grune & Stratton.

Naidoo, S. (1972) *Specific Dyslexia.* Bath: Pitman.

NAGC (National Association for Gifted Children) (1984) *Survey Report on the Needs of Gifted Children.* London: NAGC.

Neagley, R. L. and Evans, N. D. (1967) *Handbook for Effective Curriculum Development.* Englewood Cliffs, New Jersey: Prentice-Hall.

Neale, M. D. (1958; revised edn, 1966; 1989) *Analysis of Reading Ability.* London: Macmillan.

Neisser, U. (1967) *Cognitive Psychology.* New York: Appleton-Century-Crofts.

Newton, M. and Thomson, M. (1976) *The Aston Index.* Wisbech: LDA.

NSPCC (National Society for the Prevention of Cruelty to Children) (1986) *Survey Report on Child Abuse.* London: NSPCC.

NUT (National Union of Teachers) (1984) *Corporal Punishment: the Case for Alternative,* 2nd edn. London: NUT.

Nuttall, G. and Snook, N. (1973) 'Contemporary models of teaching'. In Travers, R. M. W. (ed.) *Second Handbook of Research on Teaching,* ch. 2. Chicago: Rand McNally.

Ogilvie, E. (1973) *Gifted Children in Primary Schools.* London: Macmillan/Schools Council.

O'Leary, K. D. and O'Leary, S. C. (eds) (1973) *Classroom Management: The Successful Use of Behaviour Management.* New York: Pergamon.

Olson, D. R. (1977) From utterance to text: the bias of language in speech and writing. *Harvard Educational Review* **47**(3), 257–281.

Ornstein, R. (1977) *The Psychology of Consciousness,* 2nd edn. New York: Harcourt Brace Jovanovich.

Parrant, H. (1986) Unpublished thesis, Kingston Polytechnic.

Pearson, L. and Lindsay, G. (1986) *Special Needs in the Primary School: Identification and Intervention.* Windsor: NFER-Nelson.

Pearson, L. and Tweddle, D. A. (1984) 'The formulation and use of behavioural objectives'. In Fontana, op. cit.

Peck, R. R. and Havighurst, R. J. (1960) *The Psychology of Character Development.* London: Wiley.

Peel, E. A. (1963) *The Pupil's Thinking.* London: Oldbourne.

Peter, M. (1988) 'The National Curriculum. Will it cure learning difficulties or create them?' Paper to Kingston Polytechnic Learning Difficulties Conference.

Peters, M. L. (1967) *Spelling Caught or Taught?* London: Routledge & Kegan Paul.

Peters, M. L. (1970) *Success in Spelling.* Cambridge, UK: Cambridge Institute of Education.

Peters, M. L. and Smith, B. (1986) In Root, op. cit.

Phillips, J. L. (1975) *The Origins of Intellect. Piaget's Theory,* 2nd edn. San Francisco: Freeman.

Piaget, J. (1952) *The Origins of Intelligence in Children*. New York: International University Press.

Piaget, J. (1953) How children form mathematical concepts. *Scientific American* **89**(5) (November), 74–79 (offprint 420).

Plowden, B. (chair) (1967) *Children and their Primary Schools* (The Plowden Report). London: HMSO.

Pollack, M. (1979) *Signposts to Spelling*. Fulham: Helen Arkell Institute.

Poteet, J. A. (1977) *Behaviour Modification: A Practical Guide for Teachers*. London: University of London Press.

Pringle, M. Kellmer- (1973) *Able Misfits*. London: Longman/National Children's Bureau.

Pumfrey, P. D. (1977) *Measuring Reading Abilities*. London: Hodder and Stoughton.

Pym, D. (1980) Towards the dual economy and emancipation from employment. *Futures* (June), 223–237.

Quicke, J. (1984) 'The role of the educational psychologist in the post Warnock era'. In Barton, L. and Tomlinson, S. (eds) *Special Education and Social Interests*. Beckenham: Croom Helm.

Rawlings, A. (1989) In Mongon, D. *et al.*, op. cit.

Raybould, D. A. (1984) 'Precision teaching and pupils with learning difficulties'. In Fontana, op. cit.

Read, C. (1971) Pre school children's knowledge of English phonology. *Harvard Educational Review* **41**, 1–34.

Read, C. (1975) *Children's Categorisation of Speech Sound in English*. Urbana, Illinois: National Council for the Teaching of English.

Read, C. (1986) *Children's Creative Spelling*. London: Routledge & Kegan Paul.

Roberts, M. (1986) 'The infinite capacity of the young child'. Conference Paper, World Education Fellowship (Great Britain section), Kingston Polytechnic.

Robertson, A. H., Henderson, A., Robertson, A., Fisher, J. and Gibson, M. (1983) *Quest: Teacher's Manual*. Oxford: Pergamon Arnold Wheaton.

Robins, L. (1966) *Deviant Children Grow Up*. Baltimore: Williams & Williams.

Robinson, F. P. (1962) In Robinson, F. P. (1962) *Effective Reading*. New York: Harper & Row.

Robinson, M. (1981) *Schools and Social Work*. London: Routledge & Kegan Paul.

Root, B. (1986) *Resources for Reading: Does Quality Count?* London: UKRA/Macmillan. (Proceedings of 1985 UKRA Conference.)

Rosenthal, R. and Jacobson, L. (eds) (1968) *Pygmalion in the Classroom*. New York: Holt, Rinehart & Winston.

Royce-Adams, W. (1977) *Developing Reading Versatility*, 2nd edn. New York: Holt, Rinehart & Winston.

Rutter, M. (1975) *Helping Troubled Children*. Harmondsworth, Middx: Penguin.

Rutter, M., Maughan, B., Mortimore, P. and Ouston, J. (1979) *Fifteen Thousand Hours*. London: Open Books.

Rutter, M., Tizard, J. and Whitmore, K. (eds) (1970) *Education, Health and Behaviour*. London: Longman.

Rutter, M. and Yule, W. (1973) 'The concept of specific reading retardation'. In Mann, L. and Sabatino, D. (eds) *First Annual Review of Special Education*. Philadelphia: Burntwood Farms.

Sassoon, R. (1983) *The Practical Guide to Children's Handwriting*. London: Thames and Hudson.

Sayer, J. and Jones, N. (eds) (1985) *Teacher Training and Special Educational Needs*. London: Croom Helm.

Schiffman, G. and Clemmens, R. (1966) *Observations on Children with Severe Reading Problems Learning Disorders*. Seattle, Washington: Special Child Publications.

Schonell, F. J. and Schonell, F. E. (1946; 4th reprint 1970) *Diagnostic and Attainment Tests*. Edinburgh: Oliver and Boyd.

Schools Council (1980) *Study Skills in the Secondary School*, pilot edn. London: Schools Council.

Scott MacDonald, W. (1971) *Battle in the Classroom*. Brighton: Intext.

SED (Scottish Education Department) (1978) *The Education of Pupils with Learning Difficulties in Primary and Secondary Schools: A Progress Report by HMI*. Edinburgh: HMSO.

Shannon, J. (1987) Unpublished thesis, Kingston Polytechnic.

Sharp, R. and Green, A. (1975) *Education and Social Control: A Study in Progressive Primary Education*. London: Routledge & Kegan Paul.

Shuard, H., Rothery, A. and Holt, M. (1980) *Children Reading Maths: a working paper*. London: National Association of Teachers in Further and Higher Education Mathematics Education Section.

Sigston, A. and Addington, J. (1984) In Sigston, A. and Pinner, J. (eds) *Children in Transition* (1986) London: Waltham Forest School Psychological Service.

Simmons, K. (1986) Painful extractions. *Times Educational Supplement* (17 October).

Simon, C. (1986) 'Written language'. Unpublished manuscript, NFER.

Skinner, B. F. (1953) *Science and Human Behaviour*. New York: Macmillan.

Skinner, B. F. (1971) *Beyond Freedom and Dignity*. London: Cape.

Smith, B. M. (1985) 'Using the word processor to help children think about writing'. In Potter, F. and Wray, D. (eds) *MicroExplorations No. 2*. Ormskirk: UKRA.

Smith, F. (1971) *Understanding Reading*. New York: Holt, Rinehart & Winston.

Smith, F. (1973) *Psycholinguistics and Reading*. London: Holt, Rinehart and Winston.

Smith, F. M. and Adams, S. (1972) *Educational Measurement for the Classroom Teacher*, 2nd edn. New York: Harper & Row.

Smith, P. A. P. and Marx, R. W. (1972) Some cautions on the use of the Frostig test. *Journal of Learning Disabilities* **5**(6), 357–362.

Snow, R. (1973) In Travers, R. M. (ed.) *Second Handbook of Research on Teaching*. Chicago: Rand McNally.

Snowling, M. (ed.) (1985) *Children's Written Language Difficulties*. Windsor: NFER-Nelson.

Snowling, M. (1987) *Dyslexia: A Cognitive-Developmental Perspective*. Oxford: Blackwell.

Solity, J. and Bull, S. (1987) *Special Needs: Bridging the Curriculum Gap*. Milton Keynes: Open University.

Southgate-Booth, V. (1985) In Root, op. cit.

Southgate-Booth, V. (1987) 'Making the most effective use of reading time'. Paper to Kingston Polytechnic Learning Difficulties Conference.

Southgate-Booth, V., Arnold, H. and Johnson, S. (1981a) *The Effective Use of Reading Project*. London: Heinemann.

Southgate-Booth, V., Arnold, H. and Johnson, S. (1981b) *Extended Beginning Reading*. London: Heinemann.

Spache, G. (1940) Characteristics of good and poor spellers. *Journal of Educational Research* **34**(3).

Springer, S. P. and Deutsch, G. (1981) *Left Brain Right Brain*. San Francisco: Freeman.

Steed, D. (1985) Disruptive pupils, disruptive schools. Which is the chicken? which is the egg? *Educational Research* **1** (February), 3–8.

Stenhouse, L. A. (1975) *An Introduction to Curriculum Research and Development*. London: Heinemann.

Stephens, T. M. (1976) *Directive Teaching of Children with Learning and Behavioural Handicaps*, 2nd edn. New York: Merrill.

Stephenson, J. (1981) Unpublished thesis, Kingston Polytechnic.

Stevens, M. (1976) *The Education and Social Needs of Children with Severe Handicap*, 2nd edn. London: Edward Arnold.

Stillman, B. (1932). In Gillingham and Stillman, B., op. cit.

Stonier, T. (1979) *Knowledge and Technology: The Impact on Society, Employment and Education*. Southampton University Conference Papers.

Stonier, T. (1982) 'Changes in western society: educational implications'. In Richards, C. (ed.) *New Directions in Primary Education*. Brighton: Falmer.

Story Chest. London: Edward Arnold.

Stott, D. H. (1981) Behaviour disturbance and failure to learn: A study of cause and effect. *Educational Research* **23**(3).

Swann, M. (chair) (1985) *Education for All* (The Swann Report). London: HMSO.

Swann, W. (1982) *A Special Curriculum: E241 Special Needs in Education*. Milton Keynes: Open University Press.

Swann, W. (1985) Is the integration of children with special needs happening? *Oxford Review of Education* **11**, 3–18.

Swann, W. (1987) In Booth, Potts and Swann, op. cit.

Taba, H. (1962) *Curriculum Development: Theory and Practice*. New York: Harcourt Brace Jovanovich.

Tansley, A. E. and Gulliford, R. (1960) *The Education of Slow Learning Children*. London: Routledge & Kegan Paul.

Tansley, P. and Panckhurst, J. (1981) *Children with Specific Learning Disabilities: NFER Report*. Slough: NFER-Nelson.

Taylor, P. H. (1962) Children's evaluations of the characteristics of a good teacher. *British Journal of Educational Psychology* **32**, 258–266.

Taylor, P. H. (1968) In Kerr, J. F. (ed.) *Changing the Curriculum*. London: University of London Press.

Taylor, P. H. (1970) *How Teachers Plan Their Courses*. Slough: NFER.

TGAT (Task Group Assessment and Testing) (1988) *Report* (The Black Report). London: HMSO.

Thomas, D. (1978) *The Social Psychology of Childhood Disability*. London: Methuen.

Thomas, D. and Smith, C. (1985) In Sayer and Jones, op. cit., ch. 6.

Thomas, G. (1985) Room management in mainstream education. *Educational Research* **27**(3).

Thomas, L. and Harri-Augstein, S. (1972) *Reading Behaviour Research. A Report*. Uxbridge: Brunel University.

Thomas, L. and Harri-Augstein, S. (1984) 'Learning conversations: self organised learning'. Paper to SCEDSIP/COPOL Conference, Kingston Polytechnic.

Thomson, M. (1984) *Developmental Dyslexia*. London: Edward Arnold.

Tizard, B. (1987) Parent involvement. *Times Educational Supplement*; (4 March).

Tizard, B. and Hughes, M. (1984) *Young Children Learning: Talking and Thinking at Home and School*. London: Fontana.

Tizard, J., Schofield, W. N. and Hewison, J. (1982) Collaboration between teachers and parents in assisting children's reading. *British Journal of Educational Psychology* **52**, 1–15.

Topping, K. J. (1986) *Parents as Educators*. London: Croom Helm.

Trickey, D. (1987) Dyslexia conference report. *Times Educational Supplement* (July).

Turner, M. (1990) Positive responses: dramatic results of a corrective reading programme. *Times Educational Supplement* (19 January).

Tyler, R. W. (1949) *Basic Principles of Curriculum Instruction*. Chicago: University of Chicago Press.

Vargus, J. S. (1972) *Writing Worthwhile Behavioural Objective*. New York: Harper & Row.

Vargus, J. S. (1973) In Vargus (1977) op. cit.

Vargus, J. S. (1977) *Behavioural Psychology for Teachers*. New York: Harper and Row.

Vellutino, F. R. (1979) *Dyslexia: Theory and Research*. Cambridge, Massachusetts: MIT Press.

Vellutino, F. R. (1987) Dyslexia. *Scientific American* **256**(3) (March), 20–27.

Vincent, T. (1983) Unpublished thesis, Kingston Polytechnic.

Wade, B. and Wedell, K. (eds) (1974) *Spelling: Task and Learner*. Educational Review Occasional Paper No. 5. Birmingham University: ICAA (Invalid Children's Aid Association).

Walkerdine, V. (1982) 'From context to text: a psychosemiotic approach to abstract thought'. In Beveridge, M. (ed.)

Waller, W. (1932) *The Sociology of Teaching*. New York: Wiley.

Waterland, E. (1985) *Read with Me*. Stroud: Thimble Press.

Watzlawick, P., Weakland, J. H. and Fisch, R. (1974) *Change: Principles of Problem Formulation and Problem Resolution*. New York: Norton.

Webb, J. (1962) The sociology of the school. *British Journal of Sociology* **13**(3), 264–272.

Webster, A. and McConnell, E. (1987) *Children with Speech and Language Difficulties*. London: Cassell.

Wechsler, D. (1974) *Wechsler Intelligence Scale for Children – Revised*. New York: Psychological Corporation.

Wedell, K. (1973) *Learning and Perceptuo-motor Disabilities in Children*. London: Wiley.

Wedell, K. (1977) *Orientations in Special Education*. New York: Wiley.

Wedge, P. and Prosser, H. (1979) *Born to Fail?* London: Arrow Books.

Wellings, G. A. (1980) 'Teaching mathematics to slow learners/assessment'. Course notes, Portsmouth Teachers' Centre.

Wells, G. (1981) *Learning through Interaction*. London: Cambridge University Press.

Welton, J., Wedell, K. and Vorhaus, G. (1982) *Meeting Special Educational Needs* (Bedford Way Papers no. 12). London: University of London.

West, D. J. (1982) *Delinquency*. London: Heinemann.

West, D. J. and Farrington, D. P. (1973) *Who Becomes Delinquent?* London: Heinemann.

Wheldall, K. (ed.) (1981) *The Behaviourist in the Classroom* (Educational Review Offset Publications No. 1). Birmingham, UK: University of Birmingham.

Wheldall, K. and Merritt, F. (1984a) *Positive Teaching: The Behavioural Approach*. London: Unwin Education.

Wheldall, K. and Merritt, F. (1984b) *BATPACK Positive Products*. Birmingham, UK: Birmingham University.

Wheldall, K. and Merritt, F. (1986) Looking for a positive route out of poor class behaviour. *Special Children* (2), 26–27.

Wheldall, K., Morris, M., Vaughan, D. and Ng, Y. Y. (1981) Rows versus tables: an example of the use of behavioural ecology in two classes of eleven year old children. *Educational Psychology* **1**, 171–184.

Wheldall, K. and Riding, R. (eds) (1983) *Psychological Aspects of Teaching and Learning*. Beckenham: Croom Helm.

Williams, P. (1970) In Williams, P. *Children and Psychologists*. London: Hodder and Stoughton.

Willis, P. E. (1977) *Learning to Labour: How Working Class Lads Get Working Class Jobs*. Farnborough, Hants: Saxon House Press.

Wilson, M. (1981) *The Curriculum in Special Schools*. London: Schools Council.

Wilson, M. and Evans, M. (1980) *Education of Disturbed Pupils*. London: Schools Council.

Wisbey, A. (1984) Preventing waste. *Industrial Society* (June), 22–24.

Wisbey, A. (1987) 'Overcoming dyslexia'. Paper to Learning Difficulties Conference, Kingston Polytechnic.

Wiseman, S. (1972) *Intelligence and Ability*. Harmondsworth, Middx: Penguin.

Witkin, H. (1959) The perception of the upright. *Scientific American* (February).

Wolfendale, S. (1987) *Primary Schools and Special Needs: Policy, Planning and Provision*. London: Cassell.

Wolfendale, S. and Bryans, T. (1979) *Identification of Learning Difficulties: a Model for Intervention*. Stafford: NARE.

Wolfendale, S. and Topping, K. J. (eds) (1985) *Parental Involvement in Children's Reading*. London: Croom Helm.

Womack, D. (1984) Step this way. *Times Educational Supplement* (5 October).

Wood, S. and Shears, B. (1986) *Teaching Children with Severe Learning Difficulties: A Radical Reappraisal*. London: Croom Helm.

Wragg, E. C. (1981) Paper to IT-INSET Conference. Cambridge, UK: Institute of Education.

Wragg, E. C. (ed.) (1984) *Classroom Teaching Skills*. Beckenham: Croom Helm.

Wragg, E. C. and Kerry, T. L. (1979) *Classroom Interaction Research* London: Macmillan.

Wright, D., Taylor, A. *et al.* (1970) *Introducing Psychology*. Harmondsworth, Middx: Penguin.

Ysseldyke, J. E. (1987) Annotation. *Journal of Child Psychology and Psychiatry* (January).

Ysseldyke, J. E. and Salvia, J. (1974) Diagnostic–prescriptive teaching: Two models. *Exceptional Teaching*, 181–186.

Yule, W. (1967) Predicting reading ages on Neale's Analysis of Reading Ability. *British Journal of Educational Psychology* 37, 252–255.

Yule, W. (1988) Dyslexia. Not one condition but many. *British Medical Journal* 297, 501–502.

Name Index

Subject Index